GOD UNDERNEATH

GOD UNDERNEATH

Spiritual Memoirs of a Catholic Priest

Edward L. Beck

IMAGE BOOKS

DOUBLEDAY

New York   London   Toronto   Sydney   Auckland

AN IMAGE BOOK
PUBLISHED BY DOUBLEDAY
a division of Random House, Inc.
1540 Broadway, New York, New York 10036

IMAGE, DOUBLEDAY, and the portrayal of a deer drinking from a stream
are trademarks of Doubleday,
a division of Random House, Inc.

God Underneath was originally published by Doubleday as a hardcover in
July 2001.

Book design by Lynne Amft

The Library of Congress has cataloged the hardcover edition as follows:

Beck, Edward L., 1959–
God underneath: spiritual memoirs of a Catholic priest/Edward L. Beck.—1st ed.
p. cm. 1. Beck, Edward L., 1959–
2. Catholic Church—United States—Clergy—Biography. I. Title.
BX4705.B43 A3 2001
271'.6202—dc21
[B]
00-065734

ISBN 0-385-50181-1

PRINTED IN THE UNITED STATES OF AMERICA

August 2002
First Image Books paperback edition

3 5 7 9 10 8 6 4 2

For my parents,

Geraldine and Eddie,

for the ways in which they have

always made God underneath come

to the surface.

Music I heard with you was more than music,
And bread I broke with you was more than bread.

—Conrad Aiken

ACKNOWLEDGMENTS

Whenever authors write: *This book could not have been written without* . . . and then list a bunch of names, I sometimes think to myself, "Yeah, right." Now I know it's true—especially a book of this nature. I wish to thank the many people whose lives have intersected with mine with enough force and memory to warrant inclusion in the following pages. Thank you for letting our stories be told.

There are, of course, other people whose lives have also impacted mine in ways that filter into the following pages, but perhaps their names are not explicitly mentioned in the narrative. So thank you to: Patrick D'Amelio, Natalie Binversie, O.S.F., Michael Eschmann, Maurie and Bob Flanagan, Héctor Lozada, Ken Mabe, Robin Mathiesen (Blue), Huguette J. McKenzie, Honora Nicholson, R.S.M., Karen and Ed O'Neill, Marilyn Perlman, John Sawicki, C.S.Sp., Peter Schubart, Melvin Shorter, C.P., Norman Simon, Paul Wadell, Elizabeth Walter, and Wendy M. Wright.

Thank you to John Shea, mentor and gifted theologian, for writing the Foreword of this book.

Thank you to Francesco Scavullo for his artistry and generosity.

Thank you to Peter Friedman, teacher and scholar, who made numerous and valuable suggestions, and to the writing group that he shepherds, whose members never hesitated to tell me what they thought.

Thank you to my literary agent, Denise Marcil, who believed

viii / Acknowledgments

in this book from the beginning, and who put her talent and resources behind making its publication a reality.

Thank you to my family for its love and encouragement; and to my religious family, the Passionists, for their willingness to support me and for giving me the space and freedom necessary to write this book.

Finally, thank you to Eric Major, my editor at Doubleday, for his invaluable suggestions and for always being able to hear the heartbeat of this book. Perhaps an island on which we both have been "sheltered" holds the key to this rewarding collaboration.

CONTENTS

ix

A SACRED STRING OF BEADS

When we tell our experiences as a series of stories, they become a string of beads, a necklace we wear that expresses who we are and introduces us to others.

And when these stories are memories of people, places, and times that awaken us to our own spirit and to the surrounding darkness and undeserved light we call God, then we have fashioned a sacred string of beads, a life story told as both resistance and response to the subtle invitations of grace.

This book is Edward Beck's sacred string of beads.

In the Introduction he tells us clearly, "Spirit does not desire to be separate from earth and flesh, rather, it desires to suffuse it more and more." In the twenty-one vignettes that follow we watch this suffusing Spirit at work both in Edward and in the people he meets:

> in his Poseidon father pulling him and his cousin from the
>   undertow of the Atlantic;
> in the lingering spirit of his feisty grandmother;
> in a pen-wielding, frightened teenager fending off some
>   bigots;
> in a Marlboro-smoking priest who steps between Edward
>   and a sexual predator;
> in a homeless person who persistently asks him, "Change
>   today?" until he finally gets it;
> in a wounded jogger and unflagging social activist who re-
>   fuses to give up;

in a man who passionately believes God has a "Bruce Lee" side;

in an unflappable scholar-sister who urges him to be transparent;

in a woman who wants more than he is willing to give;

and then there's mama—complaining, funny, unpredictable—the secret source of his own zest for life.

The context for these random and pushy spiritual teachers is the contemporary circus of Catholicism—liturgical squabbles, the role of women in the Church, official positions on homosexuality and personal conscience, conservative and liberal ideologies, celibacy and boundaries, saints and healing, etc. But this is not a book of issues, and these concerns are not treated in an abstract and argumentative way. Instead we see the startling ways they play out in actual experience.

We watch Edward's classmate lie in order to have a song and singer excluded from a vow ceremony.

We watch a pastor nudge out a nun on the way to the pulpit.

We watch a serendipitous happening on retreat force Edward into a long and honest look at the official Church and homosexuality.

We watch a pastor cancel a mission because he judged it too "liberal," and then hide in the rectory with the lights out as the parishioners bang on the door.

We watch a woman "stalk" Edward from city to city, forcing him into the question of the extent of priestly caring.

We watch Baptist parents use a relic of St. Martin de Porres to contribute to the healing of their child.

Most of all we follow a committed, honest, post–Vatican II priest on his way to his fortieth birthday, holding on to his underlying supposition—"the spiritual is infinitely more significant and empowering than the physical."

In the play *Shadowlands* a student tells C. S. Lewis, "We read to know we are not alone." *God Underneath: Spiritual Memoirs of a*

Catholic Priest is that type of reading experience. As in all suffi-ciently perceptive autobiography, we see ourselves in Edward, his people, and his situations. Edward Beck's story becomes an invita-tion into our own. Our memories are jogged, and grandparents, parents, friends, colleagues, and the humiliating and exhilarating incidents of our lives come into view. Under the impact of Edward Beck's telling, we begin to fashion our own sacred string of beads.

—John Shea

Old paint on canvas, as it ages, sometimes becomes transparent. When that happens it is possible, in some pictures, to see the original lines: a tree will show through a woman's dress, a child makes way for a dog, a large boat is no longer on an open sea. That is called pentimento because the painter "repented," changed his mind. Perhaps it would be as well to say that the old conception, replaced by a later choice, is a way of seeing and then seeing again.

That is all I mean about the people in this book. The paint has aged now and I wanted to see what was there for me once, what is there for me now.

—LILLIAN HELLMAN, PENTIMENTO

My mother arrived in New York from her Florida home one week after I had moved into my first Manhattan apartment. After having been a Catholic priest for fourteen years, I had been given the gift of a sabbatical rest, during which time I resided alone and wrote this book. I am a Passionist *religious* (noun used to describe men and women who take vows in religious communities), and my community had generously offered me this time, after my years of serving as an itinerant preacher. Traveling the country to lead parishes in retreats and missions had depleted me in ways I hadn't even realized. I sensed I needed a break from the constant movement and lack of rootedness, and my community concurred. My mother, intent on making sure my priestly vocation remained intact during my year "in the world," had deemed it her maternal duty to come and inspect the priest's "bachelor pad."

My diminutive New York City studio (350 square feet), of which I was very proud, had a tiny sleeping loft and lots of character—my own urban hermitage. I had done everything possible before my mother's arrival to transform this small but charming apartment into a presentable domicile: fresh flowers arranged in ceramic vases, summer fruit strategically placed in matching bowls, and minimal furniture polished to a self-reflecting gloss.

After I picked up my mother at the airport and was forced to maneuver luggage that sent me back to the chiropractor, we arrived, sweaty but not defeated, at my Manhattan studio. I eagerly opened the door to my newfound Shangri-la. My mother stepped in gingerly, glanced around with a Leona Helmsley "out on bail" visage, and said, "It's so small in here, I couldn't even change my mind."

So began our week of cohabitation in space I soon began to agree seemed very small. Surprisingly, however, it was a fitting way for me to begin my sabbatical year. It became an opportunity, as Hellman suggests, "of seeing and then seeing again." Viewing my relationship with my mother and weighing its spiritual relevance proved to be a rare chance for me to see "what was there for me once, what is there for me now." It also highlighted the theme of this book even before I began writing it.

Hellman's quote suggests a metaphor for my life: a multilayered fresco that is altered with each added layer. Perennially beginning again, I can change my mind and express myself, as I never have before. The underneath layers, while perhaps covered up for a time, occasionally may bleed through to reveal their persistent presence. With a fresh perspective and distinctive flair, I can add new layers, forging my own "pentimento," replete with people and places I hold close in memory—and those I have yet to discover. I can make way for an open sea when tired of thrashing around in the same old river. I can be created anew.

Being created anew is a desire of many of us. We want to start fresh, do it better, transform our lives, live more deeply. But we get stuck and lose our way. We yearn to live more meaningful lives, but we get co-opted by the superficial values of our society, which communicate that only the physical matters: what we look like, how much money we have, how big our house is, what position we hold in the firm, and how our sexual prowess measures up against the people in the Certs breath mint commercial. We not only lose our way; we are indeed, at times, led down the wrong path.

The challenge is to peel back the much-touted superficial layers and to discover if something more interesting and satisfying lurks underneath. This is where we find the world of Spirit. The surface experiences, while they may appear ordinary, even mundane, have the potential of denoting something deeper and more meaningful than may be apparent at first blush.

I had had high expectations for the week spent alone with my mother, often imagining such time, if the opportunity ever presented itself. We would take long walks down the bustling streets of the city and talk frankly, isolated from the censoring gaze of relatives and friends. Satisfying our common penchant for savory cuisine and exemplary service, we would linger at tables in esoteric restaurants, mindless of the cost, since Dad would be getting the credit card receipts. Plays by Ibsen and O'Neill would offer fodder for post-theater conversations, while the many museums, galleries, and shops would thrill us during the day.

So much for great expectations. The anticipated long walks turned into griping sessions about "how far everything is" and "how it would have been better if you had kept a car in the city." As we strolled through bucolic Central Park on a sparkling, cloudless day, my mother's refrain managed to mar the idyll: "I've gotten so dirty in two blocks, I could already take another shower. Terrible." Appraising the high-tech apparel of the joggers whizzing by us on Central Park South, she asked longingly, "Do people wear those headphones to block out all this noise? Where can I get one?"

The dream of feasting on haute cuisine while waiters pirouetted around us proved a nightmare. New York apparently lacks what is ubiquitous and prized in Florida dining: "Early Bird Special Menus." It doesn't seem to matter that the Southern nosh-ers are also in bed by 8 P.M. After finally tiring of the endless spa and California nouveau cuisine dishes proudly heralded on Manhattan menus, my mother boldly queried one waiter, "Doesn't *anyone* make simple veal cutlet parmigiana anymore?" He peered at my mother with disdain, as if she had just suggested he give up his acting career.

But our excursion into the arts proved the most interesting. We were enjoying an Off-Broadway comedy, with the first act clipping along nicely. Out of the corner of my eye, I could see my mother smiling, even chuckling at all the right places. At last, she seemed to be having a good time. I settled into my seat, breathed a sigh of relief, and joined her in savoring the *bons mots* of the witty new playwright. Then out of nowhere, as if the gods were intent on sabotaging this one ray of sunshine on an otherwise bleak horizon, an actor onstage precipitously dropped his pants and stood before us naked while my mother sat in the second row with her mouth wide open—a compromising posture, to say the least.

"So this is the kind of play a priest brings his mother to?" she said. "Terrible. Terrible."

I heard the word *terrible* a lot during a long week. In retro-spect, it was an appropriate word, derived from the root "to frighten." My mother was indeed frightened; almost everything about the city seemed to make her afraid. Her distance from an ur-ban environment, the repercussions of a benign brain tumor, and the constrictions of growing older have all contributed to chang-ing my mother, changes that I find hard to accept.

My struggle during our week together prompted me to reflect on spiritual themes that my relationship with my mother had sur-faced. "Loss" headed the list. I was reminded of the approach that I take in the retreats I give around the country, where I encour-age the viewing of ordinary experience as a gateway to spiritual revelation. I realized early in my ministry that, if my preaching was effective, it was because of the stories I incorporated to illustrate the salient points. Those stories, used to highlight the spirituality beneath the experience, were what people remembered and asked me about after the presentations. Most effective of all were the personal stories from my life that seemed to resonate with my listeners.

The story of my mother's visit seems an apt example, because there is another story underneath it. Hoping to fulfill my own dream for my time together with my mother, I failed to inquire about my mother's dream—or the loss of it, due to variables that now shape her in ways I sometimes find unacceptable, sometimes embarrassing. I think it's because I have to let go of *my* dream, and I resist that. I want my old mother back. I want the fearless mother who used to take me to Rockefeller Center by subway each Christmas and proudly watch me skate circles around the other novices. I want the mother who encouraged me to try sushi and exotic vegetables and who suggested I read Jane Austen and Sidney Sheldon because they *both* could teach me something about life.

But deep down, I want even more than that. I long to feel her maternal embrace, like the time she comforted me when I was beaten up by Chris Thomas, the neighborhood bully, and embarrassed in front of my classmates. I yearn for her to assure me that the life I have chosen makes her proud, when sometimes I think she would have preferred that I had married and had children. I desire for her to mother me again, to take care of *me* more than I take care of *her*. But it's just not that way anymore. I have to learn to let it go, for her sake and for mine. But it's hard.

The internal conflict that I experienced, however, also produced some spiritual lessons. My longing for the mother I once knew caused me to confront a similar void that I experience in our religious tradition. It put me in touch with the God for whom I long, one who is more than "Father." As a result of our patriarchal religious roots, we have been accustomed to relating to a male God, a "Father" God. Yet the penchant in my own Catholic tradition for making Mary into a goddess reflects an innate desire to connect also with a feminine aspect of the Divine. We want a God who can mother us, too.

I am heartened in recalling that, even in the midst of the strongly patriarchal Hebrew ethos from which our male images of God emerged, feminine images of God also broke through, unable to be suppressed even in a society in which women often were. In the first book of the Hebrew Scriptures we read, "God created humankind in His image; in the Divine image He created him; male and female He created them" (Genesis 1:27). The Divine image is seemingly described by the author of Genesis as incorporating male and female, the totality of all that we are, and then much more.

The psalmist writes, "I have stilled and quieted my soul like a weaned child. Like a weaned child on its mother's lap, so is my soul within me" (Psalm 131:2). The mother brings peace and comfort, just like God. In the book of the prophet Isaiah we read, "Can a mother forget her infant, be without tenderness for the child of her womb? Even should she forget, I will never forget you" (Isaiah 49:15). God's love is compared to that of a mother's love for her child, and the feminine imagery serves to highlight the care of a God who, while superseding our anthropomorphic designations, is not diminished by them.

My account of my mother's visit is, therefore, also a story about a deeper longing. I have learned to trust stories to communicate spiritual wisdom, believing that stories can relay spiritual and theological truths, because they speak of the world of experience. It is in the details of our experience that we encounter God. Stories can also inspire and heal, because they connect us with the loving vitality of soul in each of us and make it conscious to us. We all have such stories. People can therefore make my story, or anyone else's, their own if they find meaning and truth in it, because, ultimately, we all share the same story.

A truism in spirituality states: Authentic spiritual life begins where we are. It is the only place where God can meet us. Is it possible that we are being relentlessly pursued by a power wanting only our happiness and fulfillment, but that we sometimes fail to allow that sovereignty take hold of us, because we don't know where or how to find it? For so long, many of us have been told we must go beyond the parameters of our everyday lives to encounter God. So we go to church or temple, or travel to holy shrines or mosques, or traverse the hallways of monasteries and convents, hoping to absorb the holy through osmosis. Yet, Spirit does not desire to be separate from earth and flesh; rather, it desires to suffuse it more and more. We need not go anywhere else to find God. God is in the midst of it all.

What about discovering the sacred where we are (as I did, surprisingly, in the visit of my mother)? What about the twenty-four hours a day, seven days a week of daily, at times mundane, living, including the eight hours or more of work we do each day? And what about those who don't have the luxury of *going* anyplace else to find God: housewives homebound with kids and the demands of caretaking, the aged, no longer mobile, the sick who stare at the same four walls daily, the poor who lack the resources to "leisurely contemplate"? Might not our most profound experiences of God be located in the everyday rhythms of our lives?

While not a novel concept, Incarnational Spirituality is perhaps worth exploring more fully, because we have not always sufficiently reverenced it. Incarnational Spirituality believes that God chooses to be revealed in the people and events of our lives. (*Incarnate* comes from the Latin *incarnari*, to be made flesh.) Thus, this spirituality is of the very stuff of our lives. God becomes incarnate, a God with skin.

Unfortunately, rather than highlight this fleshy spirituality, the Church has often promoted a disembodied and rarefied one, relegated to the privileged few. We have been encouraged to suppress the physical, in order to be released into the spiritual. But spirituality is not an esoteric discipline reserved for those who can leisurely pursue it in the cloister, or for the mystic who can effortlessly transcend the constraints of physicality. Rather, it is in the realm of all of us; there is no escaping it. It is the stuff of our lives: our families, marriages, and friendships; our losses, joys, work, and sexuality. These are the places where God is revealed to us, where the possibility of transformation hovers. While we may choose not to partake of the inherent power available or to plumb its depths, it is always there, moving with stealth, underneath.

My hope is that the stories contained in this book speak to your heart and open it more to this world of Spirit; that they encourage you to take journeys in your heart that you have heretofore resisted, to worlds you have previously avoided. I trust that you will see yourself reflected in these stories, because I'm confident that, ultimately, our stories are the same.

While we live in a physical world, we are also privileged to have citizenship in a spiritual one. Although some of us may never choose to have that passport stamped, the border remains open for us to cross over anytime we wish. Those who learn to negotiate dual citizenship may discover how to have the best of both worlds. Passports in hand then, let us make that crossing together—lifting up the surface of experience and mining the deeper layers. Pentimento. To allow the surface to become transparent; to see through the original lines; to see and then see again; to see what was there for us once, what is there for us now—underneath.

CHAPTER ONE

NAME RECOGNITION

See, upon the palms of my hands I have written your name.
—Isaiah 49:16

I was supposed to be named Adelaide . . . if I was born a girl. My
mother gives thanks to this day that the first thing she saw while
lying on the delivery table was a penis. The doctor held me up all
bloody, squirming, and screaming and moved to lay me on my
mother's chest.

My mother winced and said, "Oh, thank God, a boy. But,
please, clean him up first." She is still saying that in one way or another. Who could have predicted the lasting power of that first
breath metaphor?

My parents married young—three times, each time to one another, and with no divorces. That must be a record somewhere.
The first wedding occurred after an evening of revelry spent with
friends at Frankie and Johnny's pub in Flatbush, Brooklyn. The
magic of that evening and the lowering of inhibitions provided by
enough beer and whiskey sours made an expeditious marriage
seem inviting. My parents hopped into a 1955 Chevy Impala and
headed toward the Mason-Dixon line. My mother called her
mother from Maryland (a state known to marry you within
twenty-four hours, no questions asked) to tell her where she was
and what she was planning.

"Momma, I'm in Maryland with Eddie and we're going to get married."

"Well, I figured that was coming sooner or later. He's a good guy and he seems to treat you well. It's just too bad he doesn't have money. You know love goes out the window when the bills come in the door."

"Oh, Momma!"

"You can learn to love anyone who treats you well, but you love them even more when they have money and can treat you *really* well."

"Momma, we'll be fine, and I do love him—money or no money."

"O.K., but don't you come home here unless you two get married. If you stay out all night with a man, you had better be married to him."

"Momma, we *are* getting married. That's why I called you. I'll see you sometime tomorrow."

Once the inspiring phone call had ended, my mother anxiously sought out a priest, because she wanted to be married in the Church. Religious affiliation was not yet paramount for my father. A justice of the peace would do just fine for him. But late in her teens my mother had discovered her Catholicism anew and she fell for it mightily, making novenas three times a week and never missing Mass. It was important to her that the Church from which she received so much solace and meaning bless this marriage.

They finally found a priest willing to sit down with them after ringing the doorbells of a few rectories. The seasoned cleric listened patiently to this young woman's story, touched by her desire to make this marriage sacramental, but not touched enough.

"Are you pregnant?" he asked her.

"No, no, of course not," she said.

"Then go home and forget about this nonsense. It will never last. Take your time; plan a proper wedding. Do this right. It's too important to rush through on a whim."

But my mother knew they couldn't go home. It was too late.

It was already well into the night and Nanny's words echoed in her mind—she had better be married to him.

Left with no other alternative, my parents sought out a justice of the peace, who performed a no-frills nuptial in a private chamber with people they met that night serving as witnesses. Geraldine, a twenty-year-old red-haired knockout with a dazzling smile, and Eddie, a twenty-two-year-old blue-eyed charmer with a gelled pompadour, exchanged rings and promised forever. The obviously overworked justice flatly said words he probably uttered in his sleep, "I now pronounce you man and wife." The newlyweds spent their first night in a prosaic Maryland hotel which offered them congratulatory free beer as a toast to their legal but not yet sacramental bond.

During the drive home, my mother began to consider the priest's question: "Are you pregnant?"

"He had some nerve asking me that. Is that the only reason people elope? It did get me to thinking though about when we do finally have a child. What will we name it?"

"Gerri," my father said, "that's quite a ways off. Do we really need to talk about it now?"

"Well, I mean just for fun. I already know anyway. If we have a son, I want to name him Christopher Michael after my stepfather and real father, and if it's a girl, I think, Maureen, a nice Irish name."

"Fine, whatever," my father said, more intent on worrying about where they were going to live.

Once they had secured a modest apartment and had gotten settled with the details of newly married life, the call of the sacrament returned with an insistent beckoning. My mother still earnestly wanted to be married in the Church, and my father had gradually become convinced of its value. My parents went to see another priest. After listening sympathetically to their Maryland odyssey, this priest finally agreed to marry them.

"You know, of course, that this is a serious sacramental commitment," he said to them in hushed tones. "You must invite God into this union if it is to perdure. And you must work at it. I'll do this wedding, but you are the ones that will have to make it last."

They accepted the priest's counsel, ready to agree with whatever he said, and were elated that someone was finally willing to marry them. A small wedding was planned. My parents felt some embarrassment at having to repeat the nuptials, but they trusted that this time would be qualitatively different. With family and friends gathered, pungent lilacs placed at the high altar and in front of the Mary statue, and the organ playing a melodious Bach cantata, the priest leaned over to my father, who had on a flattering charcoal gray suit, and requested the marriage license. My father looked at my mother in her beige, lace-sleeved dress. She turned and looked at her red-haired sister, who didn't know to whom to look. Then everyone looked horrified. No one had realized my parents would need a New York State marriage license and blood test after having already been married in Maryland. The wedding was off. With sacramental connubial bliss evading my parents once more, the disgruntled guests retired to a local bar to await word of the next ceremony.

After attending to the New York legalities, some weeks later my parents returned to the church and were married in an unceremonious wedding, witnessed by only my aunt and grandfather and a few friends at a side altar in St. Edmund's Church in Brooklyn. Others who had attended the first aborted Church wedding passed on this one, sure that another mishap would dictate a further delay. They had better things to do with their Saturday afternoons. With New York State license and blood test in hand, the young couple said, "I do," again, this time before God; thus making the legal bond a sacramental one as well. With God finally giving His stamp of approval, my parents were determined to live up to their end of the bargain.

For years this escapade has remained a running joke in my family, especially at the time of my parents' anniversary each year. "Now, which one are we celebrating anyway?" My mother is not amused.

Oh, yes, but about my name. It all came down to money. My parents struggled financially in the early years of their marriage. My mother had heeded Nanny's advice in marrying a man who treated her well, but unfortunately not one who had money. My father worked three jobs at one time to keep them afloat, including driving a taxi in New York City, which in itself merits praise and extra life insurance. When not bartending at Monahan's, he would do odd handyman jobs, like fixing leaking sinks or helping to remodel outdated kitchens that no longer satisfied Flatbush housewives. He was dexterous with a hammer and screwdriver, prompting people to remark how lucky my mother was to have a husband who could do things around the house.

But about the name. I learned late in life that I wasn't my parents' first child. They had endured a miscarriage a few months after their marriage. In addition to the obvious sadness, this also put them in a delicate position. Because the pregnancy was interrupted, no one was able to accurately chart the date of conception. My mother got wind that some were concluding that she and my father "had to get married."

"They have some nerve," she said to my father. "They should only know that I wouldn't even let you kiss me the wrong way because the priest told me it was a sin."

My mother took a protective stance toward the next pregnancy, the one that ultimately resulted in my being born. She maintains that she hardly went out of the house for the nine months for fear of miscarrying again. She ate a lot of Breyer's ice cream and Nathan's hot dogs, watched Lucy and Desi on TV (Lucy was also pregnant), and ballooned to 175 pounds from a svelte 135 pounds. Liver spots covered her face and the red hair dye she used wouldn't take. She says it wasn't pretty.

Because of my parents' limited resources, the costs of having a child so soon proved daunting. Perceiving my imminent arrival, Grandpa Beck saw an opportunity. An overweight man with a chin that doubled down to his chest, he was a dinner guest most Sundays. He was also a wonderful cook, holding culinary secrets to savory German meals, secrets he often shared with my mother, if she agreed to execute the meal as he directed. He was a tough tutor, though, always correcting, subtly putting down even her most earnest of efforts. He also had trouble with gambling, losing large amounts of money at the racetrack, including my father's share of a taxi business they owned together—something my father won't talk about to this day.

"Well," Grandpa Beck said one day as he lowered himself onto the sofa in the living room for the beginning of a TV ball game. "I know you two are kind of strapped financially and you have a baby on the way, so I'd be willing to help out. I'll buy you a beautiful baby carriage, so it's one less thing you'll have to worry about."

"Gee, that's very nice of you, Pop," my father said. "Thank you. We appreciate it."

"There's just one thing," my grandfather continued. "I'd like to be able to name the baby in exchange for me getting you the carriage."

"Name the baby?" my mother said warily. "What would you name it?"

He said, "Well, if it's a girl, I'd like to name her after my deceased wife, Eddie's mother, Adelaide."

My mother choked on her rye and club soda and dropped her handful of peanuts back into the dish. *"Adelaide?"*

"And if it's a boy, I'd like to name him Edward Leon Beck III. We may as well continue my and your husband's name. It has served us well all these years."

My mother was able to swallow her drink on this one, but barely. She saw her dreams of Christopher Michael and Maureen being dashed more quickly than my father could mix another drink. She also resented being bribed, but she needed a carriage. "After all," she reasoned, "this probably wouldn't be their only child." The names would still be there. She could live with Edward III; at least it had a regal quality to it. She didn't know, however, if she could forgive herself if forced to name a daughter

Adelaide, who she was sure would be called "Addy" for short. The mere thought of it gave her stomach cramps well before the onslaught of labor. But having little choice, she entered into this Mephistophelean agreement, albeit reluctantly, with the hopes that Adelaide would never be a name she'd have to put on a birth certificate. So, that day in the delivery room, as she prayed up a storm and held her medal of Saint Gerard close to her chest, she was never so happy to see a penis.

I have always preferred Edward to Ed or Eddie, partly because my grandfather was Ed and my father, Eddie. I wanted my own version. I like the sound of my name being called, probably because it signals that the one calling has some connection with me. As a child, I could tell the caller's emotion by the mere intonation used. The "Edward!" screamed by my mother when I had inadvertently crayoned the living room wall as a child sounded like a different language from the "Edward" cooed when I brought home a self-made Mother's Day card complete with kisses and hugs. Of course, this is a universal experience. The name uttering you might welcome in moments of unselfconscious lovemaking is worlds apart from the name sputtering you surely dread when it is discovered that you mistakenly left the water running in the bathtub, ruining the freshly painted ceiling of the den below. Whole sentences are spoken in one word, the name.

There is also power in a name. When someone calls me Edward, as opposed to the various derivatives, I know that person has a part of me not everyone does, however small it may seem. They know me well enough to be familiar, and to respect my preference. This is the reason ancient Israel never said or wrote the name of God. They believed that to say or write the name gave one power over the Deity. It was too familiar. Ancient Israel presumed no such power. When needing to refer to God, YHWH was written, which cannot be uttered without the vowels that render YAHWEH. Today one often sees G-d, also unspeakable.

The Scriptures do, however, refer to a God who calls *us* by name, sometimes suggesting a lover whose hands are all over us.

The God who has written our names on the palm of God's hands (Isaiah 49:16) is the One of whom the psalmist sings, "Truly you have formed my inmost being; you knit me in my mother's womb" (Psalm 139:13).

From the moment I was conceived, I am confident God has been whispering, "Edward," beckoning me forth into a fullness of life that only God can ultimately provide. God calls me by name because God knows me that intimately, the most intimately anyone can know me. And when God speaks my name, it is always as lover—never as angry parent or disgruntled spouse. God makes rainbows out of the crayoned wall and waterfalls out of the overflowing tub.

CHAPTER TWO

THE WAVES IN WHICH
WE TUMBLE

*Suddenly a violent storm came up on the sea, so that the boat
was being swamped by waves; but Jesus was asleep. They came and
woke him saying, "Lord, save us! We are drowning!" He said to
them, "Why are you so terrified, O you of little faith?" Then he
got up, rebuked the winds and the sea, and there was great calm.*

—MATTHEW 8:24–26

Why was my father—alone—taking my cousin Denise and
me to the beach? I still can't figure it out. Even at ten years
old, I was suspicious of the arrangement. I was hardly ever alone
with my father. He was usually working two or three jobs, and
when he was home, he needed to catch up on sleep or attend to
house projects that my mother had dreamed up. When my
brother, Chris, and I were left alone with my father, the house felt
unfamiliar and the comfortable rhythms broken. Even television
was different. We liked having my mother around, because she
usually let us watch whatever we wanted. My father, on the other
hand, could watch sports all night and still not have his fill; I had
mine after the national anthem was sung.

So I'm not sure how this beach sojourn came about. Nor do I
have a clue as to where my mother and brother were, or how my

father had possibly agreed to this. He hated the beach—too much sand and too many flies.

I was glad it was Denise who was coming with us, though. She was my closest cousin, probably because we were only a year apart in age. When we were young, our mothers would drag us with them to Nostrand Avenue, in Flatbush, while they went to Trunz's butcher to get the meat for that evening's meal, and to Ebinger's bakery for fresh rye bread and delectable fruit pies. Denise and I often lagged behind, and once out of the view of our mothers, we would torment some of the shop owners, like Max, the dry cleaner who worked in the back of his store, cleaning the clothes. Denise and I would open his front door, step on the entrance buzzer that served to alert him to customers, and then run away. We would do this repeatedly, until poor Max thought he was going crazy. Once, after seeing us, he chased us halfway up the avenue with a cigar hanging out of his mouth and sweat beading down his puffy cheeks.

Our mothers would get their hair done every week in Miss Beauty, a beauty parlor on Nostrand Avenue, where Denise and I would be subjected to the asphyxiating smells of hair permanent solution, dyes, and toxic sprays. We maintain that our shared propensity to upper respiratory infections is due to our hours spent in beauty parlors, to say nothing of the smoke we inhaled endlessly from our mothers' cigarettes.

Sometimes, as a reprieve from the beauty parlor pollution, we would sit outside on the sidewalk and play games or with our G.I. Joe and Barbie dolls, even in the coldest weather. (We didn't tell my father that I had a G.I. Joe, because he didn't think that boys should play with dolls.) Concerned mothers would pass by with their well-bundled younglings safely ensconced in carriages and look at us sympathetically.

"Where are your mothers?" they would coo.

"Inside, getting their hair dyed," we would respond. And they would shake their heads in disbelief, their expressions betraying disgust that any mother could leave her child unattended in such cold weather.

Once, an alarmed woman who happened to be passing by saw us sitting outside and marched into the beauty parlor on a crusading hunt for the delinquent mothers.

"Are these anyone's children out here?" she inquired with repugnance to the whole beauty parlor.

Netted, curled, and teased heads turned toward the door to investigate the commotion. My mother and aunt were sitting under the dryers, oblivious to the child advocate's query.

"Carol! Gerri!" the well-coiffed receptionist screamed to my aunt and mother under the dryers. "She wants to know if they're your kids out there in the cold."

"Tell her to mind her own business, unless she wants to take them home with her for a few hours," my aunt responded.

"The cold is good for their resistance," my mother offered.

The chastened champion stormed out of the beauty parlor, "Oh, well, I never . . ."

"Well, you have now," said one of the wags sitting by the front door, her head full of pink curlers wrapped with black netting, and a cigarette hanging out of her mouth.

But on the day of our beach excursion, our mothers must have been getting their hair done without us. An unlikely trio: my father, Denise, and I were packing a cooler full of Mountain Dew, Dr Pepper, and Schaeffer beer and putting it into the red Pontiac, preparing to go to Jones Beach—a special treat, since Riis Park was usually the shore of choice for us Flatbush dwellers. We left Nostrand Avenue on a sparklingly clear July day and made the trek to the suburb of Long Island, the peninsula to which many former Brooklynites fled with hopes of a better life. As kids, we knew it as the place that had the "beach with the big waves."

During the car ride, my father was mostly silent, while Denise and I sat in the back seat, comparing notes on another fast approaching school year. The mere thought of its proximity gave her shivers, while it brought me delight.

"I don't get it," she said. "I can't wait to get out of there, and you go home and *play* school. What's the matter with you?"

"Well, I like playing it with Poppa [our grandfather] because I can be the teacher and tell him what to do. I also get to practice what I learned that day in real school."

"Practice?" she said. "Who wants to practice it? I want to forget about it as soon as I get out of there. You know, you're a little weird. Uncle Eddie, do you ever play school with him?"

My father looked at us in the rearview mirror. "No, that's your Nanny and Poppa's job," he said, and continued driving. Silently, I think he worried about me, too.

When we arrived at the beach, my father scouted out a spot far from the other parents and their screaming kids. If he had to come to the beach, he at least wanted a peaceful site. We spread out our blanket, careful not to kick the dreaded sand on it, and placed our shoes on the corners to hold the blanket down from the brisk wind that had begun to blow. Denise and I wasted no time clamoring that we wanted to go into the water. My father retrieved a green container from the striped beach bag and told us to sit on the blanket. I can still remember the smell of the suntan lotion, Sea & Ski, as he rubbed it on us. My mother swore by Sea & Ski. Even in her absence, my father knew he had better use it, or risk having to explain to my mother blistering shoulders and howling cries later that night. She decreed that it had to be the *green* container, because "that was the only one you could be sure would keep you from burning." My father rubbed the white, familiar-smelling stuff on our backs and shoulders, arms, legs, and stomachs with the determination of a chef greasing soon-to-be-cooked chickens.

"There, that should do it. Let it dry a little while before you go into the water and then I'll put some more on when you come out. Just stay where I can see you."

Sufficiently ultraviolet-basted, Denise and I ran down to the water's edge with our shovels and pails. We played on the shore for a while, building sand castles that collapsed as fast as we could mend them. Finally, no longer able to resist the lure of the foaming surf, we moved slowly into the water, until it reached our navels.

"Edward, this water is freezing," said Denise.

"I know, but it feels good," I said, splashing her, causing her to cringe and then laugh. She had a great smile, made more interesting by her broken two front teeth that formed a perfect, upside-down V. She had broken them while roller-skating and tripping on a cracked concrete sidewalk. I still remember her Confirmation picture that hung in our apartment for years. She wore a red satin, graduation-like gown, supplied by the Church, and a matching skullcap. Her long brown hair hung limply, parted in the middle, with the front cut shorter, "Mary Hartman, Mary Hartman" style. A light smattering of freckles danced on a face displeased at having to smile for the camera. Her smile was forced and stingy, intent on hiding the broken teeth, but it was a futile effort. To this day, it's probably her least favorite picture of herself, followed only by the pictures of her taken at her sister Carol's wedding when she overdid it with the purple eye shadow and red rouge. "What *was* I thinking?" she bellows.

"Let's try to dive into the waves," I said.

"No, let's ride them back to shore," she countered.

As we turned our backs on the sea churning before us, in an unforeseen reversal of gravity, I found my feet in the air and my face on the bottom of the ocean floor. My aquatic somersault left me unmoored, and breathless. I could barely see Denise doing her own circus act—a large and terrifying wave had caught us both unawares. We were pulled under with heart-stopping speed and ferocity, as if inside a boundary-less washing machine. I tried to keep my eyes open, searching for anything familiar, something to hold on to, but there was nothing, no one except Denise. I could feel my beloved cousin enduring the same spin cycle as I.

After we had been violently pushed to the ocean floor, the tide began to take us out. Then the truly acrobatic somersaults began. Pulled out to sea together, miraculously side by side, we were captives of an ocean that had seemingly morphed from washing machine to vacuum cleaner. After tumbling for some time, I remember being thrown against Denise, feeling her flailing body next to mine, and thinking, "At least we're together."

I swallowed water in my fright; my lungs ached; and sand forced my eyes shut. My body stopped resisting, and yielded to what seemed an inevitable ride. No longer feeling Denise next to me, and alone in the cloudy sea, with my consciousness slipping away, I began to give up the fight.

Then I felt them—hands all over me, struggling to take hold. Hands that had so carefully slathered Sea & Ski over my body earlier were now grasping to deliver me from the water. My father lifted me up by the back of my neck, and when I opened my eyes, I saw him holding me by the neck in one hand and Denise by her hair in the other, she and I choking back seawater and tears.

He carried us tenderly back to shore, attempting to hush our cries and soothe our fright. "It's O.K., calm down, you're fine now. Nothing's going to happen. I'm here, it's over." Then he plopped us on the shore like two baby birds that had strayed too far from the nest.

After allowing us some moments to rest and catch our breath, and seeing that we were unharmed, his consoling tone took a holiday. "I told you two to stay closer to the shore, where I could see you! Don't ever do that again. Pack up your stuff. We're going home."

Beneath his anger was obvious relief. As a crowd gathered, the lifeguards at last appeared, asking if they could help, but they were too late. Our unintended foray into the briny deep had ended, and we were packing up with our tails between our legs. It would be some time before I would attempt to spread my nautical wings again, and when I did, it was with a newfound fear of the sea.

I still don't know why my father took us to the beach alone that day, but if someone else had been there instead, the seas may have claimed Denise and me. His presence was essential that day for our survival. It made up for the times when I resented his presence, like the Sunday Bingo nights when my mother would abandon us and take her pennies and markers to the local synagogue with my aunt and grandmother, leaving my brother and me alone with my father, whom we perceived to be a tough negotiator, especially when it came to TV. Sunday was a bad television night anyway, with Walt Disney or Lawrence Welk the only alternatives to my father's cherished sports. I wanted no part of squeaky Mickey Mouse and ballroom music depressed me. Since my father wanted no part of playing "school," what were we to do together?

He also appeared to be sterner than my mother, insisting that we go to bed on time and not creep out from our bedrooms, complaining that our stomachs hurt, and asking, "Could we please have some hot cocoa?"

"You should have thought about that earlier" would come my father's unwavering reply—not mean, just firm.

That day at the beach, though, he came through with a lot more than hot cocoa. The harried concern he revealed betrayed caring feelings not usually visible or accessible. Reared in the tough alleys of Brooklyn, he had learned early that real men don't show their feelings. Because of that cultural indoctrination, I had no way of knowing what he felt about anything, including me. I remember one time asking him, "Dad, how come you never cry?"

"Men don't cry," he said. "And in a few years, you're going to have to stop, too."

I remember thinking sometime later, "Where do the tears go if they're no longer allowed to come out?"

Though we never evolved to having common interests (or television viewing habits), we did learn to respect one another's differences. He allowed me freedom to do what I wanted with my life and to pursue my aspirations, even though he was often doubtful of them. When I finally told him I wanted to be a priest, after years of considering every career imaginable, from being a jockey to a famous actor, he listened quietly, said he didn't think I'd make it, but that he would support me. It was enough.

He also mellowed somewhat as we both matured. I grew to

accept that he loved in his own distinctive way, unspoken and re-moved, but nonetheless heartfelt. While I still wish it were more, he is who he is. Abandoned by both parents by the time he was seventeen, and forced to live alone in a furnished room, where could he have learned the nurturing skills and intimacy that I felt were lacking? It's hard to give what you've never had. Certainly, he has given *me* more than *he* ever received. And I am confident that he still stands ready to pluck me from turbulent seas if they threaten to drown me—just as long as we don't have to talk about it afterward.

Denise remains a kindred spirit with whom I've tumbled many times throughout the years, knees touching, and hands reaching out. She has gotten her teeth fixed and today has an appreciation for education she once lacked. She struggles to pass on that hard-earned lesson to twin boys she hopes will finish college and to a younger son she'd like to see get through grammar school. She re-mains united with me in the hope that survival is always just be-yond the next riptide, if we can manage to hold on long enough.

Denise has had her share of undertows through the years, with a husband who is a recovering alcoholic and a son (one of the twins) who anguishes with Tourette's syndrome. I have tried to be there for her, an ear to listen, and a dinner companion on those infrequent occasions when she can steal away. We still laugh to-gether easily, and reminisce about those times when life seemed simpler and our mothers better coiffed. More important, we help keep each other afloat when the vicissitudes of unexpected tides threaten to pull us under again.

Finally, our day at Jones Beach reminds me of the unantici-pated waves that surprise us all at various times in our lives: a se-rious illness, the ending of a marriage, the loss of a child, the betrayal of a friendship—all threatening to drown us. And how people who care pull us from those waves, sometimes by the scruff of the neck, long after we have given up hope, and lead us gently back to shore, or perhaps simply help to remove the sand from our eyes, until we can once again see more clearly.

CHAPTER THREE

A HEBREW REVELATION

> He came to his native place and taught the people in their synagogue. They were astonished and said, "Where did this man get such wisdom and mighty deeds. Is this not the carpenter's son? Is not his mother named Mary and his brothers James, Joseph, Simon, and Judas? Are not his sisters all with us? Where did this man get all this?" And they took offense at him.
>
> —MATTHEW 13:54–57A

It is not easy for me to write about my father. Though his lifeguard skills are not to be faulted, there is much about him that I don't know or understand. Taciturn by nature, he communicates an air of reserve and privacy that few attempt to break through. Much has gone unspoken over the years, words that perhaps should have been said, but they simply weren't available to him—nor to me.

My mother reasons, "Your father's not a talker. Never has been. He doesn't even talk to me, except maybe after a few glasses of wine."

Perhaps this is why I have a need to write about him—to fill in some of the missing pieces never spoken. I wonder if they ever will be spoken.

The little I know about his childhood comes from his siblings, my Aunt Joan and Uncle Charlie, and the stories told by Aunt Mae (my father's aunt) at family gatherings where alcohol flowed freely, releasing tongues and inhibitions. Before my Aunt Mae died, such holiday gatherings at her apartment proved most reve-latory.

"Well, you know, of course, that your grandmother, Adelaide, was Jewish," Aunt Mae said matter-of-factly one day as I was mix-ing a drink in her narrow kitchen for one of the adults busy con-versing in the living room.

"Jewish?" I said, incredulous. "My father's mother was Jewish? He never told us that."

"Sure. I mean, she eventually converted and became Catholic. But her maiden name was Rubenstein. Can't get much more Jew-ish than that." Aunt Mae laughed with a smoker's cackle, the re-sult of too many years of Parliament 100s.

I ran into the living room and said, "Dad, your mother was Jewish? How come you never told us?"

Even with a few Scotches in him, he didn't welcome this ex-posure.

"Mae!" he shouted to my aunt, who was still cleaning up some glasses in the kitchen. "What are you telling him? Are you crazy?"

"Oh, Eddie," she shouted back, "it's no big deal. What's the harm?"

My Uncle Charlie sat on the couch under an oil painting of a scene from the Battle of Gettysburg that looked as if it had been painted by numbers. It was prescient of the ensuing battle to be waged in the living room of Aunt Mae's apartment.

Uncle Charlie lifted his Scotch (in those days, he was still drinking) and proposed a toast: "To my mother, Jewish, Catholic, but one beautiful woman. And I still . . . miss her."

He then started sobbing uncontrollably. Everything in the room stopped. My father looked down, shaking his head. Aunt Mae came to the doorway of the living room to see what had hap-pened. Surmising that Uncle Charlie was getting melancholic, as sometimes occurred when he drank around the holidays, she put one hand on her hip and produced a sly smile across her pouting pink lips.

She finally said, "Now, Charlie, don't tell me that you never knew either?"

Everyone laughed, even my father and Uncle Charlie, diffusing the tension that had floated in the air, as if deciding which way to turn. And I had one more piece of a puzzle that seemed to grow more Byzantine with each holiday gathering.

Finding out my grandmother, whom I never knew, was Jewish, delighted me. Not only was it information that my father had suppressed, but it was an exotic detail. We had lived among Jewish people in Flatbush our whole lives, but I never imagined that, in some way, I was one of them. They had always seemed so different from us. My mother played mah-jongg with my aunt and four or five Jewish women each week and often came home with tales that made her game partners seem eccentric and foreign.

"Do you know that Molly goes topless in front of her children?" I heard my mother whisper to my father one day.

"Topless?" my father said.

"Yes," my mother assured him. "And the husband takes showers with the children. Disgusting."

What was I to make of this bare-all information? Was this what it meant to be Jewish? It sounded more interesting than our religion. All we had were fully clothed statues and some candles.

"But I have to tell you," my mother continued, "that home is immaculate. You could eat off the floors. But of course, she has help. You could eat off mine, too, if someone came in here every other day and washed them for me . . . I just wish they were as clean about themselves."

Though the remarks were laced with unconscious anti-Semitism, it wasn't vindictive, just ill informed, as most prejudices are. The religious and cultural differences shrouded the Jewish neighbors with a mystique not penetrated merely by socializing, because that occurred frequently enough.

It was always a treat for me when it was my mother's turn to host the Jewish ladies at our apartment for the mah-jongg marathon. Because my mother and her sister (my Aunt Carol) were always served delectable fare at the homes of the Semitic sirens, they needed to match the array of noshing choices when it was their turn to host. My father, my brother, and I were the ancillary beneficiaries. As the peanut cluster chews and pistachio nuts were carefully arranged on silver platters, we would offer to transport them to the card tables arranged in the living room for the impending match. Not all of the eatables made it to the tables. Then when the ladies arrived and the cacophony of clicking tiles began, we were sequestered to the bedroom to await the conclusion of the interfaith council.

I learned a valuable piece of Jewish tradition from one of these women.

"Mrs. Goldstein, I found out my grandmother was Jewish," I quietly reported one evening when she was the first to arrive for the weekly match.

"You vhat, dahlink?"

"Found out my grandmother was Jewish, you know, like you."

"Vell, I'm quite sure she vasn't Jewish like me, dahlink, but who ever told you such a think?"

"My Aunt Mae. She said my grandmother's name was Rubenstein."

Mrs. Goldstein appeared to ponder the implications of the name and its authenticity, then put her hand to her mouth and said, "Vhich grandmother?"

"My father's mother," I replied.

"Vell, dahlink, you know vat that means, don't you?"

"No, Mrs. Goldstein, what does it mean?"

She smiled broadly, revealing a golden incisor that shone brightly. "It means your father is Jewish."

"What?" I asked quickly, sure that I had misunderstood.

"Yep, that's vat it means, dahlink. If your mother vas Jewish, zen you are Jewish."

I was sure she wasn't getting this right, so I said, "But you don't understand. My father is a Catholic. He's been baptized. He goes to Mass and receives communion. He wears a cross."

"Doesn't matter," she shot back, dismissing me with a wave of her hand. "He can practice vhatever religion he vants. Once a Jew, always a Jew."

She had given me something no Gentile ever could have. I decided to save this newly discovered theological pearl for the appropriate moment of disclosure.

That moment came one day as I walked down Flatbush Avenue not far from our home. I was a teenager and had been shopping with some friends at Kings Plaza Mall. I got off the bus and started to walk toward our house, when I passed a coffee shop my family frequented. It was a typical neighborhood joint, selling the *Daily News* and the *Post* and offering breakfast specials for ninety-nine cents that included juice, coffee, eggs, potatoes, and toast. As I passed the large window that flashed a neon Coca-Cola sign, I looked in and saw my father seated at a green and white faux-marble Formica table with a man I had never seen before. My father was dressed in a suit, the attire of his clandestine detective work, while the other man was all in black, including a large black hat that sat on his head like a misshapen sack. He had a beard and long banana curls that extended down his face in front of his ears. Tassled white fringe peeked out from the top of his pants, a sharp contrast to the severe black.

In the street in front of the coffee shop was a dilapidated red Impala with a torn white vinyl roof in which sat a woman in a turban and some kids. I noticed them, because the woman was fanning herself with a newspaper and yelling at the kids in the backseat. "Stop fighting, or when your father comes out here, he's going to give the three of you something to fight about."

When I walked into the coffee shop, the man seated with my father rose from the table and extended his hand to him. My father stood up and shook his hand, and the man turned and walked past me out the door, looking dejected and sullen, like a man who had just found out that the lottery ticket he thought was a winner had missed by one number. My father seemed surprised and embarrassed to see me.

"Hi, Dad," I said. "Who was that?"

Ignoring my question, my father sat back down at the table and picked up the diner-like menu, which had so many choices on it, I used to think I could go there every day for a year and still order something different to eat.

"Do you want something to eat?" he said. "I'm hungry."

"No, I ate at the Plaza. Dad, who was that?"

My father continued looking at the menu, and then, realizing that once I wanted a question answered I was like a dog with a bone, finally said, "Oh. You mean that guy? That's someone I have to arrest later."

My father had been a New York City fireman and then went on to become a fire marshal. Basically, that meant he was a detective for the fire department, investigating arson and often having to arrest suspected arsonists or their accomplices.

"Arrest later!" I practically shouted across the table. "What are you talking about? He was right here! You had him!"

This interchange was severely testing my "NYPD Blue" image of my father throwing someone behind bars for a mere infraction of the law. I knew him to be a tough guy and a well-respected fireman and marshal-detective. So what was this "later" business?

I could tell that he was annoyed with my persistence, and he finally looked up from his menu and said quietly, "Edward, what did you want me to do? Arrest the guy in front of his wife and kids?"

I turned to the window and saw that the red Impala with the woman and children was gone. Then I turned back to look at my father, as if seeing him for the first time, suddenly privy to an aspect I hadn't seen before. Others, whose fathers are policemen, have told me that the "compassionate arrest" is not an uncommon occurrence. My memory of this incident was jogged when the theologian John Shea told a similar story about his own Chicago policeman dad. I remember John saying, "My father passed on faith to me that day." I knew what he meant.

The event in the coffee shop excited me because a layer of my father had surfaced with no smoke screen, no shield of secrecy or modesty. "Where did this man get all this?" [Matthew 13:57] *Isn't this the cabdriver's son?* Catching him in an act of compassion that some may have termed weak or soft was a real coup. He would have never spoken of it; but now there was no denying it. It caught me unawares because for so much of my life he appeared to be the stern one, the disciplinarian who often had to play the bad guy, especially when my mother's leniency threatened anarchy in the house. I took it personally because I perceived him to be particularly stern with me as a result of my iconoclastic tendencies as an adolescent. I felt as if I didn't measure up to his priorities: I wasn't much of an athlete; I didn't like to go fishing; and I liked my hair long instead of in a crew cut. Three strikes and I was out. Yet I wanted so desperately to be "in," but I didn't know how to get there. Now, in a coffee shop on Flatbush Avenue, I saw an aspect of a man that arrested me, not with handcuffs, but with compassion. I almost didn't recognize him. This was the place to which I really wanted entry.

As he was paying the check for the omelet he had ordered, we stood by the cash register in silence while the Pakistani owner doled out my father's change. I saw an opportunity to capitalize on a vulnerable moment. We turned to walk out the door and I looked up at my father and said, "Mrs. Goldstein says you're Jewish because your mother was."

Pausing for the briefest of moments, all he said was "Tell Mrs. Goldstein, if she ever needs someone to sit shiva, she knows who to call."

We walked onto the street and turned toward home. I wasn't exactly sure what his response meant, but I never felt the need to bring it up again.

Sometimes that's how it happens. God uses the people closest to us to reveal things we couldn't learn from any book or theology course. Although I know intellectually that a compassionate response is always more life-giving, and that sometimes it comes from unexpected places, experiencing it that day made me believe it. I suppose the same was true of those who witnessed it in Jesus. The familiarity of those closest to Jesus caused them to dismiss His power and potential. He was too near for them to see it. Not accepted in His native place, He had to go elsewhere to fulfill His mission. Once He left Nazareth, compassion flowed out of Him like an open fire hydrant on a hot day in summer, refreshing those wilted by the swelter of injustice and the torridity of oppression. The familiarity that had bred contempt was transformed into novelty that proved life-giving. Similarly, I needed objective distance from my father to see who he really was, and to be able to drink more fully from the wells that ran deep in him.

In the coffee shop that day I saw more clearly than I ever had before that my father was a righteous man who had always strived to do what is honorable. It was as if he had suddenly moved from the shadows of judgment into the light of undeniable truth. I resented that he hadn't let me see it more often. His unwillingness to reveal salutary aspects of his personality and his hesitancy to be emotive piqued me. Sure, I had glimpsed it our day at the beach when he had saved me from drowning, but it wasn't enough to satisfy my craving. Too often, the emotional distance I perceived made me feel that I had done something wrong, something to cause him disappointment. Although he didn't intend it, it hurt nonetheless.

But occasionally, an unanticipated tear, which he always quickly wiped away and attributed to allergies, would surprise me. It revealed there was more to him than he allowed any of us to see. Or he would do something like that day in the coffee shop on Flatbush Avenue, and it transcended being an isolated, individual act, because it caused *me* to want to act like him. *I* then wanted to cut someone a break. He made me want to be liberator of someone's pain, to release the shackles. It was contagious, a rippling circle. That's what good people do for us—they cause us to be better than we would be without them by modeling for us a superior way of acting and being. And they make us want to get to the place they seem to inhabit so effortlessly. Even a cabdriver's son can do that.

CHAPTER FOUR

STUBBORN POWER

And behold, I am with you always, until the end of time.
—MARK 28:20B

As a quiet rain fell against my bedroom window, my eyes opened and I immediately thought of Nanny, who lay in a hospital room. A week earlier, she had resisted going to the hospital with all of the strength left in her.

Dr. Segal stood by Nanny's Murphy bed in her and my grandfather's one-and-a-half-room apartment and said, "Carol, you cannot stay here anymore. You're too sick. You have to be admitted." He wore a smart business suit and carried the little black bag, obligatory when doctors still made house calls.

"No, I'm not going to any hospital, damn it. Now get the hell out of here and leave me the hell alone! I'll be fine. My husband will take care of me."

"Carrie, Chris can't do it anymore. Your daughters can't do it anymore. You need more help than they can give you. You have—"

"I'm not going, I said, and that's it." She opened her steely blue eyes, revealing an intensity not to be messed with.

"Momma," my mother said, putting her arm on my grandmother's body, which was wrapped in a white sheet like she was being laid out at an Orthodox wake. "You have to go. You'll get better and then you'll be back here in a week or two. Please let . . ."

"If I go in that hospital, I won't be coming home. I'm telling you! I'll die there and it will be all your faults!" She waved her index finger close to my mother's face.

"Come on, Carol," said Dr. Segal. "I'm calling the ambulance now and they'll be here in fifteen minutes. That's it. I'm not giving you the choice. You're going. Chris, pack a bag for her. Girls, you get together whatever you think your mother might need."

My grandmother turned to the wall, angry and defeated. She wasn't going to make it easy for them. When the ambulance arrived and the paramedics tried to put her on the stretcher, she gave them whatever fight she had left.

"Get your hands off of me, you morons! Don't touch me! Chris, you bastard, I'm going to kill you for letting them do this to me! And you two, what kind of daughters allow their own mother to be treated like this?" She wiggled and kicked like a woman who had bugs crawling all over her.

My mother and aunt began to cry softly, their faces turned toward a wall that was filled with chotskas that my grandmother had collected throughout the years. One was a Pluto clock that chimed and stuck its tongue out every hour. Next to him sat Peggy, a favorite doll of my grandmother's; one day I had taken a scissor to Peggy and cut off all her hair. My grandmother chased me down two flights of stairs after that tonsorial mishap.

My grandfather looked confused and heartbroken as he watched his wife struggle with the paramedics. His head moved from side to side in disbelief that this was happening. Previously during their marriage, he had simply done whatever she said, except when he drank, and then he didn't do what anyone said. But now he was a traitor. Although he knew that she had to be admitted to the hospital if there was any hope for her, he felt as if he were siding against the team for which he had always promised to play.

"Hon, please. Stop it," he said. "I'll be going with you. And I'll spend all day at the hospital with you until you can come home. Don't be that way."

She ignored his plea, stubborn in her defeat, remaining turned toward the wall while she lay on the stretcher. Somehow, they had failed to strap her hands, and as they wheeled her out through the narrow corridor to the door, she began grabbing at anything in their path. She pulled down a wooden, freestanding coatrack, which landed on one of the paramedics. "Ouch! Would you calm down, lady?"

"Good for you," she said. "You bastard."

In the hospital they began treating her for a variety of ailments, some of which we were surprised to discover she had. Worst of all was a severe case of diabetes that she had never monitored. It had produced a growth in the corner of one of her eyes, a running sore that resisted healing. She had had it for years and we simply grew accustomed to it as part of her lined face. It had, however, foreshadowed a gradual and irreversible descent into blindness. As kids we missed the seriousness of her failed vision and thought it fun that she couldn't always make us out from a distance.

"Who's there?" she would yell from her chair in the living room, situated close enough to the TV that she could decipher the various characters of her favorite soap opera, "Secret Storm."

"It's Edward. No, it's Chris. No, it's Denise," we would tease, attempting to disguise our voices to confuse her even further.

"Bastards!" she would shout back.

Sometimes she would be leaning out from her third-floor window, resting on two pillows, watching the cars and pedestrians below, and we would sneak in behind her like prowling cats until we were flush with her rear end. Then we would yell or goose her, and she'd jump, startled, and hit her head on the windowsill while we turned and ran out of the apartment giggling.

She'd run after us with her fist clenched in her mouth. "You louses. If I catch you, I'm going to kill you."

Although we tortured the poor woman, our mischievousness was rendered in the name of love. In addition to our antics, there were many tender moments that exhibited that deep bond we felt with her. "I can stand it" was a ritual game we played with her, whereby we would lean against her as she put her arms around us and tickled us.

"I can stand it," we would say quickly, "I can stand it, I can stand it," until we couldn't any longer and we had to break loose from her sturdy grasp. Then it was the next grandchild's turn. The grandchild who could "stand it" for the longest period of time, according to her count, won. She knew each of our weak spots and zeroed in on them like a heat-seeking missile.

Some of our fondest memories were of bus trips she and my grandfather took us on to Sheepshead Bay to eat at Lundy's Restaurant. We would walk along the piers looking at the fishing boats bring in their daily catch.

"Soon you're going to be eating that crab," she would say. "And if they don't cook it enough, it's going to cut your tonsils out with its claw, so you better make sure it's dead."

We would stare back, wide-eyed, not sure what was apocryphal and what was true, because she said everything with the same poker-faced seriousness. Entering the restaurant, she would request a table by the water and proceed to orchestrate the meal, shelling the crabs and lobsters, and then feeding us the delectable crustaceans by hand.

"Here," she would say, "taste this part. It's the sweetest." Then she'd drop the succulent morsel into our mouths, like a mother bird that had found the fattest worm for her young.

Long before the lure of the ersatz casinos and their clanging bells made Atlantic City a gambler's haven, my grandmother and grandfather would take us there to walk on the boardwalk and eat cotton candy and freshwater taffy while the waves of the New Jersey shore lulled us to contentment. My grandmother, a strikingly tall woman with flaming red hair (not her own, of course), would stand at the edge of the boardwalk and stretch out her arms from her sides, like a cop giving traffic signals. Without the lure of any food, pigeons and seagulls would land on her arms, proudly perching themselves as if in the shelter of an old oak tree. I remember looking up at this sight of Nanny, who resembled some kind of beneficent ornithologist, and thinking, "Is she God?" If any of *us* attempted to touch one of the birds, it would retreat or peck at us for our intrusion. Only Nanny had the power.

Where was all that power now as she lay in a hospital bed, looking so helpless, so defeated? I had never seen her like this. As the week passed and she realized her only hope of release was cooperation, her incendiary temper mellowed, though occasionally her formidable discontents made an appearance.

"I'm not eating that crap you're trying to feed me. Get it away from me," she said one day, as she pushed a platter of food so close to the edge of the table that it nearly toppled to the floor.

"But, Mrs. Taraboch," the patient nurse reasoned with a smile, "if you don't eat, you're going to grow weaker, and you'll never be able to go home."

"Yeah, tell it to your sister. Maybe she'll believe you. Or better yet, give it to her to eat."

"Nanny, here, let me," I said. "I'll feed you." I took the utensils and began to spoon-feed my grandmother the applesauce and mashed carrots that looked more like Gerber's baby food than a grown woman's dinner. Obviously hungry, she ate all of it. In retrospect, I was taking my turn feeding the woman who had fed me my whole life, the woman who had nourished me fat with love and determination. I decided I needed to feed her as many meals as possible, so that she would eat and grow stronger.

So on this particular Saturday morning, with rain steadily descending from a gray and ominous firmament, I awoke hearing a clarion call to go to the hospital to feed her breakfast. I could make it in time if I skipped my shower and rode my bicycle fast enough. I dressed quickly, put on an oversized blue Giants football rain poncho, and snuck out of the house. Navigating my black Royce Union through puddles and overflowing sewers, I arrived at the hospital twenty minutes later, wet but undefeated.

When I walked into my grandmother's room, she looked the

worst I had seen her. Her usually coiffed tangerine hair was matted to her head, the result of restlessness and of not being washed in days. Her deeply etched face appeared sallow; her nicotine-stained mouth was open, as she breathed laboredly.

"Nanny, Nanny," I whispered, shaking her slightly to rouse her.

She didn't move, continuing to breathe in gasps.

I went outside and found one of the nurses I had seen caring for her.

"Hi," I said. "I'm Caroline Taraboch's grandson. I came up to feed her breakfast, but she doesn't seem to want to wake up. And she looks really bad."

"Yes, I know, sweetheart. We've done everything we can for her, but I'm afraid your grandmother isn't doing too well. I'm sorry." She touched my shoulder gently. I didn't like it. It felt condescending, not comforting.

Walking back into the room, I pulled the chair close to the bed, feeling helpless. Not ready to say goodbye to her, I tried to will her well. I began thinking about the many ways that her ribald example had encouraged me to retain a distinctive voice, even when others tried to silence it.

"Who cares what they think?" she would say of people whose opinions she dismissed with the wave of a hand. "They're not paying my rent."

She had taught me it was O.K. to be different, to value my instincts, to resist intimidation. "What, did they go to Harvard?" she once said when she thought I was deferring too easily to the opinions of some classmates with whom I disagreed. The student wasn't ready to lose the teacher.

I leaned over the safety railing on the bed and got close to her ear. Grasping onto her arm like a life preserver from which I feared being parted, I said, "Nanny, don't leave."

She opened her eyes, a glimmer of ice blue light on an otherwise pallid countenance.

"I'll never leave," she said clearly and distinctly. "I'm too stubborn."

Then she closed her eyes, her head fell away from me, and she died.

The wake was typically Irish-Catholic in an inebriated, celebratory way, with skilled raconteurs holding court in each corner of the viewing room. My grandmother lay in a coffin too small for her looming frame, in a powder blue dress she would have never worn in life. Lack of money and minimal insurance had dictated a no-frills wake and burial, for which the church was absorbing the total cost. I walked around the room listening to what people were saying about this woman who had made such an impression on all who knew her.

"Dirty Carol, that's what we used to call her," said a woman who had lived across the street on Nostrand Avenue. "She had such a mouth on her, but you know what, she told it like it was. I remember the time she told the butcher in Trunz that he should get a job as a mailman because he certainly couldn't cut meat. I thought he was going to take the cleaver to her."

Ann, a cosmetician from Royal Drug Store, which my grandmother, mother, and aunt had frequented, stood on the right side of the coffin, underneath a heart-shaped bouquet of red roses. She tousled her jet-black hair forward toward her pancake made-up face and smiled a gap-toothed grin with perfectly lined and colored lips.

"Well, *I* loved the fact that she never wore any underwear," she said as she batted her false eyelashes. "And she didn't care who knew it! I just wish I could be as free as she was. Do you know, I would catch her standing over the subway gratings outside of Wolfie's with a smile on her face? And I'd say, 'Carol, what are you doing?' And she'd say, 'I like the breeze.' What a riot she was."

Listening to these and other stories, it suddenly occurred to me that my grandmother had kept her promise. She never left. Her spirit hovered in that room in every story, in every memory, in every heart that refused to relinquish the formative imprint she had left. We were who we were because of her, a presence that was inextricable, indelible, and stubborn.

Isn't this what Resurrection is about for the people left behind: life continuing after death, the person living on in a transformative way? While I believe that the Resurrection of Jesus was both a corporeal and spiritual experience for the disciples, the debate over "bodily Resurrection" doesn't seem relevant when I consider my grandmother. Does it really matter what happened to Jesus' body? He lived on in the hearts and lives of those left behind. Somehow, that's enough for me. "I am with you always, until the end of time" (Mark 28:20B). Period.

While I don't mean to suggest my grandmother's life has had the same impact as Jesus', her lingering spirit also lives on. And while her death was painful because she was no longer present to me in familiar ways, I learned to let her live in another way. And she does. That is the power of Spirit. It is underneath. And it, too, is stubborn.

CHAPTER FIVE

REAL LIFE IS NOT
LIKE COLLEGE

Therefore do not be afraid of them . . . Do not be afraid of those who kill the body but cannot kill the soul; Are not two sparrows sold for a small coin? Yet not one of them falls to the ground without your Father's knowledge. All the hairs of your head are counted. So, do not be afraid; you are worth more than many sparrows.

—MATTHEW 10:26, 28–31

In a commencement address at a Connecticut college, the actress Meryl Streep began her speech by saying, "Remember, real life is not like college. It's like high school."

I went to my high school because its motto was "The Best in Brooklyn." Most of my graduating class from grammar school went to Nazareth High School, a local diocesan school known for its basketball team and average students. Wanting to get as far away from many of them as I could, having no affinity for basketball, and never wanting to be classified as "average," I chose another all-boys' school that required a two-hour round-trip commute from Flatbush, which everyone said would be worth the effort. "It's a college preparatory school. You'll have your pick of colleges. You'll *love* it there." High school defies augury.

I don't remember any good times there. I do remember a lot

of pain. Freshman orientation introduced a class of about 250 students with whom I would share what everyone kept telling me "will be the best years of your life." Early in orientation week I met Philip and Joe, two Italians who had bonded quickly over stories of "gravy" their grandmothers made and comparisons of the pinochle games their relatives played on weekends. I was "the Irish one," blue-eyed and freckled, a definite minority in a school where thick gold chains with evil eye pendants and ceaseless crotch repositioning predominated.

Favored haircuts were John Travolta *Saturday Night Fever* vintage blow backs (though that movie had yet to be released), and wispy mustaches were showcased proudly by any who could. Nylon printed shirts, multicolored with scenes of Venice or distorted Picassolike women, were worn with bell-bottom pants and platform shoes. This was the '70s; "preppy" had yet to make it from Ryan O'Neal's Harvard Yard to the concrete mazes of the high schools of Brooklyn. Studio 54 and disco were the rage. The Odyssey 2001, a dance club in Bay Ridge, Brooklyn, which appeared in the movie *Saturday Night Fever*, was a precursor for many of the clubs that followed. Mary Tyler Moore, Sonny and Cher, and Carol Burnett were reigning supreme in living rooms across America, whose décors were highlighted by plastic slipcovers and lava lamps. I was fourteen years old and had no idea of the lessons in cruelty I would be taught so young.

Having done well academically in grammar school, I was liked by my teachers and presented with the graduating class's English award for outstanding student. Not as well liked by my classmates, I was a loner, prone to reading more books than was deemed healthy for an adolescent and to spending large amounts of time alone in my room pretending I was Sonny singing backup to Cher's contralto (and doing what I considered to be a better job). In short, I worried my parents a lot.

I had been counseled by my parents to be more social in high school, to get involved in more clubs and make new friends, to not be so much of a "pill"—my mother's favorite word to describe me. For her it encompassed everything from my finicky eating habits to my more esoteric, very un-Brooklynlike tastes. She wanted me to fit in more. So I was happy when Philip, Joe, and I became a fast trio, meeting early each morning before class in the auditorium to talk about the absurdity of taking three classes in a foreign language we didn't yet know (a.k.a. language immersion program) and to trade homework assignments from the previous day. During "free periods," we gossiped and played Uno when we should have been studying. Liberated from the watchful eyes of our parents and the teachers in grammar school, we liked feeling more independent, free to make our own schedules, distant enough to do what we weren't allowed. It was the beginning of early adulthood and I ran toward it.

At times I felt excluded from the kinship Philip and Joe seemed to share. Their common Italian heritage and predilection for discussing homemade pizza recipes that had been passed down in their families for generations made me feel like a foreigner in a familiar land. I was the third wheel. Despite Catholic theological claims that the Trinity is the relational perfection we all strive to emulate, my experiences in high school and later as a novice in a class of three cause me to question the veracity of those claims. Three should be left to God, who doesn't have to worry about being left out of a conversation or passed over when only one pair of tickets is available.

Joe wore high platform shoes and had a receding hairline even as a freshman. He spoke with his body, especially his hands, communicating sentences with a shrug of his shoulders and a lateral move of one hand. He would stretch his neck forward in synchronization with his shoulders and hand and say, "*Stugots*," a vulgar Italian punctuation to a thought or emotion that was never in doubt. His mother got breast cancer during our second year in high school and I remember him joking about the "fake boob" she had to wear to feign symmetry. Breast cancer was a rarity then and reconstructive surgery an unheard-of commodity reserved for the wealthy. The stigma surrounding the disease hushed conversation, except in the halls of high school where anything to do with breasts was an occasion for discussion.

Philip was shorter than Joe or me and slightly overweight. He too wore platform shoes—inexpensive ones that he purchased with his father (always a bargain hunter) in Alexander's Department Store. Philip had black curly hair that he rarely bothered to comb and blackheads that he regularly squeezed even in mixed company. He and I would meet on the #9 bus in front of Kearny High School, after I had already taken another bus for twenty minutes from my home in Flatbush. By the time I transferred to his bus, he had completed his algebra homework and was doing additional practice exercises to strengthen his mathematical muscles. While he inexplicably enjoyed mathematics, I would rather have had to read five additional novels than do more math exercises than absolutely necessary. Subsequently, I would guiltlessly copy his precisely executed algebra homework, in exchange for giving him a précis of the short story we were to have read for English class. It was an amicable agreement, contributing to making me a mathematical imbecile and Philip someone who still can't make it through a book that doesn't have the word *text* in the title.

I savored those early morning rides when Joe was absent and Philip and I had the opportunity to converse alone. Once we got to school, I felt an immediate alienation of affection, as the Italian duo were once again hand signaling their way through another *paisano* tale. I would then retreat into a book and wait for any opening to break through this seemingly impenetrable ethnic affinity.

Soon there were more important things to worry about, however. It started slowly with passing comments in the corridors and unwarranted shoves during gym class. Whether our classmates resented our friendship or simply needed targets to release their emerging testosterone, we began to become the recipients of their inchoate macho aggression. One day, as the three of us were sitting in the auditorium between classes, four students walked in and spotted us in the back row. "Hey, don't you guys ever do anything but sit around and talk like little girls," one of them said. "Faggots," said another. Their looks of disgust were frightening. I glanced at Joe and Philip to see their reactions. Joe appeared nervous and embarrassed, not sure what to say, while Philip seemed to be shrugging off the incident as if he'd seen this movie before. I was with Joe, concerned by what had prompted this vitriol and wondering whether we were soon going to have their fists in our faces. Grammar school, with its petty fights and puerile antagonisms, seemed worlds away. While I certainly had had my scrapes there with athletes who mocked my athletic ineptitude and bullies who fought with anyone who preferred books to bats, this was different. These guys were out for blood.

Luckily, a maintenance man who was checking the thermostats in the auditorium walked in at the very moment the foursome was approaching our row. Although his presence diffused the encounter, I knew it was merely a delay in what we would inevitably have to confront.

One day, after homeroom attendance was taken, as we were changing classes in the departmental musical classrooms ritual, I walked into the corridor amidst the sea of other students and saw Philip flanked by two bullies who were harassing him. "Why do you hold your books like a girl?" one said. "You're not supposed to hold your books like that, you're supposed to hold them like this." And with that he pushed the books Philip was gripping to his chest to the floor and they spread out like a deck of cards beneath the feet of the students hurrying to class before the warning bell rang. I walked over to Philip, who was busy gathering the footprinted papers and books from the floor, and bent down to help him retrieve them. When he saw me he said, "Those bastards. They're not going to get away with this." He hurried to class while I meandered pensively to mine.

With each passing week the frequency and intensity of the incidents seemed to increase. While Philip remained the primary target, Joe and I were pulled into the ring as well. Joe became ever more concerned about his crumbling reputation and began to worry about his personal safety. While I had similar feelings, I knew there was little I could do to alter this lynch-mob mentality. I simply began to avoid situations that put me in the path of our nemeses. Joe, on the other hand, began to avoid Philip and me.

Stories of what Philip was enduring told of treatment more severe than the occasional taunts and pushing I was receiving. One day in gym class, twin brothers, who had managed the odd feat of one being handsome and one being ugly, badgered Philip mercilessly. The ugly one got behind Philip in a calisthenics line and powerfully kicked him in the rear end, lurching him forward and causing him to fall flat on his face. Angry and embarrassed, Philip refused all group gym activities after that day, to the dismay of the administrators, who said, "Gym is a requirement in this school." Philip retorted, "So is Christianity, but I don't see you enforcing that." Not bad for a sophomore who was generally deferential to authority figures.

As Joe slowly distanced himself from our once inseparable triumvirate, I felt the pull of loyalty to friendship. I also realized that this wasn't all about Philip. I had no guarantees that alone I would fare any better. Besides, it was comforting to have someone with whom to share the ostracism. In an effort to avoid confrontations, Philip and I began to isolate ourselves, which only served to exacerbate the quickly deteriorating situation. In the mornings we would sit on the step landing of the third floor immediately below the residence of the teaching brothers who lived on the top floor of the school. One day the vice principal, who was a religious brother, passed us on the stairwell in his jacket and tie on the way to his office. He paused on the landing and said, "You know, this isn't going to help you two, hiding here on the stairwell. You should mingle more." He continued down the stairs as Philip and I stared at each other dumbfounded. Was this the best advice the second most powerful administrator in the school could give us? It strangely felt like they, too, were becoming the enemy.

One snowy day a week before Christmas break the situation

erupted. Philip and I were once again sitting in the auditorium, this time with two of our classmates, Bill and Tony, who were in an advanced mathematics class with Philip. I was reading *Wuthering Heights*, captivated by its narrative beauty and the breadth of its romantic sweep. Philip was sitting beside me chattering on about logarithms and fractions with Bill and Tony, until they eventually excused themselves for class. Philip and I remained, graced by another free period, or perhaps cursed. As I was being transported to the miasma of the Yorkshire moors of Emily Brontë, Philip sat next to me fidgeting with some papers shoved sloppily into one of his books, when he suddenly blurted out, "God, we're in trouble!"

I looked up to see two of our malevolent classmates walking toward us down the center aisle of the auditorium. Two other guys were going up the side aisle to our right, thus blocking both exits from the row. Turning around, I saw another two standing in the back of the auditorium, three rows behind us, by the exit doors. My heart started to pound rapidly as I considered the possible scenarios, none of them good.

"What are we going to do?" I said quietly.

Philip was gripping a clear Bic pen just below the chewed top that peeked out from his clenched fist. As the boys came closer, one said, "We're going to get you now, faggot." It was obvious that Philip was their target, but I was in the line of fire by association. What could I do to help him against six gold-chain–laden miscreants? Philip, slow on his feet, sensed the improbability of his escaping the approaching predators. He steeled himself for their pounce, pen held tightly, books strewn on the floor.

He turned to me, lithe and lightweight, and said, "I want you to jump over these rows and run as fast as you can and get help. Go now."

Without thinking I leapt like a gazelle over three rows and ran to the aisle. None of the encroaching bullies made a move to stop me, too preoccupied with their primary target. As I reached the exit of the auditorium, I turned for one final look and saw Philip raise his pen-clenched fist and strike a fierce blow to the arm of one of the guys who had just smacked him across the face. The guy yelled out in pain as I watched his shirt rip and blood begin to spew from his arm.

I ran into a corridor full of students, my eyes flashing like pin-balls from one face to the next in search of an administrator or teacher. I began to shout, "Emergency in the auditorium! Emergency in the auditorium!" Finally I saw a teacher who had heard my cry move toward the auditorium surrounded by curious students. I ran back in to find Philip sitting alone in the same seat in which I had left him, tears washing down his ashen face, one leg trembling uncontrollably. The teacher, who was by now standing next to him, said, "What happened here?"

Philip shook his head in disgust and disbelief and finally said, "The same thing that's been happening to me practically every day since I came to this damn school. And you people couldn't care less."

I later learned that after Philip had stabbed the one boy with the pen, they all became fearful at the escalation of violence and ran with the blood-soaked boy out the exit doors in back. Philip and I issued complaints in the dean's office against the perpetrators, but Philip was the one castigated for using his pen as a weapon and for not reporting the seriousness of the situation earlier. Once again we were made to feel that this was entirely our fault. Finally realizing that the administration was unable or unwilling to help or protect us, we began taking our own safety measures to ensure we weren't caught alone in harm's way. Though things improved slightly once word spread that Philip wielded a mighty pen, we both entered accelerated academic programs that enabled us to graduate in three years instead of the customary four, and we got the hell out of there. And gratefully, despite Ms. Streep's comments, real life has not proven to be like high school.

Real life has, however, caused me to confront some of the issues that Philip and I did in high school. And I am surprised to discover how many other people have also endured similar struggles during adolescence, the repercussions spreading tentacles into later life and relationships. Some of the insecurity I battle today is undoubtedly rooted in those early experiences. I sometimes wonder had they not occurred, would I feel more liberated from sentiments of inadequacy, self-doubt, and inexplicable fear? Though perhaps these feelings originate from many places, they are surely tied to being made to feel that I was never good enough.

Learning to love the parts of myself that have been so long hidden out of shame is no easy feat. The wounding opinions and comments of others have caused deep rivers with beds of resentment and anger to run through the landscape of my life. The sediment of those rivers rises from the bottom in moments of vulnerability to cloud my vision and obfuscate my direction. I have sometimes sabotaged relationships that had the potential of holding deep meaning for me by secretly questioning whether I was deserving of them. I mistakenly believed that all "they" said about me back then might be true.

But not always. In clearer moments, when the sediment remains unstirred and pristine waters refresh the parched land of my self-doubt, I know and act differently. Despite the hecklers and naysayers who threaten to muddy these waters, I feel myself emerge free of residue, unencumbered by the debris that threatens to drown my self-esteem and engulf my status as a loved child of God. I feel strong and alive and invincible. I hear another voice calling me forth, its timbre more resonant, and its pitch more perfect. It sings sweetly that I am cherished and known intimately, its arias lifting me to levels of self-worth I have rarely scaled. The waters from which this voice rises wash over me and I emerge like an athletic swimmer who has gone the distance and been awarded the medal of victory, a victory so sweet its melody echoes in my ears like the words of an old Negro spiritual, "His eye is on the sparrow, so I know he cares for me."

CHAPTER SIX

A PRIEST IN DEED

I have come that they may have life and have it to the full.
—JOHN 10:10B

I was late for an audition that promised to be a big break for me. A vice president for CBS Television was interviewing teenage actors for a pilot they were producing in the fall. My agent had secured an appointment for me after submitting my 8×10 glossy and résumé a week earlier. She relayed that the CBS executive had said I "showed promise."

I arrived at the Essex House Hotel on Central Park out of breath, having raced, with knapsack in tow, from the subway at Columbus Circle to this plush hotel. I inquired at the desk where the auditions were being held, sure that I was going to be herded into a makeshift conference room with three hundred other actors, all doppelgängers for me, vying for the same part.

A diminutive woman with dyed black hair, the color of dull coal, and shiny red lips stood behind the registration desk.

"Audition?" she said. "No, I don't think so. I haven't heard anything about it. Are you sure it's the Essex House?"

I retrieved the information that I had been given by my agent from the mess inside my knapsack and said, "Yes, the person I'm supposed to meet with is George A. This is where I was told it was—the Essex House."

She walked to some files in back of the desk and flipped

through them. Without looking up, she said, "Well, yes, Mr. A. is staying with us, but I don't see anything about an audition. Let me call up to him, sweetheart, and see if I can find out anything for you. What's your name?"

I watched her make the call and seem to acknowledge recognition, nodding her head as she looked over at me. She came back to the desk and said, "Yes, I'm sorry, Mr. A. is expecting you— Room 1012. Take the elevators to your right."

Ascending in the elevator, I wondered what kind of hotel suite could accommodate the actors and staff needed to host an audition. When George A. opened the door to his room, he was dressed in a sweatshirt and exercise pants, hardly the attire of a television executive auditioning actors for the new fall hopeful. He had silver hair, cropped close to his head, and a long, aquiline nose. He sported an L.A. tan, his skin showing the wear of too many poolside deals and convertible freeway cruising. He was George Hamilton on a bad day, minus the hair dye.

"Hi, you found it. Come in. It's great to see you. Mary Ellen has told me some good things about you and sent your info ahead to me. I'm happy to meet you."

As he extended his hand, I felt an immediate discomfort, as if I had caught someone at an inopportune moment and should excuse myself. There was no one else in the room—a standard hotel room with a king-size bed and requisite seating area, behind which loomed a beautiful view of Central Park, alive with joggers and baby carriages with nannies at the helms.

"Did I get the time wrong?" I said. "I thought there was an audition call, but maybe Mary Ellen didn't . . ."

"No, no. I was expecting you. The timing is perfect. I've just finished a long day and now I have time to give you some uninterrupted attention and to go over your stuff with you. Please sit down."

He shut and locked the door; I walked to the windows overlooking the park and sat in one of the chairs by the table. My stomach started to feel queasy as it registered this unusual setting for an audition—an unfamiliar hotel room with a man I had never met. I immediately wanted to leave, but didn't know how to do it gracefully.

"So tell me a bit about what you've done. I have your picture and résumé, but I'd like to hear you tell some of your story in your own words. Tell me a bit of your history, your family, you know, who you are."

He sat in the chair across from me, the small table between us, staring at me, waiting for my response. He leaned forward in the chair, both hands cupped beneath his chin, conveying undivided attention.

Tell him some of my story? This was supposed to be an audition. I perform a short piece, he says, "Thank you very much," and I leave. Was the procedure so different for a television pilot?

"I'm sorry, Mr. A., but . . ."

"George, George."

"Um . . . George, but I thought I just had to read for a part and that's really all I'm prepared to do. I'm sorry if you were told . . ."

"Sure, that's O.K. You can read. Whatever you're comfortable with. I just thought it would be nice to get to know you a little better first."

How could I just sit here and read? No stage, no place to move, no lights to blind me to my evaluator?

"Look, you seem a bit nervous," he said. "Why don't you just take a few moments to get yourself together and relax? It's important I get to see the real you before I can know if you'd be any good for this part. You have these beautiful blue eyes that I'm sure will shoot really well. We may have to bring you out to L.A. for a test and see. Here, let me help you relax a bit."

He got up from his chair and walked behind my chair and put his hands on my shoulders. His hands felt bony and intrusive, as if a hawk had just descended on me without warning. My body froze.

"I have magic fingers and I can release some of the tightness in your neck. You'll feel much better; I promise."

I wasn't feeling better. I was now sure this was unlike any audition I had ever been on, though I certainly had heard about ones like this. *How had my agent, Mary Ellen, gotten me into this? Didn't she check this guy out?*

I stood up. "Mr. A., I'm sorry. But I really need to go. I think you have the wrong . . ."

"I don't think that would be a good move," he said as he stood in front of me, meeting my gaze. "Look . . . I can help you. I have a lot of pull in the television industry. I'm very well connected on the West Coast. All I want to do is just relax a bit with you and unwind after a long day before we get into the work stuff. I promise you can read and I already can tell you have great potential for this part."

He was standing in front of me, blocking the only access to the door, a narrow passageway between the bed and dresser. He put his hands on my shoulders again as I looked down at the floor. I started to shake slightly, frightened I might never get out, newspaper stories of such incidences racing through my head.

In an unsteady, pleading voice, I said, "Please, Mr. A., I'm not the guy for this part. I shouldn't have even come. It's a simple misunderstanding. Please let me go. I won't say anything to anyone, not even Mary Ellen."

"Eddie, you're free to go whenever you want. I'm just trying to tell you, it's in your best interest to stay. And you can tell Mary Ellen and anyone else whatever you want. I can't help it if you're just not right for the role and you're feeling a little sad and angry about that."

I reached down for my knapsack and lifted it from the plush floral carpeting. His arms moved from my shoulders down my back. I pushed his arms away and brushed past him as he sat on the bed to allow me to pass. I unlocked the door and shut it without looking back.

I took the stairs down to the lobby, not wanting to take the chance of another encounter while waiting for the elevator. The woman behind the desk smiled pleasantly as I walked past her, no

clue of the indignity I had just experienced. I walked into the
street with Central Park calling to me as a refuge in the midst of
this unanticipated squall. As soon as I entered the park, I knew exactly where I needed to go.

I sat under the misty spray of the fountain of the Angel of
Bethesda. Tourists walked leisurely, cameras flashed, dogs lapped
the water of the fountain, and slumming bohemian artists stood at
their easels attempting to capture the moment. Behind me was the
lake, with rowboats floating past, lovers nestling together in their
bows, luxuriating in the shadows of the multicolored backdrop of
autumn foliage that framed the lake. This was my favorite spot in
the park. I had always imagined these waters to be healing, like the
biblical waters that sprang up where the Angel of Bethesda
touched down in ancient Israel.

As I sat there, I wondered what I should do. *Clearly, I should
tell my agent, Mary Ellen, what happened, but I was embarrassed. But
what if she sent someone else to this guy? She should know.* I prayed for
guidance and for peace, for a healing spirit from these waters that
I had sat beside so many other times, when absorbing sunshine and
enjoying scenery were my only concerns.

I called Mary Ellen from a pay phone on Fifth Avenue and relayed my afternoon episode. She apologized, assured me she had
no idea, and agreed she would never send anyone to him again. I
asked her not to call him, just to let it alone, and then I walked to
the subway back to Brooklyn.

When I entered the back door of my house, my mother was
standing in the kitchen by the stove making dinner. "You had a
call from that audition you went on. He left his number; he wants
you to call him back. I put it on the table in the dining room."

I felt sick again. I couldn't believe this guy was still bothering
me after our scene in the hotel room. Didn't he realize that I could
make trouble for him? Or did he sense that I was too afraid to do
anything about what had happened?

The paper on the table said: GEORGE A.—PLEASE CALL—and his
number at the Essex House.

"Mom, what did he say when he called?"

My mother stood stirring something; a green Panasonic radio filled the silence of the kitchen, tuned to my mother's favorite station, playing songs from the 1930s and '40s.

"Not much," she said. "He just asked for you and I said you weren't home yet. He said you did well on the audition and that he needed to talk to you further. Why? What's wrong?"

"Oh, nothing. I was just wondering, because I thought it hadn't gone too well. I'm just surprised he called. Where's Dad?"

"He's not home from work yet. He may be late, so we may eat without him. Why don't you go tell your brother dinner's almost ready?"

"Um . . . I have to go out," I said.

"What? What are you talking about? You just got home."

"I know, but I have to take care of something. Please, just let me eat later."

"Edward, where are you going?"

I paused briefly and then said, "I'm going to church. I told Father Zona that I would stop by yesterday and I forgot all about it. I don't want him to think I just forgot about him."

My mother turned to look at me. I sensed she knew that I was making this up as I went along, but she also knew enough to let me go.

"What time are you going to be home here? I'm not going to be cooking dinner and washing dishes until ten o'clock tonight."

"I'll come home as soon as I find out what he wants and we're done talking. Why is it such a big deal? I'll just eat later. God."

I walked out the door knowing I was indeed going to see Father Zona, the first person I thought of when needing to come up with a destination. He was the young associate at the parish who had the long hair and iconoclastic ideas. I had gone to confession to him in the past and was always touched by his warmth and understanding. I had also helped him in projects with the other youths in the parish. One New Year's Eve he invited me to the rectory with about twelve of his close friends to sit in a circle and

pray in the New Year instead of partying with hats and noisemak-
ers. I felt special that he had included me. He was different and
alive, not like most of the other priests I knew. I was confident I
could trust him and that he would receive what I said without
judgment.

We sat in a courtyard behind the rectory on redwood yard furniture under a green umbrella that was no longer needed as dusk
fell. I had interrupted his own dinner but he said it didn't matter.
He sat in a white T-shirt and black jeans smoking Marlboros and
drinking a Scotch as I relayed to him my afternoon tryst from hell.
He listened empathetically, nodding in understanding, touching
my arm when my eyes began to fill with tears, as I sat ashamed at
my stupidity.

He lifted my head up with his hand and said, "Edward, this is
not your fault. You didn't do anything wrong. You went on a
damn audition, for God's sake. This guy is the one who should be
embarrassed. How dare he put you through that."

"I know, but now he's called my house and I'm afraid. What if
he tries to come and find me, or tells my parents something, or . . .
I don't even care about the stupid audition. I just want this guy to
leave me alone."

"You have his phone number, right?" he said.

"Yeah. He's staying at the Essex House Hotel in Manhattan.
He left this message with my mother."

I handed him the piece of paper; he looked at it briefly and
then shoved it into his jeans. "Now I want you to listen to me,"
he said. "I'm going to take care of this."

He took my hands in his and looked at me straight on. "And
you're never going to have to worry about this guy again. I promise. I want you to go home and forget about it. Just put it out of
your mind. But just be more careful where you go the next time.
And tell that ditsy agent of yours to check it out more thoroughly
before she sends you somewhere."

"But what are you going to do?" I said. "What are you going
to say to him?"

"Don't you worry about it. By the time I'm done with this guy, he's going to wish he had stayed on the West Coast. And if he gives me any trouble, I know someone at CBS who will knock this guy out so fast his head will spin. And I'll make sure to tell old Georgie boy that. Believe me, this is over. Go home, and forget about it."

I embraced him and thanked him. I left the courtyard and never heard from George A. again.

In a strange cosmic synchronicity of events for which there is no rational explanation, as I write this piece, my telephone rings. My friend Robert is calling to inform me that Father Jim Zona was found dead this morning in his rectory in Long Island City. He had a massive heart attack at age fifty-one. I am shocked by the news, even more so because he has been so present to me in recent days, as I recalled the above incident. What lesson am I to learn from this?

I attend the funeral and wind up sitting at the end of the pew in the church, next to the coffin that rests in the center aisle. It's so close I can touch it, and do. Here lies this man I have had little contact with in the last twenty years. I've seen him—maybe twice. Once was when he called and invited me to go to the theater with him to see Liv Ullmann in *I Remember Mama,* a musical. We sat in the second row, on the right side of the orchestra. I remember his enthusiasm at seeing this Swedish actress, whom he had long admired in Ingmar Bergman films, come to life on a stage fifty feet from where we sat. He was like a child, glowing with excitement and wonder.

The homilist at the funeral begins by saying, "There's a wonderful scene in *Funny Girl* where Fanny Brice, the Barbra Streisand character, is having it out with her beau, Nick Arnstein, played by Omar Sharif.

"She is fed up with his playboy, philandering ways—while she seems to be doing all the work. 'What do you do, Nicky, tell me what you do?' she asks him.

"He turns to her and says, 'I live, Fanny . . . I live.'

" 'Well, what's so great about that?' she says, 'Everybody does that!'

"Nick Arnstein looks at her and says very simply, 'You're wrong, Fanny. Practically no one does that.' "

The homilist goes on to say that Jim did. He lived fully. As the homilist speaks, emotions well up in me that I didn't know were there; tears begin to stream down my face. Images of Jim linger before me: his first Mass at our parish in his sandals and long hair; absolving my mother in a school yard for using birth control after she had been thrown out of the confessional by another priest; sitting around that New Year's Eve circle as the champagne mixed with holy water; the Essex House debacle; him jumping to his feet for Liv Ullmann's curtain call.

He did indeed live fully. And somehow, he has helped me to as well. I owe part of my priesthood to him. His example and encouragement prompted me to chance this arcane life. I thought that if he could do it, and seemingly be happy, maybe I could too. He also helped me to appreciate that reverencing myself was more precious than garnering acceptance, or some part in a pilot. He stood up for me when I didn't know where else to go, convincing me that I mattered. And he affirmed my instinct to cherish my body and spirit, even when others didn't. He became my Angel of Bethesda, offering me healing waters that refreshed the aridity of my broken spirit.

I miss knowing that he's somewhere out there where I can call him and hear that raucous laugh. I miss knowing that his example of priesthood and manhood is lighting the way for others who may be tempted to mortgage their souls. But for those of us who knew him, there is still light cast by his luminous spirit. There remains the call to live fully whenever we think of his unwavering zest for life. He is somewhere out there, still calling, still laughing, still continuing to mentor me in fully embracing this wondrous life, a life he danced through with such panache.

CHAPTER SEVEN

CHANGE TODAY

*As he was walking by the Sea of Galilee, he saw two brothers,
Simon who is called Peter, and his brother, Andrew, casting a net
into the sea; they were fishermen. He said to them, "Come after
me, and I will make you fishers of men and women." At once, they
left their nets and followed him.*

—MATTHEW 4:18–20

"I'm really sick. I can't go."

"You're going."

"But I feel like I'm going to throw up. I can't. You'll be sorry
when they call you to pick me up. You'll have to come all the way
to the end of Long Island to get me."

"You're going."

O.K., so I wasn't sick, but I might have well been. I certainly
felt like throwing up. The thought of being on a weekend retreat
on some island in the middle of nowhere with forty of my bar-
barian classmates was enough to make my stomach kick. But
my *cri de coeur* went ignored, with my mother roundly dismissing
my malady-driven excuses for skipping the religious soiree. I was
going.

The high school I attended required that all students make a
weekend retreat before graduating. I wanted no part of it. If my
classmates treated me with derision in the secure hallways of the
school, I could only imagine the indignities that awaited me on a

remote island. My only protection would be two token chaperones who would probably be too seduced by the beauty of the idyllic environs to notice any attempt to throw me into Long Island Sound.

Despite my protestations, Friday afternoon found me on a yellow school bus with the above-mentioned forty cretins and two adult vacationers on my way to the east end of Long Island. When we got to Greenport, the bus boarded a ferry that shuttled us across the bay to Shelter Island. Remaining in the bus for the short trip across, we pressed our noses against the windows as the setting sun danced tiredly on the turbid sea and the sloping hills of the now-purple island. By the time we arrived at St. Gabriel's Retreat House, it was dark. We were led into a lounge area and told to take seats. The room was large enough for sixty, with comfortably overstuffed chairs, a few tables, and a lectern. Windows on every side provided a breathtaking view of Ceocles Harbor, by now a dark expanse with twinkling lights framing a perimeter that extended to Rams Head Island on the other side of the harbor.

A man in a black robe with a white heart attached to it walked to the lectern with a lumbering stoop, his torso arriving first with his legs seemingly trying to catch up. He had curly sandy hair and ruddy cheeks, the ruddiness extending down his neck like a nervous rash. He stood silently at the lectern. Taking out a small golf pencil from a folder, he brought it to his nose and began smelling it. We had been given packets on our seats that contained paper and a similar pencil. Finally he spoke.

"You know, these are very special pencils. They are banana wood pencils and you can still smell the banana in the wood. It's amazingly fragrant."

We began retrieving our own pencils from the packets to accompany him in this olfactory exercise. As we smelled the pencils and eyed each other inquisitively, it soon became apparent to us that wood and lead were the only scents emanating from the writing implements. A bunch of pencil-mustached suckers. When I looked up at the black-robed priest, he was laughing so hard, his face was red and his body was bouncing in spasms of laughter. We had a jokester on our hands.

After laying down the rules for the weekend, he led us outside to a small chapel set on a hill about fifty yards from the retreat house. A beautiful white-shingled building, it had a pitched roof and a steeple with a carved metal cross looming above the entrance. The stained-glass windows, illumined from the inside by dim lights, emanated soft blues and reds onto the black lawn. As we filed in the front door of this edifice that resembled a Currier & Ives etching, I wondered how many other kids had made the unlikely passage through this portal. It felt like we were entering a place that held its own holy secrets, perhaps whispered in the prayers and yearnings of others who had traversed this doorway—kids my age praying to a God they needed to know loved them. I was now part of that prayer.

We were told to lie down on the floor of the sanctuary. This was a first for me in church. Kneeling, standing, sitting, yes—but lying down? The priest told us to close our eyes as soft music began to float from the stereo speakers positioned throughout the chapel. And then he took us to a place I had never been. With a serious and resonant voice, hardly the comedian any longer, the banana-pencil-smelling priest asked us to imagine a place of beauty and peace that was totally ours, a place containing whatever we wanted, whatever made us feel most at home, most safe, most loved, most alive—our paradisal Eden. And then he introduced us to God in this place. The priest told us to silently speak with God about whatever was on our minds and in our hearts, just as we would with someone close to us. And so I spoke with God as if He was my best friend, sitting on the floor of my bedroom after a winning baseball game (or, in my case, losing game). I told Him about my struggles in school, my concerns about my future, and about my raging hormones. God had never been more real, or more understanding.

Each event of the weekend seemed to surpass the previous one. In small group discussions, hardened classmates, who had slammed me into lockers just for the fun of it, were now crying openly about parents who abused them and girlfriends with whom they felt pressured to have sex. During a penance service, after asking forgiveness for unspeakable transgressions, these guys were hugging the priests who had helped to untie knots that had held them captive. And then they embraced anyone else available in the path back to their seats. What kind of magic did these guys with the black robes wield? I wanted to revel in their sorcery for just a bit longer.

When I left St. Gabriel's on Sunday afternoon, I took a part of it and the black-robed religious with me. Graduating from high school that year, in 1976, I proceeded with my plan to study theater arts at Brooklyn College and to work on Wall Street full-time in a brokerage firm. It was not a good beginning. Externally, my life seemed to be racing on the fast track toward success and fulfillment of my dreams. Internally, I felt empty.

After a full morning of classes, I would take the #4 subway train at the junction in Flatbush to Bowling Green in Manhattan. While walking to the plush offices of Bear Stearns on Water Street, I often passed homeless people sitting on the subway gratings to keep warm.

"Change today?" one would say. "Change today?"

I usually hurried to the deadening monochrome of the office building, attempting to drown out the pleas with soundproofed windows that looked out upon a city that appeared more forgiving from fifty-two floors up. Once inside the money-producing monolith, I busied myself with my job of clearing the option trades that had been made on the exchange that day, but I remained curiously detached from the rising and falling numbers I systematically charted. Frequently, my mind drifted back to the streets, back to the subway gratings, and to the calls for "change."

In February of my first year of college, I was walking to work as a snowstorm was beginning to descend with fury on a gray and already desolate Manhattan. When I rounded the corner where Delmonico's Restaurant loomed as the bastion of noontime power

lunches, there sat Smiley, one of the homeless men I passed periodically on my daily treks to and from the subway. I had stopped
to talk to him a few times, learning he still had family in Alabama
he hoped to see again one day. He spoke of a daughter he hadn't
seen since she was five days old and of a brother he had slashed
with a knife for stealing money from him while Smiley slept in the
barn they shared as a bedroom.

"Edward, how you doin'?" he said. "Change today?"

I stopped with the snow swirling around me in a blinding
whirlwind. His words hit me like an avalanche. For the first time,
I heard them, not as a request for money, but as a command for
altering my life. Change today. *I* had to change, or this world of
greed-inducing numbers and the trading of stocks, wives, and
worst of all, dreams, would surely consume me.

I rummaged in my pocket for whatever money I had, gave it
to Smiley, shook his hand, and said, "Thanks, Smiley. Thanks a
whole bunch. You better get out of this cold, though, before this
snow buries you. Why don't you go to the Port Authority or
something?"

"Edward, if I go to the Port Authority, all I think about is going somewhere else but here. So, until I'm ready to get on one of
those buses myself, I ain't going there. But don't you worry none.
I'll be fine."

That was the last time I ever saw him. I like to imagine that he
took my advice and went to the Port Authority and got on a bus to
somewhere else. But even if he didn't leave, I knew that I had to.

Later in that week I called St. Gabriel's Retreat House, eight
months after my memorable retreat.

"Hello, St. Gabriel's."

It was a familiar male voice, sounding vaguely like one of the
priests I had met on the weekend retreat.

"Hi, um, my name is Edward Beck and I made a retreat there
last year with my high school and it was a really great experience
and I was just wondering if there was any way of reconnecting
with the place because I was so impressed with it."

"You mean you'd like to make another retreat?"

"Well, no, not exactly. I guess I was just wondering if maybe you have some kind of follow-up programs or something for people who may want to continue the experience, or just come back again and maybe . . ."

"Why don't you come out this weekend?"

"You mean like in two days from now?"

"Yes . . . isn't that why you're calling?"

"Well, yes, but you see I have this Duster for a car and it's been not running well recently, and I just don't know if it would make it all the way out there and back, so it might . . ."

"Didn't you ever hear of the Long Island Rail Road? It's a great ride and they take you right to the ferry. We'll see you this weekend. What was your name again?"

"Edward . . . Edward Beck . . . But I don't know if . . ."

"See you then, Edward."

And before I could say anything else, he hung up the phone.

What could I do? After all, I had called him. I convinced myself it might not be too bad. I could just blend in with whatever group was on retreat and have a quiet weekend for myself in a beautiful spot. It would also give me the opportunity to sort out what I wanted to do with my life.

Friday afternoon found me in Pennsylvania Station boarding a Long Island Rail Road train to Greenport. When I arrived at the same ferry that I had ridden on eight months before with my classmates, I felt a connection I couldn't quite articulate. Strangely, it felt as though I was going home. I stood on the ferry, with an icy wind lashing against my cheeks and spray from the water coating my eyebrows and eyelashes with frost. A Carly Simon song, "Never Been Gone," played in my head: "Seagulls cry and the hills are green. And my friends are waiting for me. Miles from nowhere, so small at last, in between the sky and the sea. I'm bound for the island. The tide is with me . . . I'm going home. And it feels like I've never been gone."

When the ferry arrived at Shelter Island, the banana-pencil

priest was waiting in a green station wagon to pick me up and drive me to the retreat house.

As we drove along Route 114 on this tiny island, he turned to me when we passed George's IGA Supermarket not far from the retreat house and said, "Did I mention to you on the phone that there's no retreat on this weekend?"

"No retreat? No, um . . . I wasn't even sure it was you on the phone."

"Oh, well, it's just that it's a free weekend for us, so it will just be you and the Passionists who live here for the weekend. You'll have us all to yourself."

My stomach bubbled like a watercooler. *What had I gotten myself into? What was I going to do with four priests and a brother on an island for a whole weekend?*

"Well, that's great. It will be nice to get to know you guys a little better. I'm not sure, by the way, if I can stay till Sunday. I may have to leave tomorrow afternoon, because my aunt needs help moving. But I'll know after I call home in the morning. My parents are working on getting someone else to help." It was the quickest safety net excuse I could fabricate, just in case I had to hightail it out of there.

"I'm sure it will work out," he said. "It's a long trip for just one day. And I think you're supposed to be here." *Why?*

The weekend was ordinary, unremarkable, yet perhaps the most significant of my life. For a few days, I simply shared the life of these men. I ate with them, prayed with them, helped them to clean the kitchen, played cards, watched TV, and—I watched them. I observed them intently, every move, every nuance. In some ways, the veil of mystery was lifted. Out of their black robes, they seemed like ordinary guys who sometimes used foul language and seemed to have the same inconsistencies as the rest of us. But there was another veil less opaque, yet still discernible. Something was different about them that I couldn't quite put my finger on. They carried peace around with them like a mother who comfortably straddles an infant on her hip. Content with the familiar rhythms of their lives, they weren't in a hurry to get anywhere. It was O.K. to simply be where they were, so unlike the people on Wall Street and the theater people I knew, who lived rushing to get to someplace else as if it might hold more promise or fulfillment. Not impressed with the striving peripatetic existences that surrounded me, I longed for what these priests and brothers had instead. But I didn't know how to get it.

Of course, I stayed the whole weekend. Sunday afternoon found me sitting alone in the same lounge of the retreat house that I had sat in months before with my classmates. As the sun set over Coecles Harbor, I sat facing water that was calm as a skating rink. A crucifix hung on the wall between the windows, and I found myself staring at it as the room turned tawny gold. My eyes filled with tears, to which I cannot attach simply one emotion. I felt so full. I looked at the crucifix and audibly said, "O.K., yes, O.K.," without fully knowing at the time what my words meant or how my life would be transformed.

As the priest drove me back to the ferry on Sunday evening for my trip home, he said, "So have you ever thought about doing something like this with your life?"

"Something like what?" I said.

"Like this, like what we do. Make a difference in the lives of people, serve God."

"No, no, I haven't. I'm pretty set with what I'm going to do. But thanks for asking."

"Oh," he said. And that was all he said: "Oh."

I left the island and went back to my world of numbers, school, and auditions, but his words reverberated like a haunting mantra: "So did you ever think about doing this with your life, did you ever think about doing this with your life . . . ?" They were like the resounding words, "Lowenstein, Lowenstein," that Tom Wingo hears in the Pat Conroy novel *Prince of Tides* when he leaves behind his life in New York and is driving home over the bridge in South Carolina, ready to start a new life with his family. "And I said it like a prayer," he says.

By April of that year, I was calling the priest at St. Gabriel's again, this time to ask what would be entailed if *maybe*, someday in the future, I were to *possibly* think about doing "something like this with my life." By the following September, I was transferring colleges and moving to a state I had never visited, to live in a house I had never seen, with guys whom I had never met, to discern if *maybe* I was being called to be a Passionist and to do "something like this with my life."

I used to think that if I hadn't joined religious life and hadn't become a priest, God would have been mad, or at the very least, disappointed. I don't think that anymore. I think I could have chosen to be a truck driver and God would have been just fine with it (my mother, I'm not so sure about). Don't get me wrong; I think God is happy that I've chosen to do this with my life, but something else may have been just as tickling. The requisite is my happiness and my ability to contribute to the happiness of others. I think that's what gets God to do back flips. *How* that happens is relatively immaterial to God.

Of course, this questions the notion of vocational call and discernment, as we understand it. We consistently employ language that betrays an understanding that God calls certain people specifically to a religious vocation. "When did you receive your calling?" is a question I am often asked. I like to respond, "I'm still receiving it." The calling is to fullness of life and to facilitating fullness of life to flourish. For me, that happens to be as a religious and priest. I know that from my experience of doing it. But it's not the only way I could have done it—though I'm certain that Wall Street wouldn't have been a way. For me to have stayed there *would* have made God sad, to say nothing of how I may have felt.

The call by the lake that Simon and Andrew received from Jesus was a call to discipleship and a call to be "fishers of men and women." All of us receive the same call today, no matter how we choose to live it. Truck drivers and mailpersons unite. Like Simon and Andrew, I got my call by the water, too. The nets I left behind to pursue that call were ones that had entangled my life in

destructive and selfish ways. Leaving them behind freed me to follow in a way not possible while tethered in their web. But "Come
follow me" weren't words I heard once, and then the path was set.
I keep hearing them. And now there are other nets from which I
must cut myself loose.

CHAPTER EIGHT

GOD IS FRIENDSHIP

> *God is love, and whoever abides in love abides in God and God in him/her.*
>
> —JOHN 4:16

"Y ou've got to come hear this deacon preach. He's really terrific." The year was 1977 and my parents were still giving advice. I had just turned seventeen and had begun my first year at Brooklyn College. Attending classes in the morning and then traveling to Wall Street in Manhattan to work all afternoon and evening was taxing, though being sent home by the firm in a private car after working late made me feel like a Wall Street whiz kid. My disenchantment with the Wall Street ethos was increasing, however. Even as a teenager, I perceived that fidelity to making money at any cost and infidelity to one's spouse whenever possible was a skewed worldview.

My disenchantment with the institutional Church had set in even earlier. Eleven years of enforced Catholic school religion had caused me to long for something more than rules. Although I continued to attend Mass on Sundays, it had begun to feel like excessive verbiage with little heart. I longed for a more intimate community and a less structured religion. Although I deeply wanted to be connected to God, I didn't feel that connection in the Church.

Perhaps my dissatisfaction had begun even earlier. I had been an altar boy through grammar school, often having to rise at 5:30 A.M. to serve a 6:30 A.M. Mass. (One consolation was getting called out of class to serve funerals, hoping that the grieving families weren't too distraught to remember to tip us altar boys $5.00 for missing math class.) But the enforced routine of frequent serving, along with having to attend precisely to unbending rubrics, took their toll, and I grew numb, even to the Eucharist, which I was told was supposed to be the high point of my religious experience.

I almost didn't make it to the altar anyway. The requirements to be an altar boy were surprisingly stringent when I was in the fifth grade. Although my parents and teachers assured me that serving as an altar boy would be "good for me and bring me closer to God," they failed to mention that I'd have to pass two written tests and one practicum exam before I could *get* "closer to God."

"Why do I have to take a test to serve God?" I asked. "I thought He loves me no matter what grade I get."

Mrs. Holz, my fifth-grade teacher, who slicked her hair back like a '50s greaser and had the gait of a football player, said, "Well, of course, He does, dear, but He loves you even more when you don't embarrass Him at His holy altar."

After studying for weeks the names of various liturgical paraphernalia and learning the Latin terms for sundry ecclesiastical accoutrements, I and about thirty-five other students took the first part of the written test. We sat in the pews of St. Vincent Ferrer Church in Brooklyn and were monitored by a balding, uptight priest assigned to train the altar boys. Peering over his round, wire, priestly glasses, he said, "Any attempt to look at your neighbor's paper will be immediate disqualification—and a sin." *What wasn't a sin?*

Three days later the results were posted on a bulletin board in the vestibule of the church where two lists hung alphabetically: Passes and Failures. My name headed the pack of the latter. "69" might have well been flashing in neon next to my name, when "70" was needed to pass. One measly point had made me a "Fail-ure," a classification not missed by my mother, who stood beside me and said, "That's terrible. He could have at least let you know before posting it for the whole world to see . . . And why did you only get a '69' anyway?"

Luckily, I passed the second part of the exam and the practicum with a healthy margin, and when the final list of new servers was posted on the same bulletin board two weeks later, my name was included. Thus my parents and I were spared the public embarrassment of my flunking out of "Altar Boy 101."

Many years later I was watching a newsmagazine show on television, when an image and name flashed on the screen that I immediately recognized. It was the priest assigned to train the altar boys and who had administered the qualifying exam. He was on trial in Florida for sexually molesting young boys, after having already been convicted once and sentenced to twenty years in prison. I considered myself fortunate to have received only a failing grade from him.

St. Vincent Ferrer was the church in which my parents still worshipped when I began college. It was here that the young deacon, who they said preached so charismatically and whom they had encouraged me to hear, was assigned. I had begun going to other Catholic churches for variety, often attending Mass at the historic St. Elizabeth Ann Seton, in the Wall Street area, or at Our Lady Help of Christians, a small church in Brooklyn to which I was attracted because of its intimate setting and an engaging priest who moonlighted as chaplain to the New York Mets baseball team. But St. Vincent Ferrer remained my parish and held ties not easily severed. I had attended grammar school there for eight years and it felt like home. After agreeing to meet my parents there for a Saturday evening Vigil Mass on Halloween weekend, I was eager to hear the deacon about whom they had spoken so effusively.

As we sat near the back of the church, the Mass began with Father Jim Zona presiding. (He was the young priest with the long hair and unorthodox ways whom I had gone to see when the Essex House debacle reared its head.) The cantor for the Mass was an anachronistic, heavy-set, guitar-playing alto, whose long brown hair cascaded down her back, like that of the many flower children of the '60s. A churchy Joan Baez, she sang with the religious fervor of one who revered the transcendent nature of the gathering. With a yellow peace button attached to the strap of her guitar, and Birkenstock sandals on her measure-tapping feet, she led us in singing the treacly folk song "Sons of God." (Inclusive language had not yet made its way into our Roman Catholic liturgy.) "Sons of God, hear his holy word. Gather round the table of the Lord."

Father Zona announced we would be having a guest homilist, our deacon. An unfamiliar voice full of youth and resonance began to read the Gospel. It was hard to see from the back with everyone standing, but the reader appeared to be short with curly blond hair and a pleasing, open face. I don't remember which Gospel he read, but I remember clearly what happened next: the whole church burst into laughter and applause. The young deacon had donned a rubber Halloween horror mask. Standing prominently at the pulpit, he began his homily with the mask intact. As the church quieted, he slowly removed it and then gave an inspired homily about the masks we wear in our lives and about God's desire to help us peel them off so that our true selves may be revealed. It was a masterful blending of the secular Halloween celebration and the religious Eucharist we were gathered to memorialize. More important, he was funny, articulate, and real, enlivening what was often a deadly juncture in the liturgy.

As we filed out the doors of the church, my parents looked at me expectantly, awaiting my appraisal.

I finally said, "You were right. He's very good. I liked him. I just wish there were more like him."

"Ah, you're all talk," my mother said as she waved her hand dismissively.

We rode home in the car in silence while I pondered the ambiguous response of my mother and remained preoccupied with the preacher, who had made an indelible impression.

Months later, after reconnecting with St. Gabriel's at Shelter Island, I discovered that the young deacon was a member of the Passionist community, who ran the retreat house. After my memorable return weekend and innumerable consults with family and friends, and a lot of hand wringing, I found myself in the Rectory of St. Vincent Ferrer requesting a letter of recommendation from my pastor to the Passionist seminary in Worcester, Massachusetts. I had decided it was time to put some of the "talk" my mother chastised into action. Though I had considered a religious vocation earlier in grammar school, by eighth grade I had abandoned seriously pursuing it. Fame and fortune seemed sexier. But my retreat at Shelter Island and my introduction to priests and brothers with whom I could identify had resurrected the appeal of a religious vocation. Its allure reignited, I moved on instinct.

While I was waiting for the pastor in the Rectory, the blond-haired deacon passed by and saw me waiting.

He extended his hand and smiled. "Hi, I'm Bob. I hear you're thinking about joining us."

"Yes," I said. "That's . . . if I get accepted. I think I'd like to enter the seminary next fall and transfer to college up there."

"I'm sure you'd like it if you decide to give it a shot," he said. "Hey, if *I* can make it, you can. It'd be great to have you."

Another Passionist priest appeared behind him, an older man who had come to St. Vincent's every year for as long as I could remember to give the traditional Lenten mission. A kindly gentleman, he preached on the tip of his toes, accentuating the word *God* with a Bostonian accent and an actor's flair. There was hellfire and brimstone in his message, but softness in his heart. (My mother might take issue with this assessment, as he was the priest who had angrily refused her absolution that day when she had confessed to using birth control.)

"So," he said, "you're the new recruit. Wonderful. I've lived this life for forty years and I thank *'Gawd'* for it every day. I'm so happy to be a Passionist. And look at Bobby here. Doesn't he look happy?"

Robert rolled his eyes and smiled. "Most of the time, Leander, most of the time." I left the rectory with my letter of recommendation in hand and my heart in my mouth, wondering if I could really do this.

April of that year found me accepted to the Passionist seminary and beginning to disengage from my life of Wall Street and theater, and everything else that had become familiar. The following month I and 150 other parishioners boarded three buses that St. Vincent Ferrer had chartered to attend Robert's ordination to the priesthood. In an inspiring ceremony, the bishop rubbed the holy oils into the hands of Robert and his four classmates, and then more than one hundred concelebrating priests laid hands on their heads, invoking the Spirit to descend upon the ordinandi. The mystery and majesty of the Church were on full display with incense smoking, trumpets blaring, and choirs lifting their voices in jubilant praise, all drawing me deeper into the calling I had begun to hear in the guarded lockbox of my heart. I tried to imagine myself one day kneeling in front of the bishop, and all those priestly hands being laid on my head. I couldn't conceive I'd ever make it that far.

When I arrived in Massachusetts to begin my studies, and was informed I had to choose a "spiritual director," I requested Robert, who, in his first assignment, had been conveniently stationed only an hour away in West Springfield. My formation director counseled me to choose someone "more seasoned," but I was tenacious. Robert and I began to meet monthly to talk about my prayer and my blossoming relationship with God. Often we would walk on the property of Spencer Abbey, a Trappist monastery not far from the Passionist Residence. There was a beautiful fieldstone church and monastery surrounded by fifty acres of land, where the fall colors of rolling fields framed by mountains created an agrarian kaleidoscope that variegated with each movement of the light. The sound of the wind as it rushed through the valleys, carrying the chants of the monks observing the liturgical hours in their stark chapel, was haunting. It was the perfect place to discuss the call of God I was discerning in my heart.

"I just don't know if I'm cut out to do this," I said one day as we walked down a pebble path not far from the monastery.

"What makes you say that?" asked Robert.

"I don't know. I don't feel holy enough. I look at some of you and I think, 'I'll never be that.' "

"I do the same thing, though, Edward, and I'm already ordained."

"Yeah, but it's different. Sometimes I feel like God is saying to me, 'You've got to be kidding. Go back to New York and resume your life. You'll never make it.' It's as if I'm pretending I can do this, but soon I'm going to be found out." The monastery church bells tolled in the distance.

"But, Edward, we're all pretending, all the time. The secret is to ask God to help us to pretend less, to gradually become more our true selves. That's what conversion is. But it's a lifelong process. Give yourself a break, Edward. You're just starting out."

"But what if I never get there?" I said. "What if I *never* feel worthy enough to embrace this vocation?"

"Then, I'd say, you'll probably wind up being a great Passionist. Because if we ever feel totally worthy of it, maybe we *should* say goodbye to it." He stopped walking, looked at me, and put his hands on my shoulders. "Please don't be so hard on yourself. Try to see yourself as God sees you, and as I see you. If you can do that, you'll realize you're exactly where you're supposed to be."

I wanted to trust what he said. The God who seemed present in the landscape also seemed to be speaking through Robert, whose conversance with the deeper world of Spirit encouraged me to go there as well. His laughter, his understanding, his non-judgmental listening, all communicated a God who accepted me as I was—a God I began to slowly trust. Up to that point, my relationship with God had been rather formal: I said my prayers, kept the rules, and expected the results. But Robert and I talked about a different God, one who wanted to befriend me, and one who wanted a deeply personal relationship with me. He introduced me to a God I could wrap my arms around.

Robert remained my spiritual director during my three years in the Residence in Worcester, but when I left to continue my studies at the monastery in West Hartford, that relationship ended and another began. The spiritual foundation of our relationship had paved the way for a vital friendship. In retrospect, it was an ideal path for any friendship to have taken. Soul friends require affinity with each other's souls, and Robert and I had been graced early with the opportunity to make that acquaintance. And we have been graced with many years since to allow it to deepen.

Now spanning twenty-three years, my friendship with Robert has, of course, not always been idyllic. Moments of anger and hostility and occasions of misunderstanding and lack of communication have, at times, contributed to making God feel as far away as a Caribbean island in the middle of a winter blizzard. But when those experiences have been endured successfully with grace, the bond has emerged as sturdier, unbroken by the vicissitudes of circumstances and fluctuating temperaments. The moments of the heightened awareness of God's presence and activity have simply been more durable. Sitting in a nursing home with Robert while visiting his mother, who was debilitated by Alzheimer's disease; my preaching the funeral Masses of both of Robert's parents; his vesting me when I was ordained a priest; his being my primary support during my mother's brain surgery and subsequent convalescence. These were turning points in my life when our deep friendship shone like a beacon illumining the way home. These were moments when God became tangible for me, when I tasted fully just how loved I am.

I've come to realize that intimate friendship is imperative for my life as a celibate. Being known, accepted, and loved—warts and all—is salubrious for my spirit. And it's an indispensable reflection of the way God loves me. My friends have been my most prodigious gift because they've enabled me to see what is often invisible: transformative love rooted in a power beyond my understanding. The twelfth-century monk Aelred of Rievaulx, in an arresting reinterpretation of the text from the letter of John, writes, "God is friendship and the one who abides in friendship abides in God" *(Treatise on Spiritual Friendship)*. That's pretty powerful stuff. It's theology I can touch, positioning God in the midst of my human experience of friendship. The love of God and the love of friends are one, says Aelred. And even though friendship may not always feel Divine, at its heart is the pulsating power of a love that is boundless if I play it right.

If I hadn't accepted my parents' invitation years ago to go and hear the young deacon preach, I might never have met Robert, and subsequently, I might never have become a Passionist. It's that tenuous, and that easily missed. The people who have enriched my life have often been my way to God. If I had passed them by, I'd have missed aspects of the face of God that provided texture and depth to an otherwise potentially superficial existence. Love is of God. Fragile as that love may be at times, were it absent in my life, I would know God less.

CHAPTER NINE

POVERTY, CHASTITY, OBEDIENCE . . . AND PETTINESS, TOO

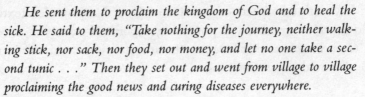

He sent them to proclaim the kingdom of God and to heal the
sick. He said to them, "Take nothing for the journey, neither walk-
ing stick, nor sack, nor food, nor money, and let no one take a sec-
ond tunic . . . ." Then they set out and went from village to village
proclaiming the good news and curing diseases everywhere.

—LUKE 9:2–6

It was supposed to be the happiest day of my life. One year and
a day had been spent preparing. This was, finally, the culmination of months of prayer, study, and washing of bathroom sinks. I
was to take my first vows as a Passionist, thus advancing from the
plebeian status of novice to the venerated one of professed religious. I would say yes to being poor, chaste, and obedient and also
to keeping alive the memory of the Passion of Jesus, our fourth
vow. Although it might not sound like the most scintillating way
to spend one's life, it was what I wanted. While it surprised some
who knew me as a *bon vivant* of the New York theater scene or as
the kid who would one day take Wall Street by storm, I sensed religious life was right for me. Despite some glaring contradictions,
it fitted me like a warm mantle.

I had two classmates, who had exclusively bonded with each
other early in the novitiate year, leaving me to fend for myself.

Not that I minded, but it became tricky when we needed to work together as a class. The planning of liturgical ceremonies and the waxing of the monastery corridors became "group-building" exercises that built little more than resentment. Having previously huddled to plan their strategies, often my classmates outvoted me and we wound up doing things their way. Two against one became a theme of the year.

I was determined not to let this happen with the planning of our vows ceremony. This was to be as much my ceremony as theirs and I was resolved to have equal say in the planning. We had prepared and studied for this day all year, and I wasn't going to be railroaded this time. When we met in the novices' recreation room for our initial meeting, the topic was music and I was armed for combat.

"Well, I'd like to have a mix of traditional and modern music in the ceremony," said John, one of my classmates, a diminutive man who walked like a penguin. "After all, there'll be a lot of people there who won't appreciate guitar stuff." He sat smugly stroking a beard that made him look more like a little rabbi than a soon-to-be Catholic religious.

"Yeah, I agree with that," said Don, my other classmate, a portly fellow with hair like disheveled hay.

"Well, I'm not opposed to having a mix of music," I said, "but a friend of mine who plays the guitar has offered to play during the ceremony and I'd like to have her participate. She plays and sings beautifully."

"Who's that?" asked John.

"Joanne," I said. "She's worked on a lot of the retreats next door and everyone raves about her music."

"I just thought we'd keep it simple," said John, "and have the retreat house organist play, and use their cantor. We don't want to make it a big production. After all, it's only first vows."

"I know what vows we're taking, John. I've been at this the same amount of time as you. I still think we can make the ceremony as beautiful as possible, and music is part of that." I was trying to keep my cool, but felt my face beginning to flush.

Don, who had been silent up to this point, finally said, "Well, maybe we could have Joanne sing *one* song. That would get her to participate but still not overdo it."

"What do you mean *overdo* it? I don't want her to come and just sit on the side until she does her token number. That doesn't make any sense. She should participate in the whole service with the other musicians."

"Well, she is *your* friend, Edward. Don and I don't even know her. Why would *we* want her?"

"Maybe because *I* am part of this class, too. And I should have some input into what my vows ceremony is like. I don't think that's asking too much, especially since you two have gotten your way with most of what we've done the entire year." I took a breath and then said calmly, "Look, Joanne is going to play, and it's not negotiable. Now, hopefully we can work out what she'll play and how much."

Silence descended on the room like a heavy blanket, with the ticking of the cuckoo clock on the wall the only sound. My persistence had obviously irked them, but they knew better than to try to dissuade me at that moment.

"We'll work it out," Don finally said. "Let's just pick the other music we're going to have."

John didn't say anything. He fussed with papers in front of him, seemingly oblivious to my comments. We worked a bit longer choosing other songs before the meeting ended with the echo of my edict still reverberating in the room. I called Joanne and told her that we'd be happy to have her partake in the ceremony and that she should prepare something appropriate to sing for a solo as well.

The remaining planning sessions were cordial, though tense, with each of us trying hard not to step on sensitive toes. I informed my classmates that Joanne would be singing a thanksgiving meditation song after communion and that she would assist wherever else the music director thought she could be helpful. They didn't respond, though I caught them making eye contact that I interpreted as subversive. Music was never brought up again—until the day of the ceremony when we gathered in the chapel for the rehearsal with our Novice Director, Fr. Raphael.

"O.K., guys, I'd like to carefully go through what's going to happen this afternoon so that there are no surprises," said Raphael. "I want you guys to look like you know what you're doing."

He was a splendid director, kind and bright, with a vast vocabulary and a razor-sharp wit. I liked him. Three times a week for a year, he had given us classes, sharing with us his wisdom about religious life in an inspiring yet down-to-earth manner. He spoke realistically about what we could expect as vowed members, attempting to temper our idealism that, at times, bordered on "Maria von Trappism." He had also been my spiritual director for the year, meeting with me biweekly to help me make sense of the inner labyrinth called religious discernment. With the vows ceremony only hours away, I had obviously decided that God was calling me to religious life. I'm not sure my classmates would have agreed.

Raphael stood in the center of the chapel, holding the program for the ceremony, which I had not yet seen. John had had the responsibility of doing the final mock-up and of getting the programs printed in the retreat house. He had then hoarded the copies in his room like prized manuscripts.

"We'll talk through everything step by step," said Raphael. "And then we'll rehearse the vows part. You'll be the most nervous then, since you'll have to recite them alone."

Raphael began the run-through, including the part when we would kneel in front of the Provincial to profess our vows. He eventually came to the instructions for communion, but failed to mention Joanne's meditation hymn.

"I think you skipped something, Raphael," I said. "After communion, my friend Joanne is going to be singing a meditation hymn."

"Oh?" he said, once again consulting the program. "It doesn't seem to be in here. Are you sure that's where it's supposed to be?"

I glanced at John, who was looking at his shoes, refusing to meet my gaze.

"Can I see the program, Raphael?" I asked.

He handed it to me and I began to peruse it, looking for the meditation hymn or any mention of Joanne in the list of musicians and "thank-yous." Nothing.

"John, where's the meditation hymn that Joanne is singing?" I said.

His eyes bore into me and then he exploded, "Look, this isn't just your ceremony! Don and I talked about it and we don't want Joanne singing. She has no connection to us and we didn't even like the song! We're tired of you trying to control this ceremony. And we're not letting you."

I was speechless—a rarity.

"Guys," said Raphael, "this is no time for this. You should have worked all of this out before now. We have to rehearse. You need to be in a good psychological and emotional space today. Now let's go ahead with the rest of what we need to do, and you can work out the stuff about the song before this afternoon."

I tried to pay attention, but my mind was reeling, filled with venom and plans of sweet revenge. The Dalai Lama once said, "My true religion is kindness." I was an atheist that day. *How could these bastards do this? Me control the ceremony? What a switch this is. I'm not letting them get away with it.*

"Edward . . . Edward?" said Raphael.

"Um, yes. I'm here."

"Edward, it's your turn. We're going over the vows formula. Come here and kneel in front of me. I'll stand in for the Provincial, and you just read from this card the way you will this afternoon."

Moving from my place in the choir stalls, I knelt before Raphael, who sat in the presider's chair that the Provincial would occupy in just a few hours. I reverently placed my hands in his and began to read from the card. I got to the third line, "I, Edward of Christ Crucified, vow poverty, chastity, and obedience, and also . . ." I broke down, unable to continue, my voice breaking from the anger and sadness overwhelming me. It all seemed like such a charade. I stood up and hurried out of the chapel into the monastery bathroom on the second floor, irate that I had let my classmates witness my display of weakness. Standing in front of the urinals, I blew my nose into paper towels and wiped my wet eyes.

When I heard the bathroom door open, I tried to compose myself, not wanting any of the priests or brothers to find me like this. But it was Raphael. I spotted him through the little window in the door that separated the commodes from the common wash sinks and toiletry boxes. He walked through the swinging door toward me until his face was only inches from mine. Putting his hands on my shoulders, he peered at me through his outdated black, plastic-rimmed glasses.

"Edward, are you going to let those jackasses ruin this day for you? This day that you have worked so hard for. This day that is your gift to God. Are you going to let *them* ruin it?"

I looked at the floor, embarrassed that it had come to this. "No, but I just can't believe that we've allowed such pettiness to mar the beauty of what's going to happen."

"Get used to it," Raphael said. "The bullshit's often part of the beauty. But I have a feeling you'll be able to separate it. Now, I want you to go and take a walk by the Stations of the Cross outside and get yourself together. Then you and I will meet in the chapel to finish going over your vows. O.K.?"

I nodded docilely, appreciating his seeking me out and seemingly taking my side.

As he was leaving, he looked back at me when he reached the bathroom door. "Oh, and by the way, get on the phone and apologize to Joanne that she's not in the program, but tell her that we're looking forward to having the gift of her music enhance our celebration this afternoon."

Before I had the chance to say anything, he walked out. I remember thinking that, if I could be half the religious he was, God would do a handstand.

My classmates and I reached a détente shortly before the service began. I wondered if Raphael had spoken to them or if they too were just tired of all the bitterness.

All John said was "Sorry for all the confusion. Let's just enjoy the day." He had no argument from me.

The vows ceremony came off beautifully that afternoon. As I knelt before the Provincial to take my vows, for real this time, I started to choke up again, no longer because of anger or sadness, but so much joy. When I came to the part "I give myself with my whole heart to this religious community," I felt it so purely that I could hardly say the words. The Provincial, Father Brendan, squeezed my hands tightly and nodded his head, as if to communicate that he knew what I was feeling. I guess he couldn't have known too well because a few years later he left the community and the priesthood to marry a former nun. It was ironic that he had accepted my vows and then decided that he could no longer accept his own.

Joanne never sounded lovelier; even my classmates seemed moved by the prayer she sang on our behalf. At the conclusion of the ceremony, we processed out of the chapel clothed in a black habit that now bore a white heart, identifying us as professed Passionists. It was the beginning of allowing an external plastic heart to become a heart of flesh marked with the sign of faith.

Many people don't understand the arcane world of a "religious." When I say I'm a religious, they say, "a religious *what*?" There is little comprehension of how my priesthood differs from that of a diocesan priest. Most think we're all the same. But we're not. My primary vocation is to the religious life. I live in a community with other men that enables me to enflesh the vows to God of poverty, chastity, and obedience that I have taken. Ordination to the priesthood was a secondary consideration for me— a vocation within my vocation. Some others, with whom I live in community, religious brothers, choose not to be ordained, yet they live the same Passionist religious life that I do.

Diocesan priests (most often parish priests), on the other hand, take no vows to God. They make a promise to the bishop of obedience and that they will remain celibate and not marry. They get a salary, have personal bank accounts, and are responsible for their own finances. In some ways, they have it tougher because they must plan for financial security and retirement with limited resources and a salary that is hardly compensatory. I have diocesan priest friends who like to joke that "Religious take the vows and *we* keep them."

This raises, however, the conundrum of the witness value of religious in today's society—an issue with which I struggle. Traditionally, the vows have been a means by which we "witness to the kingdom." In other words, I agree to live in accord with these Gospel values, and I externally vow myself to them, as a sign that I believe in their power to transform me and our world. It's a nice theory, but it doesn't always translate effectively in our contemporary world. While the vows have remained the same throughout the centuries, the world has continued to change and religious life to change with it. We have, unfortunately, failed to allow our religious language to adequately reflect those changes, thereby diminishing the witness value.

For example, vowing "poverty" in the twenty-first-century United States of America is not the same as it was in the eighteenth-century Italy of our founder, Saint Paul of the Cross. I hardly live a "poor" life. All of my physical needs are addressed: I eat in good restaurants; I wear nice clothing; and I attend the theater with some regularity. I even drive an SUV. In other words, I live a middle-class life, albeit not an extravagant one. So when people hear that I took a vow of "poverty," they sometimes look at me with the tilted head of a confused dog—and rightfully so.

In actuality, "poverty" for me means that I live a relatively simple life and share everything I have with others. Since I have no private bank or checking account, no salary, or no portfolio, I am totally dependent upon the Passionist community for my livelihood. I cannot inherit for my own gain, nor can I disburse funds made available to me by anyone to whom I minister. While these choices may be admirable, and indeed do make me more available for ministry and service, I'm still not "poor." There's also a welcome benefit in not being bound by the strictures of financial entanglements—to say nothing of how great it is not to have to file taxes. My married brother is fond of saying, "Are you sure *I* can't take the vow of poverty you took?"

The other two vows, chastity and obedience, could likewise use some updating to speak more relevantly to a contemporary culture, but that's another chapter. Unique to the Passionists, however, is a fourth vow that only we profess: "To keep alive the memory of the Passion of Jesus in the hearts of all." Some in our community maintain that this should be our *only* vow, for it alone distinguishes us. It means that our gift to the Church is our willingness to be with those who are suffering. Since the time of our founder, this charism has been the hallmark of our community. It was known that the Passionists in Italy would go where no one else would, to minister to those shunned by family and society. Today, it means we are called to stand with the outcasts, the poor, and the marginalized. When they can find a home in us, we are truly "religious." This fourth vow, therefore, continues to resonate with meaning for me.

The day I took my vows as a religious, I was twenty-one years old and had little understanding of the implications for my life. In fact, I really didn't know what I was doing at all. Does anyone at twenty-one? I was convinced, however, that I was no better than those sitting in the pews who had come to witness the ceremony—that my vocation was no loftier. Lord knows, I've been proven right there. The altercation with my classmates was a glaring reminder that religious life did not exempt me from the pettiness and fragility of being human. That is a lesson I have been taught repeatedly through the years, humbling reminders when I'm tempted to think that religious life or priesthood is the cat's meow. There's an old Leonard Cohen song that says, "There are cracks in everything; that's how the light gets in." My religious life has been bathed in light.

I still don't understand completely what this life is supposed to be. Through the years, I've needed to repeatedly profess those vows I took; to grow into them like one does a new shirt that only becomes comfortable after many washings. As vocations decline and society evolves faster than microchips can keep up, religious life must transition to meet new needs emerging in modern contexts. It's our only hope of survival. Otherwise, we will surely pass into the night, which some feel is unavoidable no matter what we do.

But for now, I remain grateful that, so far, there has been much giftedness and beauty along the way. I get to do a wonderful ministry of service and to live with men who inspire me every day. It doesn't get much better than that. But Raphael was right: A lot of bullshit has been thrown in with it, too. Most times, as he predicted, I've been able to sift it out, but sometimes I've found myself knee-deep, wondering: "What have I gotten myself into?" I sometimes romanticize what it would have been like if I'd stayed on Wall Street, especially in the bull market of the turn of this century. Or who knows, maybe I'd be on "All My Children" by now, leading a wonderfully vapid and superficial life.

As for my two classmates who made my profession day more memorable than I had wished, both left during theological studies before taking their Final (Perpetual) Vows. One married a divorced woman with two children and is now divorced from her himself, and the other went West in search of the cowboy of his dreams. And in the words of a favorite Stephen Sondheim song, "I'm Still Here." (And, as you can see, so is the pettiness.)

CHAPTER TEN

RUNNING FOR JUSTICE

Jesus came to Nazareth, where he had grown up, and went according to his custom into the synagogue on the Sabbath day. He stood up to read and was handed a scroll of the prophet Isaiah. He unrolled the scroll and found the passage where it was written: "The Spirit of the Lord is upon me, because he has anointed me to bring glad tidings to the poor. He has sent me to proclaim liberty to captives and recovery of sight to the blind, to let the oppressed go free, and to proclaim a year acceptable to the Lord."

—LUKE 4:16–19

He was the first person I saw after the eighteen-hour drive from New York to Chicago. I had taken my vows as a Passionist religious less than one month before, and was arriving in Chicago to begin four years of theological study that would culminate in my ordination to the priesthood. Five of us pulled up in a U-Haul truck and a car, on a gray day in late afternoon, spent from the travel and eager to get settled in the converted hotel, which now served as the school of theology and residence for some of the religious communities.

As we walked to the front door of the building, after parking the vehicles in the lot across the street, he was stretching his legs on a handicap-assist bar at the entrance. Wearing gray nylon running shorts and a black, burgundy, and gray tank top that revealed a well-exercised physique, he pointed his New Balance running shoes high on the black bar, stretching his hamstrings and lowering his head toward his knee. His straight brown hair hung limply in his eyes, shielding a face soon to be revealed as handsome and open, with green eyes and a wide smile that housed numerous large teeth.

Looking up from his dancerlike position, he said, "Hi, you guys just arriving?"

"Yes, from New York," answered John, my classmate. "We're Passionists."

"Hi, I'm Michael," he said, extending his hand to each of us, and smiling broadly. "I'm a Franciscan student here. Welcome. Do you need any help in with your stuff?"

"No," said Robin, another of our students. "We have it all in the U-Haul across the street. We'll get some of the guys from our community to help us later. Thanks, though."

"Anyway, you look like you were just about to go for a run," I said.

"Yeah, I am. I'm training for the marathon, trying to be disciplined. Need to do ten miles today. Do you run?"

"Yeah," I said, "I run. Not marathons—but I do run."

"Well, we'll have to get out there sometime then. There's a great running path that I use along the lake. I can show it to you. I have all the mileage mapped out precisely. Any other takers?"

Michael looked around at the four who had arrived with me. They looked like the last thing they wanted to be talking about, after the marathon drive, was running a marathon.

Only Robin responded, "Yeah, I run, too. Maybe we could go out sometime, but for now I think we just want to get settled. I'm sure we'll see you around though."

He and the others walked through the door, leaving me standing with Michael, who was finishing the last of his stretches.

"Well, I hope we can set up a time to go running," he said. "I live on the seventh floor. Stop by. And have fun settling in. It's nice to have you here."

He took off down the street, sturdy legs carrying him to the lake, where he would put in his miles in preparation for the marathon, still a month away at the time. I walked into the lobby of the building I would call home for the next four years, feeling alone and disoriented, yet pleased to have so quickly met someone friendly who made Chicago seem less foreign.

The ensuing days were filled with the details of moving and adjusting to a new environment: setting up my room, meeting new members in the community, getting information on the classes for which I was registered, and acclimating to the multicultural Hyde Park neighborhood. Hyde Park is located on the south side of Chicago and is considered one of the most ethnically diverse neighborhoods in the country. Up to that point, I had lived in primarily white, middle- to upper-middle-class communities. Suddenly surrounded with unfamiliar sounds, exotic foods, and ethnically mixed people, I relished the diversity. Walking the streets provided immersion in a cultural and ethnic mix that proved enlightening, augmenting the education I'd soon receive in the classrooms of the Jewish Community Center that the Catholic theology school rented.

A week after I had arrived, Michael was rushing around the corner of the hallway, and we nearly collided.

"Hey, how ya doin'?" he said, extending his hand. "Ed, right?"

"Well, Edward, actually. I prefer my full name."

"Oh . . . Edward then. Well, I'm Michael, Mike, whatever. I answer to all of it."

"How's your training going?" I said.

"Oh, fine. It's more time and work than I anticipated, but it's going fine. We still have to take that run together."

"Yeah," I said, "we'll have to do that sometime."

"How about this afternoon?" he said.

"Well, I don't know. I'm still trying to get settled and . . ."

"Come on, it will be good for you. All work and no exercise . . . makes for one out-of-shape seminarian."

"Well . . . O.K.," I said, "but I won't be able to go for too long. I . . ."

"Oh, don't worry about that. I'll set the pace and go easy on you. We'll do five miles, tops. I'll meet you in front of the building at, say, three o'clock?"

"Um . . . O.K., three o'clock."

I took a deep breath, wondering how I was going to run five miles when the most I had run in that past year had been three—and that was five months previous.

I considered not showing up, offering some excuse about being needed to drive the community's standard transmission Volkswagen, because no one else was around who could. Thinking that excuse as lame as the others I contemplated, I put on my New Balance running shoes and began stretching in my room, a cautious precursor to the stretching I would do downstairs with Michael, who I assumed was more limber than I and would require less stretching.

By the time we reached the lake, I was already winded, praying that my body would quickly adjust to this uncustomary burst of activity. Lake Michigan loomed large to the right of us, blue and choppy, a few large tanker vessels visible at a distance. We were running on a concrete path that, for years, had been the lure to many in this struggling neighborhood. It served as a refuge from the paint-peeling, dilapidated buildings many called home. Michael ran with determination, his mind focused and his body steeled to resist the temptation to run halfheartedly. I soon learned that he ran like he did everything else, stubbornly, with no hint of concession.

"How ya doin'?" he said as we passed under an overhead walking bridge. "That's two miles. You O.K.?"

"Yeah, I'm fine," I managed to say, without sounding like I was going to die.

How can I run three more miles at this pace? We're going to have to slow down, or I'll never make it.

"Michael, how about if we take it a little . . . bit . . . slower," I said between breaths. "I'm not used to running on concrete like this and it's harder on me than grass or dirt."

"Yeah, I can slow it down a bit, but you should actually find yourself running faster on the concrete—less to hold you back. If we go too slow, it won't be a real workout."

"Yeah, right. Wouldn't want this not to be a real workout."

I somehow found the stamina to keep up and finish the run, but my body started to revolt as soon as we ended. Winded and sweating, we walked toward South Cornell Avenue, where the theology school and Residence were located. At the corner, there stood a large maple tree with yellow chrysanthemums rounding the trunk. I walked over to the tree, bent over, and threw up. Never an activity at which I've been particularly adept, I reflexively stomp my feet a lot, alarmed by the sensation of everything rushing forth, preventing my breathing. Determined to keep the embarrassing histrionics in check, I nonchalantly did my business, wiped my face with my T-shirt, and said matter-of-factly, "I knew I shouldn't have eaten that burger and milk shake right before running."

Michael was smiling and shaking his head. Both amused and flummoxed by my arboreal aside, he stared at me and said, "Do you always end your runs with such dignified panache?"

"Only when I run with people I like," I said.

Resolved never to fertilize the tree on South Cornell again, I began running regularly the next day.

About a week after our ill-fated jog, Michael called me and invited me on another kind of expedition. Jesse Jackson was holding a rally in downtown Chicago calling for the release of Nelson Mandela from prison in South Africa, and Michael was going to join the protesters. He wanted to know if I'd be interested in going. It sounded intriguing; I'd never been to a protest before. But after I said yes, he informed me that there was the possibility of our being arrested, should the protesters decide to chain themselves to the embassy building. I hesitated on the phone. While I agreed with civil disobedience in theory, I had never had my hands cuffed to demonstrate my solidarity.

"Edward? . . . Are you still there?" Michael said into the phone.

"Yes, um . . . I'm still here. Michael, I don't know if I'm prepared to go to jail two weeks after arriving in Chicago to begin my theology studies."

He paused for a moment, then said, "I can't think of a better way to put the theology you're going to study into practice. But if you're not comfortable . . ."

I cut him off and said, "I'll meet you in the lobby. Should I bring a toothbrush?"

When we got to the office building, there were a couple of hundred shouting protesters outside with placards. They were chanting, "Free Mandela! End apartheid now! Free Mandela!" Michael knew many of them, obviously a network of collaborators who moved from cause to cause with the fluidity of trained dancers. Social justice was their rallying call, mobilizing them to put themselves on the line for their beliefs. Michael joined their ranks seamlessly, while I felt like an outsider, ignorant to the language and customs, and not sure I wanted to be indoctrinated.

"How did all these people even find out about this rally?" I asked Michael soon after we had arrived.

"Edward, this protest has been going on for weeks. There's finally real hope that we're being heard. We have to push really hard now."

"But what if they *do* try to arrest us?"

"I hope they do," he said. "It'll give us more coverage on the news, and maybe even allow our voices to be heard nationally."

"But what would our religious communities say?"

"Edward, if my religious community wouldn't back me in this, then I wouldn't even want to be a part of them. This is why I became a religious. There's no other reason to do what we do but to try to make this world more just for people."

I heard him, but wasn't sure I understood the implications of everything he said. Although we didn't get arrested that day, it was an opportunity to watch Michael thrive in a milieu he inhabited like a comfortable Gap shirt, and I witnessed his passion bubble with a contagious intensity. Respecting his commitment and admiring his courage, I began to wonder how such fervor was cultivated—and if I'd ever acquire it.

Michael and I quickly became close friends, the relationship developing with a rapidity and ease I had not known in previous relationships. My esteem for him increased as I observed him minister selflessly, particularly in the African American community. Consumed with the fight for the disenfranchised, he spent his energy waging battles for those who had no voice, those left behind by the Reaganomics of the 1980s, who never received the boon promised from the "trickle-down" effect.

I got caught up in the fight with him, discovering a world I never knew existed and wondering how I had missed it all those years. While I had certainly heard about people living on the fringes of society, and had seen news reports, it now all came to life, and, paradoxically, life is what was lacking most. People were struggling to merely survive in neighborhoods where poverty and drive-by shootings were as familiar as the drug pushers and rats that roamed the dark alleys. It just didn't seem right.

Michael brought me to St. Sabina, an African American parish on the south side of Chicago, renowned for its commitment to better the plight of those in the community, and for its white pastor, who was regularly featured in the news and on television, speaking out against the injustices pervading the oppressive system. He got arrested a lot, too. Suddenly, I was in a world of incarceration aficionados, and I had never even been sent to the principal's office.

"Michael," the pastor said one day as we sat in his office, "I want to do something to hurt the advertisers of alcohol and tobacco in the African American community."

"Sure, that's a great idea," said Michael. "Studies show that they target these communities more, hoping to capitalize on people's vulnerability and hardship."

"Why is that?" I asked. "You would think since there's less money here, they'd focus their attention where they could make more profit."

"It's part of a systematic plan to lessen the impact of the African American," said the pastor. "Kill them off with alcohol and nicotine. It's just another slow genocide. They know exactly what they're doing."

I shut up, but the pastor's response seemed extreme to me. *Did he really believe this was a premeditated plan to kill the black man?*

"Did you agree with what he said?" I asked Michael later.

"Edward, whether or not what he said is true is irrelevant. The point is alcohol, nicotine, and other drugs are doing serious damage in the African American community, and are depleting it of one of its most valuable resources, its young people. Now, if that's not enough reason to fight it, I don't know what is."

Energized by their commitment, I soon found myself joining the fray. Desiring to become more conversant with the group for whom I was fighting, I immersed myself in the African American experience with a previously untapped zeal: reading some of the history, listening to jazz and the blues, and eating collard greens and ham hocks. I slowly began to see through different eyes—eyes that gradually opened to a new world.

More important, I began to see that such exposure is what had been lacking in my experience of faith and in the cultivation of my Christian vocation. Sure, it was nice that I felt called to religious life and that I lived a "holy" monastic existence, praying in common and wearing the religious getup, but the primary message of Jesus was about doing something for people who had fallen through the cracks. When he stood in the temple and unrolled the scroll of the prophet Isaiah, he announced not only his mission but also all of ours. Now was my chance to not just talk about being a follower but actually to do something that resembled the actions of the man who had so captivated me. The poor, the oppressed, the disenfranchised were right in front of me, and I was in a position to proclaim glad tidings and liberty by my willingness to work with them toward a better future. I began to fancy myself an urban missionary.

But it wasn't all flag-waving. "All social justice and no play . . . makes for one dull seminarian," I reminded Michael, in my redaction of his earlier admonition. Fortunately, he enjoyed movies as much as I did. One evening we went downtown to the McClurg Court Theatre to see *Chariots of Fire,* a popular film about runners that was being shown on a panoramic screen. We loved the movie, Michael even more than I, and afterward, at Uno Pizzeria, we debated the moral dilemmas the film presented, and argued over the cinematic choices the director made. Michael was always up for a good fight, and I wasn't far behind.

Halfway through our pizza, Michael looked at me and said, "You know, I've decided to go to Zaire, Africa, for a year overseas training program that the Franciscan community runs." It felt like he had just thrown his glass of ice water at me.

"Oh, really?" I said, my stomach beginning to knot. "When are you going?"

"I'd leave in about three months, stay there for a year, and then come back and finish my theology studies."

"And then?" I said. "What would you do when you're done with theology?"

"Well, I'd probably go back to Zaire and work there for a few years, if everything goes O.K. I've always felt a strong call to missionary work. It's kind of in my blood. It's something I just have to do."

I sat silent, with mixed emotions, staring at my iced tea. I sensed Michael's alacrity to do missionary work, and I recognized his aptness for it, but I wasn't prepared to say goodbye to him so soon after we had met. He had made such an extraordinary impression on me, in so short a time, that I wanted to bask in that glow a bit longer. It was selfish, but I couldn't help it. He had been my mentor, introducing me to a world I was only beginning to feel comfortable inhabiting, and now I would have to find my way alone. It was a daunting prospect.

"Edward, are you O.K.?"

"Yeah, yeah, I'm fine. I guess I'm just a little bit thrown by the news. I didn't anticipate your leaving so soon. You've been such an important part of my life since I arrived in Chicago. It just won't seem the same without you."

"Well, we really don't have to dwell on that now. It's months away. Let's enjoy the time we have."

And so that's what we did—every chance we could get. After a long day of studies and community business, we would slip off to the Medici Restaurant for a midnight Earl Grey tea and pan-seared roast beef sandwiches. Well, *I* had the roast beef sandwiches.

"I'm still not really clear why you don't eat meat," I said one night. "I mean, I know it's not just a health thing, but I'm not sure why."

"Edward, do you realize that here in the United States we make up only thirteen percent of the world population, yet we consume eighty percent of the world's goods?"

"Yes, well, no, I didn't know those statistics, but I'm certainly aware that we're a consumerist society. But what does that have to do with your not eating meat?"

"We consume most of the world's meat, while one-third of the world goes hungry. It's wrong."

"But, Michael, your not eating meat isn't going to feed those people."

"Maybe not, but if there were *enough* people not eating meat, then maybe there would be excess for *those* people."

My roast beef sandwich didn't taste quite so appetizing that night. I left half of it on my plate, but then I wondered about wasting food. I couldn't win.

We lingered long into the night during our forays to the Medici, discussing religious, political, and social issues, while also making room for the more pedestrian topics of movies and seminary gossip. I continued to be inspired by his commitment, though I began to resent its luring pull to another continent. I couldn't understand why he couldn't stay here and help people. *Weren't we doing missionary work on the south side of Chicago? We had been exposed to enough need here to last a lifetime of ministry.* I came close to mouthing words I had heard my parents say since I was a child: "Take care of your own kind first." It was not my finest moment.

As the time for Michael's departure grew near, I unintentionally began to direct some of the anger and resentment I was feeling toward him. While I understood why he was going, and agreed with his reasoning, I was feeling abandoned and cheated of more time. I also minded that he was leaving to do the really heroic stuff, while I was being left behind to do the merely admirable. (Not that I had any desire, at that time, to traverse the globe.) Though it made no sense, I saw him as choosing Zaire over our friendship—and I took umbrage at his choice.

I realized later that I felt so strongly because Michael was my first real adult friend. I had maintained little contact with my New York circle of friends since I had joined religious life, and by the time I arrived in Chicago, I had accepted that the community was not going to be able to meet my need for friendships and affective relationships. Not only was the pool too small, but some of the swimmers had very different strokes. They were my brothers, but not necessarily my friends. Finally, I had met someone with whom I meshed instantly, and he was leaving just as quickly. It didn't seem fair.

It must have shown, because one day after a run by the lake, he said to me, "Is anything wrong? You've seemed kind of out of it the last week or so."

"Out of it? How do you mean?"

"Well, I don't know—somewhat distant, preoccupied, aloof, call it whatever you want."

"Well, Michael, you're leaving in about a month, and I guess I'm not feeling great about it. You've exposed me to so much, and now you're leaving me to fend for myself."

"So you're distancing yourself?"

"Not consciously," I said. "But I'm sure some of that's happening. I think I've depended on you too much. I've hardly invested in any other relationships since I arrived in Chicago. Now when you leave, there'll be a void."

"Well, I'm sorry you feel that way, but I never assumed our friendship would prevent you from establishing other relationships."

"I'm not saying it was your assumption. But this whole time, it's been like I've been Robin to your Batman, working to conquer injustice in Gotham City. And now I have to start fighting on my own. Look, I know it's my issue. I'll deal with it."

"O.K., but just don't let me feel like a stranger in this last month, because even though I'm the one leaving, I've made an investment here, too, you know."

"Yeah, but it was real short-term."

"Edward, that's not fair."

"I know, I'm sorry. It's just that I'm so sure God put you in my life to teach me something. He should know I don't learn that fast."

The remaining time before Michael left passed quickly. We tried to squeeze in a lot of runs, movies, and late-night talks, but it was like racing against an unbeatable clock. We resolved some of the issues surrounding his departure, but not all of them. I was still silently blaming him for leaving. And I couldn't understand why the need here wasn't as important as the need in Zaire. I had known him only five months, but it felt like I was being separated from a lifelong friend. I wondered: How, without him, would I negotiate the places to which he had introduced me? Would I even feel safe walking in the precarious neighborhoods we had so heedlessly roamed together? When explored with him, they felt as harmless as a well-patrolled suburb; without him, they seemed dark and ominous.

Impossible to stave off any longer, the day of his departure arrived like a persistent caller for whom you finally have to open the door. Feeling like I was sending a brother off to war, I went to the airport with his family to bid him goodbye one cold, gloomy day in January. They had driven up from Indianapolis to see him off. His mother, Aggie, and his sister, Maryann, cried.

"Michael, please be careful over there," his mother counseled. "Don't take too many chances. You know how you are."

Michael's father and brothers looked stalwart, Hoosier men keeping a stiff upper lip for the women's sake, but it was obvious they too would miss him.

Michael and I retreated to a newsstand for some final words. I tried to emulate the emotional reserve of his brothers and father, but since I was not of the same stock, tears came despite my effort at a "regular guy" goodbye.

"I'm not going to eat any meat while you're gone," I said. "It will be my attempt at solidarity with your mission over there."

"Gee, that's great, Edward. You'll get used to it, and I bet you'll find, as I have, that you'll actually like not eating it. You'll feel better." He was trying not to cry, too, but finally he couldn't hold the tears back and he sobbed: for me, for his family, for everything he was leaving behind to venture to this unknown place.

I tried to comfort him, though part of me held back because I thought the pain was avoidable. I wanted him to realize that he was causing it. And I wanted to know that it was hard for him to leave. I didn't say any of that, though. Instead I said, "About not eating meat, I don't know how much of that grade school theology I was taught that I still believe, but I'll 'offer it up,' if it means anything."

"Even if it doesn't mean anything to God, it means something to me."

As he walked down the ramp to the plane, a part of me walked down it with him, and never came back.

Slowly I began to readjust and focus again on my studies and ministry, immersing myself in the African American community, and in other concerns of justice to which he had exposed me. I kept my promise and refrained from eating meat during that time, as a sign of solidarity with those who were going hungry. Michael had introduced me to Bread for the World, an organization that monitored world hunger and asked for symbolic and actual gestures to help combat the epidemic. These pursuits made me feel closer to Michael while he was somewhere in the bush of Zaire, working against the ill effects of the Mobutu regime, which had pillaged the people and devastated the natural resources of a formerly plentiful country. I imagined him ignoring his mother's advice and taking chances, skirting arrest thousands of miles away. And I wrote lots of letters.

One day, about nine months after Michael had left, I walked into the dining room of the theology school to get dinner. I picked up an orange plastic tray from the rack and was scooping lettuce into a wooden bowl at the salad bar, when Arturo, one of the Franciscans from Michael's community, came up to me and said, "Edward, did you hear about Michael yet?"

His demeanor and the tone of his voice signaled trouble. I put the salad bowl back on the tray. "No, Arturo, what happened?"

"He's been in a terrible motorcycle accident over there in Zaire. They're not sure how serious it is. They're airlifting him home."

I immediately felt sick and flushed. Leaving the dining room without saying anything to Arturo, or anyone else, I went to my room, lit a candle, and prayed. I asked God to let him be O.K. Seeking forgiveness for questioning the validity of Michael's mission and for letting my judgment be clouded by my own self-interest, I promised I would try to never again choose myself over the needs of others.

Confirming our penchant for meeting at airports, I met Michael's parents at Chicago's O'Hare once more, this time for his unanticipated arrival home. When they finally carried him off the plane on a stretcher, he looked awful: his hair matted to his head, his face bruised, his eyes lifeless, and the growth of a scraggly beard making him appear derelict. He smiled weakly as they ushered him past us. When he saw me, he said, "Well, I guess it's going to be a while before we take any runs by the lake, but maybe a movie in a couple of weeks."

"Sure, whatever you say," I said. "But I'm not letting you off the hook with the run, either."

We discovered that Michael and another friar had been in the bush on motorcycles when torrential rains came and flooded the region. The friar in front of Michael was forced to stop short on his motorcycle, causing Michael to ram into the back of him. The tailpipe of the other motorcycle slashed Michael's leg at the knee. He had to lie there for some time while help was sought, giving dirt and microbes the opportunity to invade and produce an infection that resisted the antibiotics administered in an African hospital. By the time Michael reached the States, the leg was in terrible shape.

He was in the hospital thirty-three days, on each of which I visited him, pulling up a chair next to his bed, laughing about the good times we had had, and comforting him when tears of frustration and sadness overwhelmed him. He had also contracted a lung infection while lying on the ground waiting for help. The infection stymied the doctors and exacerbated an already difficult recovery. I had never seen him so low. Most of all, he feared that the leg would be of no use to him, and might hinder any return to Africa. It was obvious that the exotic continent had captured his heart, which seemed to be breaking at the thought of not returning.

An irrepressible will and fighting spirit had him walking again in three weeks, albeit slowly, and with a pronounced limp. The day after he got out of the hospital, we were sitting in the third row of the newly restored, historic Chicago theater, watching Liza Minnelli perform a benefit concert to a packed house. I had purchased the discounted tickets for $5.00 each, a city thank-you to the people of Chicago who had helped make the restoration of the theater possible. I was able to secure an aisle seat for Michael so that he could keep his leg outstretched, but it was obvious he was still in a lot of pain during the performance.

"Michael, we don't have to stay for this whole show," I whispered halfway through the performance. "If your leg is hurting too much, we can leave. Maybe it's just too soon."

"What are you, crazy? After lying in that hospital bed for a month, I'd rather be here, hurting, than anyplace else. Now listen to the lady sing." He was stubborn, so there was no use arguing.

He never ran another marathon. He never ran again at all. The leg eventually healed, but he was left with a limp and constant pain that sometimes required medication to lessen the severity. He did, however, return to Zaire, as I knew he would, and he remained almost until the fall of the Mobutu regime, when hope once again rose like a new sun, only quickly to be eclipsed by the corruption and greed of a new administration. Michael is currently in the States, completing work on his doctorate, teaching theology, and doing advocacy work for Africa in Washington, D.C. I'm sure it won't be long, however, before the fever bites him again and he's off to another part of the globe, raising his fist to combat his nemesis, injustice.

I've learned a lot from Michael. Although I don't see him often, we keep in touch through letters and an occasional phone call, and it's enough. While our relationship never again gathered the momentum of those early months, its legacy has been lasting. Michael made me aware of a world I knew little about, and made me care about that world. Though I never had his innate passion for social justice, and probably never will, I recognize its lack as a flaw, and battle my tendency toward complacency and indifference. I hear Michael's voice saying, "No, it shouldn't be this way. It's not right. We *must* do something about it." And while sometimes that voice prompts me to action, it always prompts me to reflection. Social justice is so primary a teaching of Jesus that one can hardly call him/herself Christian and not be committed to it. Michael has, therefore, made me a better Christian.

There are those people in our lives whose spirits hover like nudging gadflies, pushing us to places we would never chance if left to our own predilections. They call us beyond ourselves, to encounter faces shadowed by the paucity of daylight, faces no new moon ever illumines. Michael's ease in navigating this world continues to surprise me, and shame me. But most of all, it gives me hope, hope in humanity, hope that someday more of us will traverse those lightless places to banish the obscurity some have come to accept as normal. It will never be normal for Michael. And while he may walk with a limp, he continues to run with everything he's got. And he pulls me, and whomever else he can get his hands on, toward the finish line with him.

CHAPTER ELEVEN

"SO WHAT DO YOU DO?"

You are a priest forever according to the order of Melchizedek.
—PSALM 110:4

I lay prostrate, my face pressed into the cool, multicolored terrazzo floor. I could smell the lingering traces of others who had traversed this sanctuary, this holy of holies, this place where now I would be changed forever. The Litany of the Saints was being chanted by the choir. "Saint Michael, pray for us; Saint Paul of the Cross, pray for us; All holy men and women, pray for us." As I lay there, I prayed, too. Invoking the aid of these luminaries of our tradition, I prayed, "Help me to be a good priest. Help me to be happy in this life and to make a difference." A priest forever according to the order of Melchizedek. *What made me think I could do this?*

I rose from the floor slowly, carefully, hoping to avoid getting tangled in my bountiful vestments and falling on my face. The bishop was seated in the presider's chair, his own gold vestments wrapping him in a mantle of authority, his pointy hat and his shepherd's staff punctuating the aura. His face was lined; his left hand trembled slightly. Framed by gold wire-rimmed glasses, his eyes appeared flat and lifeless, betraying his absence. Perhaps he was anticipating a steak dinner and a cold beer with friends who awaited him at the conclusion of the ceremony. I walked toward his chair, wondering how many of these ceremonies he had performed,

how many other men he had "elevated" from ecclesiastical boy-
hood to manhood.

I knelt down before him, and he took my folded hands into
his. A double layer of praying hands: his wrinkled, with blue veins
crisscrossing the top like elevated tracks; mine smooth and pink,
not yet weathered by life's challenges. Clutched together, they
symbolized the need for God at this moment.

He looked into my eyes, finally here, the steak dinner on hold.
"Do you promise your Ordinary obedience and fidelity?"

"Yes, I do."

I was glad I didn't have to promise celibacy again, after having
already done so twice in vows ceremonies and once to be ordained a deacon. *Basta* with the celibacy. There was, after all,
more to religious life and priesthood than that.

The bishop's master of ceremonies, a priest in his early thirties
with a smooth face and Brylcreemed short hair, stood next to him.
He held the holy chrism, which he now passed to the bishop, as if
making a gift of liquid gold. The bishop took the crystal flask filled
with the yellow nectar and poured it carefully into the palms of
my hands. He rubbed it in vigorously, as if the harder he pressed,
the more lasting its effects would be. Its aromatic scent rose from
my hands to fill the sanctuary with its sweetness.

"A priest forever," he said, never breaking eye contact with
me, issuing the words as a command rather than an exhortation.

I nodded, feeling a rush of joy and gratitude. It was providen-
tial that I was kneeling, as I felt weak trying to absorb the enormity of this passage. The assistant then helped me to my feet and
led me to my priest friend, Robert. He stood smiling, holding the
vestments that I had designed and that a woman in the parish had
sewn. Desiring a fuller cut than usual, I had incorporated extra
reams of material into the design. Robert now struggled to negotiate the voluminous, flowing, wool-cotton blend as he slipped the
vestment over my head. I became engulfed in fabric, with Robert
attempting to align the hole in the material with my head, which
was endeavoring to find the light, a fitting metaphor. When my

head finally emerged, like a turtle that had gotten lost in its shell, I saw my mother standing there with Robert. Ever "Mom," she had come from her place in the front pew to assist in her son's liberation.

While my mother straightened the material in back, Robert, still smiling, embraced me and whispered, "You look like Omar the Tent Maker."

I walked back to the sanctuary, for the first time dressed as a priest. Sensing all eyes were on me, I walked stiffly, yet I knew that no clothing had ever fitted me better. As the choir began chanting the "Veni Sanctus Spiritus," I knelt once more in the sanctuary while the bishop rose from his presider's chair and stood before me. I could see only his shoes and the bottom of his lace-embroidered alb. He placed both his hands on my head, prayerfully invoking the Holy Spirit to descend upon me and to "ontologically" change me forever. His hands trembled as he pressed his fingers into my skull. I wished I had used less gel. Then every priest who had gathered in the church filed from his pew to lay his hands upon me also, symbolically sharing with me the power of his priesthood. My head bowed, I saw only shoes, some worn and cracked, others freshly polished, some tasseled, mostly laced. I began guessing which priest filled which shoes, and if I'd be able to fill any of them.

While kneeling there, I felt the power of hands that had absolved, hands that had consecrated, hands that had wiped away tears, hands that had sinned. Majesty and wonder reigned. I finally closed my eyes, no longer guessing, Thom McAn or Florsheim, and I prayed earnestly, "Holy Spirit, do descend. Change me forever. Make me your priest. Make me a good one."

I noticed them when I had begun the Mission because they were young and sad. They had attended the first evening session and came back the next morning—unusual, because, characteristically, retired people and stay-at-home moms attended the mornings. They listened distinctively, she with the openness of a sponge being rained upon after having been left in the sun too long; he with an arms-crossed passivity that said, "Prove to me that anything you say can make a difference in my life."

The second morning she sat in the pew alone. I supposed he had had enough and had given up. As I stood in the rear of the church saying goodbye to the exiting retreatants, she remained behind, kneeling in front of the Blessed Sacrament, her head bowed in prayer. While I was changing from my vestments in the sacristy, after pulling the alb over my head, I suddenly saw her standing there.

"I'm sorry to bother you," she said. "This might not be a good time, but I'm wondering if I could speak with you? It's important." She was pretty, small, with a high voice and shiny brown hair that waved naturally over the collar of her green plaid jacket.

"No, it's fine," I said. "What can I do for you?"

"Can we go somewhere to talk for a few minutes?"

"Well, the reconciliation room is free. It's kind of nice in there, not really like a confessional. And it's quiet. We won't be disturbed."

"Sure, that's probably appropriate," she said.

She sat across from me, the quiet lighting of the small space making her look more peaceful than she appeared in the harsh fluorescent of the sacristy. She was nervous though, fidgeting with the bottom of her coat, and unable to meet my gaze head-on.

"My husband, Timmy, and I have been coming to your retreat the past couple of days, and we're really enjoying it."

"Thanks."

"He's really the reason why I'm here."

"Uh-huh."

"Let me give you a little background, or it won't make any sense." She looked off into the distance, trying to decide where to begin.

She began speaking about her marriage to Timmy, with whom she was deeply in love. They had been married for about three years; he had also been married once before and had a daughter by that marriage. His ex-wife had gotten sole custody and moved far away with his daughter; he hardly ever saw her anymore. Although his heart ached at letting her go, it allowed the new marriage to feel like a fresh start. He was everything his new wife, Linda, could hope for. "A good man," she assured me. But one thing got in the way, casting a pall over that goodness.

"He drinks, Father, every day. And I've asked him, repeatedly, to stop, but he won't, or he can't; I don't know which. I've tried for years to get him to give it up, but nothing has worked. I've pleaded with him, I've threatened him, I've done everything."

"And so," I said, "you'd like me to speak with him to see if there's something I can do?"

"Well, no, not really. The first night of the Mission you asked us to name a grace we needed. And the whole night I just prayed for Timmy. I prayed that God help him, and solve this problem in our marriage. And I could tell that he was praying, too."

"That's good. I'm glad you were able to make that prayer."

"And . . . and . . ." She started to cry, unable to speak as the tears spilled forth and her chest began to heave slightly. I felt sorry for her pain, yet I was helpless to relieve it. Her happiness depended on the actions of a husband who seemingly refused to change.

"I'm sorry it's so hard for you," I said. "Take your time."

"Well, actually," she managed to say as her crying quieted, "I'm here because I think it may be getting better. And I wanted to tell you about it."

"How do you mean?"

"Well, I could see Timmy was really listening to you, and taking the retreat seriously."

"Yeah, but I noticed he wasn't with you this morning."

"Father . . . he's in his first AA meeting as we sit here. I just can't believe it." She started to cry again.

The sadness I was feeling for her lifted. She went on to tell me that she had been trying to get him to go to AA for years, but he had always resisted with one excuse or another. Unexpectedly, he had awakened that morning and said he couldn't go to church with her because he was going to a meeting. She knew it was a grace of the retreat.

That evening he was back in the pew, sitting beside her, his arms unfolded. He was a handsome guy, though his face showed some of the wear of too many years of hard living. He listened attentively to my talk and stopped to see me at the back of the church after the service.

"Father, that was really wonderful," he said. "You certainly do have a way of getting your point across."

"Well, thanks, Timmy, but not everyone seemed to be listening as intently as you were."

"You know what, Father? It's just that I'm ready. It's time. And you're here and I'm here and God's using it."

Linda stood beside him, beaming at him with appreciative eyes.

"I know Linda told you where I was this morning. It's a place I never in a million years thought I'd be. I never thought I had a problem. And this week, I admitted I did. And I believe it's because of this retreat."

"God can use whatever, Timmy," I said. "But the wonderful thing is that you were open to God working. That's the real grace."

"No, you're the real grace," he said.

And then he put his arms around me and embraced me.

Timmy has not taken a drink since that day four years ago, after having had abused alcohol for twenty-five years. He and Linda have moved to Florida, where they are trying to conceive a child after many failed attempts. He has finally gotten an annulment from his first marriage, and last year the Church blessed his marriage to Linda, something she and I had also talked about that first day in the reconciliation room. They call me periodically to fill me in on their lives, and to remind me that I was instrumental in helping them to get there. When I go to Florida to give retreats (preferably in January and February) or to visit my parents (ditto), I try to see Timmy and Linda. The happiness of their new life runs over like a brimming waterfall.

Such is the privilege of my life as a priest. I get to be there for some terrific moments, when the miracles of life and grace converge and transformation happens, altering lives that had crept along in shadows of darkness until unforeseen light suddenly dispels it. It has been fifteen years since I lay on that cool terrazzo floor and prayed that God make me a good priest. Although I have gone through some difficult times during that period, "priesthood" has gone through even more difficult times. Reports of pedophiles, dubious financial dealings, sexual peccadilloes, and even drug abuse have marred the image of the priest and caused many to question the healthiness of a lifestyle that can promote such aberrations. Vocations to the priesthood and the religious life are at an all-time low.

While these realities concern me, they also seem removed from me, because they don't reflect my experience of priesthood. They are not my struggles, although I do struggle. *I* struggle most with people's perceptions of priests and how those perceptions cause them to relate to me—sometimes as an alien from another planet. Society and the Church have long promoted an image of priesthood that is "otherworldly" and removed. We've been relegated to the rarefied status of holy clerics, capitalizing on the "mystery," at the expense of the human.

In her beautiful homily at my first Mass, my friend Dianne, a prominent biblical scholar, exhorted me, "Edward, be transparent. Allow those to whom you minister to see who you really are. Let them love the true you, not some image of who they think you should be." It was good advice, but not easy to follow. Some people don't want to see the real me. And it's hard to shatter people's illusions, especially when the illusions are better than the reality. Who wants to be a frog when you can be a prince instead?

Although we priests have our own P.R. work to do, I don't think we're solely to blame for the misperceptions. We're often misrepresented. Priest bashing (and Catholic bashing), like so many other kinds of bashing, is in vogue these days. It took me a while to catch on, but the trend soon became undeniable. I used to look forward to the inevitable social question, "So what do *you* do?" I'd respond proudly, "I am a Roman Catholic priest." Unconsciously, I'd wait for the applause, but disguised tomatoes came instead. "Oh . . . you're kidding . . . You mean the kind that can't have sex? Hey, now that your guys have finally admitted Copernicus was right, who's next, Martin Luther?"

If the responses are not condescending, they are often laced with ill-informed pity. "You poor thing. I didn't think anyone still did that . . . especially someone so young—and with eyes so blue!" Such myopia continues to surprise me, but maybe it shouldn't. For many, their image of the Catholic priest is stuck in fallacious cinema caricatures, somewhere between Bing Crosby's treacly Father O'Malley and Richard Chamberlain's prurient *Thorn Birds* cleric. Since most people don't know a priest personally, they allow misconstrued media images to be their gospel. When a more accurate depiction astonishingly breaks through, like Father Ray in ABC's ill-fated series "Nothing Sacred," it's gone before you can say, "Amen."

I often wish I could give the perpetrators of such folderol an inside peek at what it's like to don a white collar. Oh sure, I'd love to show them the struggles and the pain, the loneliness and the isolation. Who doesn't like a little pity thrown his way? But more important, I'd like to unveil for them the wonder, privilege, and mystery of my life. What it's like to sit in a confessional and be the instrument of reconciliation in the midst of someone's pain and dejection; what it's like to witness the marriage of young love and to help seal that sacrament with the blessing of the Church; what it's like to cradle a newborn and pour life-giving waters of initiation over a forehead yet to dream the possibilities life holds; what it's like to incense the body of a deceased loved one as the family receives comfort from the ancient Church ritual; what it's like to anoint a languid body with oil of healing and strength; what it's like to hold bread and wine that the praying community offers and to have those substances become nourishment for hungry hearts. And that's just the sacramental part. Still to be shown would be the balm of counseling, the grace of spiritual direction, the power of preaching, the solace of visiting the infirm. And the utter satisfaction and thanksgiving that takes hold when I witness someone's life turn around as a result of God working through me. But most people never get to see those aspects of priesthood.

Part of the reason the image of priesthood is skewed is due to the anticlericalism and anti-Catholicism that is present in society. It has existed throughout the centuries, rooted in the theological polemics of the sixteenth-century Reformation, the political polemics of the eighteenth-century Enlightenment, and the cultural polemics of nineteenth-century American nativism. Presently, it shows no sign of retreating. The issue made headlines during the 2000 primary campaign when George W. Bush visited Bob Jones University, a haven of anti-Catholicism. Even after the embarrassing publicity, Bob Jones, Jr., was still quoted on the university's Web site as saying: The Catholic Church "is not another Christian denomination. It is a satanic counterfeit, an ecclesiastic tyranny over the souls of men, not to bring them to salvation but to hold them bound in sin and to hurl them into eternal damnation." (I shudder to think what he says about her priests.) Yet, Bush's visit to the university was a minor bump in the road of his candidacy, with him still handily winning the party's nomination a few weeks later. As one columnist suggested, can you imagine the reaction if, instead of at Bob Jones University, he had spoken at a Louis Farrakhan event? His political career would likely have been ended.

While my experiences of people's misperceptions are legion, interestingly, often the inaccuracies levied are rooted in sex. People seem obsessed with sexual mores when it comes to the clergy. I've been called everything, from "Father What-a-Waste" to "Father Doesn't-Know-What-He's-Missing." If priests aren't being accused of somehow "getting it on the side," we are accused of being pedophiles—this, despite statistics that indicate priests are more faithful to their vows than are married people, and that priests show no greater propensity to pedophilia than does the general population.

Why does it make headlines when a priest is caught with his pants down, or accused of pedophilia? I'd like to think it's because the priesthood is revered and that, because priests are held in higher regard, the expectations are higher. And rightly so. In professional relationships, we should be held to a higher standard, just as doctors and psychotherapists are. Relationships inviting trust are sacred, and should be treated as such. When priests violate that trust, the repercussions should be as severe as for any other professional who steps outside the ethical boundaries of a cliental relationship.

But I think people's interest in the private lives of priests extends beyond what happens in priests' offices. Rather, the demythologizing attempted in salacious news articles seems to feed a prurient desire to unmask celibacy as unnatural and beyond the bounds of possibility. In a sex-saturated culture, where sex is presented as the solution to everything, people seem disturbed by anyone who professes that maybe it's not. One friend suggests that attempts are made to diminish the witness value of those trying to live vowed, chaste lives, because it makes the diminishers feel better when they succumb to their own epicurean tendencies. "Weakness loves company," he ascertains.

While I don't mean to be campaigning for "martyr" status, though that classification continues to be revered in our tradition, I think it's undeniable that priests and the Church sometimes get a bad rap. We are perceived as rigid and out of touch with contemporary society, and often, as encouraging hopelessly premodern doctrines. Our sexual standards are viewed as unnatural and hypocritical, and our liturgies as arcane, and even cannibalistic.

Now I'm the first to admit that official Church teaching is lofty in some matters, and that the Church is partly to blame for some of the erroneous perceptions. That's what happens when far-reaching ideals are more revered than lived experience. But the Church also does much good for which it doesn't get credit. In areas of social justice and human rights, it knows no parallel. Why don't we hear as much about that? And I seldom encounter priests so dogmatically entrenched that they are unable to respond with compassion and understanding to people struggling with complex moral and sexual issues. Most priests I know put the person ahead of the law, and forgiveness above judgment. For those who don't, *mea culpa* from the rest of us.

Gratefully, a *mea culpa* has also begun to come from the institutional Church at large. In the twilight of his career, Pope John Paul II has begun to apologize for the errors and omissions of the Roman Catholic Church over the last two thousand years. Perhaps this will help stem some of the anti-Catholic sentiment rooted in resentment and revenge. In calling for a Church-wide "purification of memory," John Paul has acknowledged the sinfulness that has been part of our history, including anti-Semitism, the Inquisition, the forced conversions of the people of Africa and Latin America, the Church's discrimination against women, and the Church's support of the Crusades, whose victims included Jews, Muslims, and members of the Eastern Orthodox Church. Though we still have further to go in acknowledging discrimination against homosexuals, and in admitting a less than forceful outcry against the Holocaust, it is an admirable beginning. It acknowledges that the Church, or at least, the "sons and daughters" of the Church, do make mistakes and are in need of forgiveness.

I'd like to add priests, specifically, to that list. We too mess up, big time. Some of us give boring homilies, are short-tempered, drink too much, have sex, though profess we don't, and live less than holy lives—some of the time. We're human, even though some would deny us that status.

When I lay on that terrazzo floor fifteen years ago, I didn't imagine that I was giving up my humanity in order to serve as God's priest. Rather, I supposed that my effectiveness would come from my shared human experience; that people would be helped by me because I was so much like them. Occasionally, that has been the case. But I've also found that some expect me to be what I'll never be, perfect and untainted; some are horrified when privy to my capacity for hypocrisy and mean-spiritedness. And then I feel guilty. At such times, it helps me to remember that I only promised I'd try to do my best, and that I would do it for the rest of my life. I'm still working to keep those promises. It also helps me to remember that there is a guy in Florida named Timmy who no longer drinks, and who assures me that I had something to do with it.

CHAPTER TWELVE

WOMAN PREACHER

Jesus said to her, "Woman, why are you weeping? Who are you looking for?" She thought it was the gardener and said to him, "Sir, if you carried him away, tell me where you laid him, and I will take him." Jesus said to her, "Mary!" She turned to him and said, "Rabbouni," which means Teacher.

—JOHN 20:15–16

I had so many things on my mind the day of my second First Mass. After being ordained a priest in a lavish ceremony, about which one of my friends commented, "Popes have been crowned in less time than it took you to be ordained," I presided at my *first* First Mass, a Saturday Vigil Eucharist at our Passionist parish in Jamaica, Queens. This was done to enable my parents to throw the evening party they wanted to give me at Buckley's, a favorite Brooklyn restaurant of my family.

My mother had reasoned, "If you say your First Mass in New Jersey on a Sunday morning, then we have to have a brunch for the party, or some kind of buffet lunch. That's terrible."

"Yes, Mother, but I've been a deacon in Union City for six months. The people there have practically adopted me. I was ordained in their church. Now, you want me to say my First Mass somewhere else?"

"Look, do what you want," she said. "You will, anyway. All I'm telling you is that our family will not want to cross over bridges and tunnels to New Jersey for a morning Mass, and then come all the way back over here for a brunch or lunch. And if you make it a dinner with a morning Mass, what are we supposed to do all day, sit around and twiddle our thumbs?"

So it was decided I would have two First Masses. The first would be at the Jamaica parish, in the evening, so the guests could then go to a sit-down dinner afterward. This kept everyone happy, except some of the Union City people, who were disgruntled that they'd be getting warmed-over leftovers, my priestly hands having already consecrated bread and wine at my *real* First Mass.

The Mass in Jamaica went swimmingly, with a tributary homily preached by Father Fidelis, who had been my director when I was a theology student in Chicago. He gave away too many seminary secrets, which I thought better left behind in his hallowed office where we met biweekly. I didn't think everyone needed to know that I had been fired from my waiter's job at Mellow Yellow restaurant for dropping a hot fudge sundae on a lady's white dress, or that I had taken a short detour to Rome when I was supposed to be in Israel for my theology semester abroad. But to make up for his indiscretion, he also said wonderful, complimentary things, with a twinkle in his eye and a Boston accent that made him sound more like Bobby Kennedy than the Dorchester ruffian he once was. In those days he was "Tommy," selling magazines door-to-door, charming poor widows to subscribe to "just one more."

The party at Buckley's was also a smash, with a choice of prime rib or fillet of sole; a DJ offering everything from Frank Sinatra to Cher; and a wait staff nonplussed by the number of white collars punctuating a dining room usually reserved for small-time Mafia dinners or first Communions. For those occasions maybe *one* white collar would emerge to say grace and then slip out quietly before Aunt Nina got his ear about how "everything was much better when the Mass was in Latin."

But on this particular day, the day of my *second* First Mass, my mind was filled with the details of trying to make everything extra special, so that the people in Union City would be convinced that even leftovers could be savory. The parish youth group was eager to lead the procession down the center aisle of the church with banners with swirling ribbons that they had made. I had co-ordinated the readers, Eucharistic ministers, choirs and cantors, honorary guests (the Provincial Counselor and some small-time Union City politicians), and my family, who had requested re-served seating in the front of the church. You'd think they'd have had their fill of ecclesiastical pageantry after two vows ceremonies (First and Final), two ordinations (diaconate and priesthood), and a first First Mass. But my parents say it's easier for them to pay at-tention when they're closer.

And then, there was Dianne to attend to. She had been my first graduate school Old Testament Scripture professor. A Sister of St. Agnes, her nickname was "Sister Amphetamine," because of her boundless energy and the ardor with which she taught her classes. A tall, statuesque woman, she moved rapidly, often walking from her office to class in a cape that dallied behind, its hem swirling in the lift of the Chicago breeze. She would enter the classroom, go straight to her desk, stand with one hand on her hip, the other flip-ping through the pages of a dog-eared Bible, and then finally look up over the top of her reading glasses and say, "Class, Exodus, Chapter 12. Now, what are we to make of this? And please, don't psychologize or allegorize about it. And don't give me your opin-ion on it, because I really don't care. Anything you tell me I want you to get from the text. What does the *text* say?"

She had made the most formidable impact on me of any of my graduate school professors, giving me an appreciation for the Bible that I had lacked until her class. Before graduating from Catholic Theological Union (CTU) and leaving Chicago, I had taken five Scripture classes with her, causing many to say that I read the Bible "According to Dianne."

She had also become a friend. We would meet occasionally for dinner or tea at a local café and talk about school politics or the troubled state of religious life. I even cut her hair. Having been trained as the community's barber in the monastery during my novitiate year, I gave haircuts to all my classmates and to others in the community courageous enough to befriend my scissors. When Dianne learned of my tonsorial skills, she said, "Look, if you bring the scissors, I'll bring the wine." Brave woman.

So every five or six weeks, we would rendezvous in her office for a trim. We listened to classical music on the local NPR station, poured wine into stubby water glasses (except for those times when Dianne remembered to bring stemware from home), and I cut away, while we chatted about world events, and while Dianne held a bowl of water in her lap, which I used to rewet her quickly drying, baby-fine hair. Once, I poured a little too much water and it rolled down the side of her face, cascading onto the white towel shielding her wool sweater. As the water soaked through the towel, she looked up at me and said, "Edward, try to control yourself. Don't take it out on me for every nun who wouldn't let you go to the bathroom."

When I was done cutting, she would stand up, brush herself off, and walk to the mirror. Then with dexterous fingers she would shape her flat, lifeless hair into beautiful swirls of silver-gray, scrunching the hair toward her scalp and then twisting it in a circular motion with her fingertips. And before you knew it, *voilà*, Dianne's tresses were lifted and coiffed, and she was once again the nattiest nun-exegete in town.

Because she had made such an impression on me as a teacher and as a person, I decided to ask her to preach the homily at my First Mass. She was honored and delighted, though she seemed to sense more than I that my request wouldn't be met with universal acceptance. "Are you sure you want me to do this?" was her first response. I was the newly graduated theology student, confident that the progressive theology and ecclesiology that we had imbibed in graduate school would easily translate to the ministry we would do in the trenches. Wrong. While CTU may have taken a liberal stance toward women in the Church, parishes back

East, and the majority of our community members, for that matter, weren't exactly leading the vanguard of a dawning age of feminine ecclesial participation. In fact, nobody had bothered to tell them that there even was a new age.

On the day of the Mass in Union City, I was dashing from the church to the Rectory and back, making sure everything was in place and that the people involved in the ceremony were up to speed. Though these details were the domain of the master of ceremonies, Melvin, a close community friend, he had his hands full simply trying to attend to my family and make sure they got seated. After performing that Herculean task, he then had to assist the Passionist priests who were present, attempting to convince them that their "priestly right" to concelebrate the Mass wasn't being denied them if they quietly said the words of consecration from their pew, rather than file *en masse* into the sanctuary. I owed him a dinner by the time the day was over.

I went back to the rectory to get a special vestment that some women in the parish had made for the Mass. Dianne was sitting elegantly in our squalid dining room on a water-stained, upholstered chair, beneath peeling wallpaper, the result of a flooding bathroom on the second floor. She was reading the *New York Times*, drinking coffee, and munching on a Dunkin' Donut from a box that the pastor had been kind enough to ensure was available for the arriving guests. I tried to recall this kindness when the later events of the day made me want to strangle him.

"Dianne, oh, hi, there you are," I said. "I see you got everything you need."

"Well, I wouldn't go that far, Edward. But I am content."

"Well, that's good. I'm really looking forward to your homily at the Mass. I know you'll be wonderful. Oh, and by the way, I think *you* should read the Gospel, since you're the one preaching. Kathleen [the liturgy professor] always said that the preacher should read the Gospel."

She paused momentarily. "Well, Edward, that's nice, and I

respect Kathleen's scholarship, but we're not at CTU. Are you sure it's O.K. with everyone *here*? Don't you think you should check it out with someone?"

"What's to check out? I mean, if everyone's O.K. with you preaching, that's more significant than your reading the Gospel, isn't it? What could be the problem?"

"Well, Edward, some people get very funny about the technicalities of this kind of stuff. You never know where they stand on it. I'd run it by the pastor, or somebody, just to be sure."

"All right. If it'll make you feel better, I'll mention it. See you in church."

The procession for the Mass was celebratory. Kids from the youth group and adult leaders walked down the aisle with the colorful streamers and banners; the choir lifted their voices with brimming emotion; the religious and clergy in full regalia added ecclesiastical panache to the pageantry. I was nervous, even more so than the Jamaica First Mass. I knew all the people here—and they knew me. In a sense, they had "trained" me and now was the culmination of the tutelage, when the student was graduating and assuming position in front of the classroom. It struck me as odd that an ordination ceremony, with the bishop laying his hands on my head, had suddenly changed everything—some say ontologically. I wanted to live up to the supposed metamorphosis and to do a good job for them, to make them proud.

Getting through the introductory remarks and the Opening Prayer was a relief. I started to relax and to enjoy the festive atmosphere. Youth group members did the readings, one in Spanish, one in English, attempting to respect the ethnic diversity of the parish. As the time for the Gospel approached, I realized that I hadn't spoken to the pastor, or to anyone, about Dianne proclaiming the Gospel before her homily, or, as I was told to call it, her "reflection on the readings." Once I returned to the church, the many details of preparation had distracted me, and I simply forgot to mention it. Dianne hadn't said anything to me before the Mass began, so I suppose she assumed I had cleared everything.

The choir began to sing the Alleluia, signaling preparation for the proclamation of the Gospel. I stood, along with everyone else in the church, and smiled at Dianne, who was seated in the sanctuary with a few other priests and me. She looked at me quizzically, as if to say, "Well, what am I doing?" I nodded to her and motioned with my hand for her to come forward to the presider's chair. I had planned to give her the blessing to proclaim the Gospel before she proceeded to the pulpit to read it and to deliver her "reflection."

She placed her program on her chair, and hesitantly moved toward me, visibly uncomfortable that we hadn't more carefully choreographed this part. Everyone was watching her. Most in the church had never seen a woman proclaim the Gospel, never mind preach. Standing before me at the presider's chair, she looked up at me, smiled faintly, and rolled her eyes, as if to say, "Let's get this part over with." Placing my hands on her head, I closed my eyes, and began a prayer of blessing, "Dianne, may the Lord open your heart, and touch your lips, that you might . . ."

"What are you doing?" a deep and sonorous voice said, interrupting my heartfelt benediction.

When I opened my eyes, the pastor was standing next to Dianne, who was looking down at the floor.

"I'm giving Dianne a blessing to read the Gospel," I said sheepishly.

"Oh no you're not," he said. "*I* will read the Gospel."

And he turned from me, leaving Dianne standing there, and marched to the pulpit. He lifted his arms and said to the congregation, "The Lord be with you. A reading from the holy Gospel according to Matthew."

My heart pounded nervously and my face flushed. I was mortified. *How could he do this?* I was afraid to look at Dianne, but when I did, she was poised, her head tilted slightly to one side, seemingly listening attentively to the pastor proclaim the Gospel she was supposed to be reading. She was so cool about it, a real class act. I, on the other hand, wanted to go to the pulpit and throw him out of it headfirst for embarrassing Dianne, who had flown all the way from Chicago to be part of this celebration.

When the pastor was done reading the Gospel, Dianne ambled gracefully to the pulpit, looked out at the bewildered congregation, which was still perplexed by our pre-Gospel summit at the presider's chair, and began her homily in a strong voice and with undaunted, gesticulating hands. She didn't miss a beat, and if the contretemps at the presider's chair had upset her, she didn't let on one iota.

Today, I remember her homily most for its plea for me to be "transparent," to allow myself to be known by those to whom I minister. She exhorted me to permit my priesthood to be a human one; to share the healing and liberating Good News as a wounded healer and to give the recipients entrée into my life.

Holding the congregation spellbound, she moved through the layers of her presentation with ease and contagious enthusiasm. I felt like I was back in her classroom, sitting at the feet of a master who knew just what to say and how to say it. And I felt proud to have her up there, proud to call her my teacher, and prouder to call her my friend.

When she was done, the congregation sat transfixed for a moment, not sure what to do, but soon the applause began, first timidly, and then building to a crescendo that reverberated throughout the church and caused my father to comment later, "Boy, they really seemed to like *her*."

Yes, I thought, they did like her, although I wasn't sure everyone appreciated the significance of the moment, or the bittersweet leitmotif proffered by her appearance. A woman, obviously gifted with the charism to preach, had stood before us and spoken eloquently about the priesthood and the makings of a good priest. But she wasn't permitted to be one. Though I doubt Dianne ever had any aspirations to be a priest, our Church, which still bars women from ordination, denies her that possibility. The argument waged against women's ordination, chiefly that Jesus chose only men to be his disciples ("the first priests"), limps with conspicuous palsy when failing to account for the vastly different station of women in today's society, as compared with the time of Jesus. It limps even further when one encounters a woman with obvious talent to be an effective priest—to say nothing of the fact that we don't seem to have many men who want to do it anymore.

While the Roman Catholic Church still requires that its priests be male, most other religious groups in the United States have flung their doors open wide to women. The percentage of women in the clergy almost tripled from 1983 to 1999, while enrollment of women in Master of Divinity programs has risen even more sharply, currently about 30 percent of the total student membership. These other religious denominations employ women in roles of priestly or rabbinic leadership without the church or temple being shaken to its foundation. The Catholic Church must finally begin to consider when it will treat 52 percent of the population with the respect and dignity it deserves.

To his credit, the pastor later penned an apology to Dianne for any embarrassment he may have caused her. He also indirectly apologized to me, although he held firm in his conviction that, as pastor, his responsibility was to uphold the law of the Church that only priests or deacons were permitted to proclaim the Gospel during Mass. I argued that, if he was willing to bend the rules to allow her to give a "reflection on the readings," why not bend a little further and let her read the Gospel of which she was going to be speaking? I didn't get anywhere, though. He maintained that if I had asked him first, we all would have been spared the embarrassment, because he would have simply told me no. I preferred the way it spun out, though, even with the embarrassment, because we almost got there. At least Dianne got half of a blessing. It was one step closer to what seems inevitable. "Easy for you to say," says Dianne. "You weren't the one left standing there."

Women priests and married priests will undoubtedly be issues that the next Pope will have to confront, if priests are to continue to exercise effective leadership in the community. Unfortunately, the resolution of such a paramount issue seems to lie solely with the theological leanings of a Papal administration. We must wait and see what and who comes next. However, we are not going to have enough celibate males to meet the need, if the present statistics hold and vocations continue to wane. Proactive, creative planning is needed soon, or it will be too late. Perhaps the dearth of vocations is the Spirit's way of prompting us to the next leap of faith, or as Anne Lamott likes to say, "lurch of faith." But we had better start lurching soon, or we'll need more than faith.

Dianne and I remain good friends, who today can laugh about the pastor's interception of her reading of the word of God. But through my years in ministry I have met many women who aren't laughing, women who are instead weeping like Mary at the tomb, women who have given up on a Church they perceive as sexist and misogynistic. It's unfortunate, because we're part of a tradition stemming from a man who was a champion of women. Jesus hobnobbed with prostitutes, offered "living water" to a Samaritan woman to whom he wasn't even supposed to be speaking, and chose women to appear to first after his Resurrection. I'd bet money that he wouldn't have a problem today with them proclaiming these accounts to communities who continue to thirst for that same "living water."

CHAPTER THIRTEEN

BRAIN TUMOR

After making the crossing, they came to land at Gennesaret. When the people of that place recognized him, they sent word to all the surrounding country. People brought to him all those who were sick and begged him that they might touch only the tassel on his cloak, and as many touched it were healed.

—MATTHEW 14:34–36

I had just finished a difficult session with someone who came to me regularly for spiritual direction. She was not having a good day. While speaking of her fear of abandonment, even by God, she cried about a philandering husband who had left two years before and a son who was moving to California to start a beekeeping business. He hoped to sweeten his bank account and settle in the Napa Valley with his bees. Loss seemed to fill her life.

As I climbed the stairs to my room, my legs felt heavy, like I was wearing workout weights on my ankles—too little sleep and too many appointments with people with too many problems. My eyes ached from an afternoon of attentiveness, and from intermittent reading between direction sessions. I needed a nap. As I pulled down the white comforter on the bed, the late afternoon sun danced on it through half-opened mini-blinds, making it look like a sheet of lined loose-leaf. Leaving the blinds open, I pulled the comforter over me, luxuriating in the last rays of autumn sun warming my face.

The phone rang soon after I had fallen into a deep sleep. Startled by the shrill ring, I vaulted from the bed, not wanting to be found asleep in the middle of the afternoon.

"Hello," I managed, clearing my throat.

"Hi, Edward. It's me," my father said.

He sounded different.

"Dad, what's the matter?"

"It's your mother," he said quietly, struggling with the words.

"Yeah, what about her, Dad? Where is she?"

"She's in the living room. She . . . she has a brain tumor."

He then began to sob, as I have never heard my father—uncontrolled heaving, unable to catch his breath. I sat on the floor. The phone crashed from the desk. I didn't fully comprehend what he had said.

"What do you mean a brain tumor? Are you sure? Let me speak with her."

As he composed himself, I sensed his embarrassment and surprise at his uncharacteristic display of emotion. "No, um, she doesn't want to talk now. She needs a little time. They're going to operate next week, but they don't know what to expect until they go in there . . . Can you come home for it?"

"Dad, of course I'll be there for it. But they don't know what kind of tumor it is, or how serious?"

"No, not yet. They have to go in. Look, I have to go now. I can't talk about it anymore. We'll talk later. Just pray for her."

As I hung up the phone, I felt an ache settle in my body like the onslaught of flu. Still half-asleep, I began lacing my Nike running shoes, exercise seeming as good a response as any to clear my head. I felt like I was moving in slow motion, watching myself perform this pre-exercise ritual from outside of myself. Shorts and a yellow Rolling Stones T-shirt with a big red tongue splashed across the front of it completed my running ensemble. Outside, the last hints of autumn light lingered on the dying lawn.

As I stretched my hamstrings on the front lawn, tears welled up in my eyes and fell onto the grass. My body ached with weakness; my first lunging strides on the concrete felt like I was completing a run rather than beginning one.

I started to pray: *How could you do this? How could you allow this to happen? What did she ever do but be a good mother and wife? She's only fifty-one years old, for God's sake.*

The more I ran and tried to pray, the angrier I became. The rush hour cars were now using their headlights on the darkening street, and people were scurrying past me, eager to get home after a day of work. How odd it seemed that none of them were aware of my news. I was just another runner to them. While turning onto Newton Square, I broke from that pedestrian rank, raising my fist in the air in a Joblike gesture of defiance.

"Don't you do this!" I shouted audibly. "Don't you do this!"

It was a cinematic moment. I imagine I looked like Norma Rae at the moment she demands the textile machines stop running, and that I sounded like Richard Gere in *An Officer and a Gentleman*, when he defies the sergeant to throw him out of the army. "This is my last chance, sir. Don't do this!" Despite the histrionics, I meant business. My sophisticated theological training took a holiday, and I prayed with my guts rather than my head, threatening God and then bargaining with Him. *I've done this for you. I became a damn priest. I've given you that. I'm not ready to give you my mother yet. You fix this.*

In hindsight, I'm embarrassed by my defiance, but that day I held nothing back. When I reached the block of our residence, I stopped running, out of breath and emotionally exhausted, my yellow T-shirt now sweaty, dark amber. My prayer, too, had been exhausted. But as I walked toward the house, my mind strangely cleared and the knot in my stomach released. More than endorphins, a peace came over me, a feeling of being embraced, of being comforted by warm hands—like being unexpectedly kissed. I knew at once I wasn't alone in this. Whatever the outcome, someone was with me. Someone who didn't mind my defiance, who high-fived my raised fist, was going to bring me home. Though I had preached that it was O.K. to get angry with God, it was now a case of doctor heal thyself. My anger proved cathartic because it forced me to relate to God as a person. I was telling God what to do (not unlike me). But most surprising was God's seeming response that He would do what I was saying.

I arrived home two days after getting the news, steeled to share this burden with my parents. I needed to be there for myself, too. Geographical distance, caused by my itinerant life, had precluded frequent home visits, making me feel remiss in not being more present to my parents. I wanted to be there now when they needed me. Also, I didn't trust my parents to handle the doctor negotiations on their own. I was always the one who asked the questions, exploring every angle and possible scenario. They'd rather not know.

The mood in the house was solemn, but, gratefully, not funereal. My mother was surprisingly more animated than I had anticipated.

"Hello, baby, I'm glad you're home," she said. "But you didn't have to come yet. The surgery's not till next week. You should've stayed in Massachusetts and done your work. I'm fine."

"I know you are. But I wanted to be here anyway. I'm sure Dad could use the support too."

"Yeah, he does seem kind of sad. But I don't know why. Everything is going to be fine. God will take care of me."

"Yes, God will, Mother."

I reached out and took her hand. I said the words, but I wasn't convinced. Although I was grateful for the feeling of peace that I received after my run, it wasn't consistent. At times, I was overcome with fear that my mother could die. And I wondered where God was in all of this. While as a priest I had frequently dealt with people confronting tragedy, it felt different when it was my tragedy. "Putting it in God's hands" and "blindly trusting" were advice more easily heeded by others.

But eventually, my mother's optimistic spirits buoyed my own. "Oh, Edward, don't be ridiculous. Everything is going to be fine." If *she* was able to remain confident in the midst of such horrific circumstances, it was the least I could do. I know her sanguineness helped my father too, though he had had better days. Although he didn't speak about his feelings, his expressionless, daydreaming face and long silences betrayed his fear. He paced the house from one end to the other, looking out the front door and then the back, as though waiting for some kind of reprieve.

He also went to work each day, mostly to keep his mind off the impending surgery, and I stayed at home with my mother. My father returned in the evenings, spent from a day of fire investigation and detective work. We had simple evening meals together that my mother still prepared. After dinner the three of us sat in front of the TV, silently watching detective shows and sitcoms. Although we felt like actors in a story even more unbelievable than anything we were watching, the shows provided distraction and helped us not to have to talk about what we couldn't.

The morning of the surgery, my father, my brother, and I stood at my mother's bed in New York University Medical Center. We were confident that we had enlisted one of the most renowned brain surgeons in the country. Dr. Ransohoff had consulted with my father and me the day before, to explain the surgery and the risks.

"This is a big tumor. Because of its positioning, I can't tell exactly how big, but it's amazing she has been able to function as well as she has up to this point."

A small man, he wore cowboy boots with multicolored, embroidered stitching, and he had a buzz-style crew cut. Behind him was the black and gray X ray of my mother's cranium, with the insidious tumor observable, a black mass lodged between the two ventricles in the center of her brain.

"Well, I don't understand why you can't tell us what kind of tumor this is," I said. "Shouldn't you be able to tell if it's malignant or benign from the X ray and the MRI that you did?"

"Sometimes we can tell because malignant tumors have tentacles that spread out into other parts of the brain. This one, I can't tell about until I go in because it's so large. It could have tentacles."

"Well, do you *think* it does?"

"I don't want to *think* when it comes to something as serious as your mother's life. I want to *know*. And I won't *know* until I go in. If you were asking me to give an educated guess, I'd say the tumor is probably benign. But with a tumor this big, it might not matter, because of the amount of cutting I may have to do to remove it. It's pretty deep. I'm just not sure what else is going to be affected when I try to take it out."

I kept wishing Ransohoff had been more reassuring. He may have been one of the best brain surgeons in the country, but he lacked bedside manner. His gruff personality was intimidating, not only to us but also to the nurses and other doctors who fluttered around him. He was known as "God" in the unit, a moniker probably most evident in his ability to chain-smoke in the hospital, with no repercussions.

I resented being subjected to his secondhand smoke, particularly when my mother happened to see him puffing away one day and said, "See, even the doctor smokes. It's not so bad. Why don't you all just get off my back?"

Years of trying to convince my mother of the dangers of smoking went down the drain. Undoubtedly, she would have joined him in a pre-op drag had she not been confined to her bed and held captive by her familial watchmen.

When two orderlies appeared at the door to my mother's room, we were asked to leave. Arriving to prep her for the surgery, one had an electric razor in his hand and the other a can of Nair hair remover.

"Mom, we'll be right outside," I said. "This will only take about ten minutes and then we'll come back in, O.K.?"

She nodded silently. For the first time, I saw fear and uncertainty in her eyes. No more anticipating what it would be like. The players were assembling, the game about to begin.

The three of us waited in the visitors' area while the coiffeurs went to work.

"Man, she's not going to like that," my brother offered.

"Ah, what's the difference," said my father. "Hair grows back. As long as the tumor doesn't."

"We should try to convince her not to dye it anymore," I said. "Just let it grow in naturally. She'd look good with salt-and-pepper hair."

Ridiculously, we were talking about her hair—anything to divert us from considering what came next: an electric saw to cut through the skull, metal clamps to keep it held open, nicotine-stained gloved hands probing deep inside the places that made my mother who she was, and who we hoped she would continue to be.

"You can go back in now," said the orderly with the razor.

"How is she?" asked my brother.

"Well, she has less hair," he said, attempting humor. I wanted to give *him* a haircut.

When we walked back in the room, my hairless mother sat in the bed; she was crying for the first time since this ordeal had begun. My father and brother looked at me, as if "the priest son" was supposed to know what to do. After all, didn't I visit patients in hospitals all the time in similar situations? Yeah, but they weren't my mother. I decided to try to offer her theological comfort and reassurance. I knelt next to her bed and took her hands in mine.

"Mother, you know, you can't lose it now. You've been so faithful and strong up to this point. You have to believe God is going to see you through this. He didn't bring you this far to leave you now. Trust in Him that it's going to be O.K., and I'm sure you'll be back to your old self sooner than you'd imagine."

She stopped crying and looked at me as though I was speaking in Latin.

"Edward, don't you think I know all of that? Just because you're a priest doesn't give you the edge on God, you know."

"But you're so upset. You haven't been this upset since we found out about this tumor."

"Edward, I just paid fifty dollars for that permanent. You'd be upset, too."

We all laughed, including my mother. And the laughter in that hospital room was holy, because it uncovered the holiness of my mother for all of us to see. She really was that rooted in faith, even if the outcome was not to her liking. She believed that God was present to her and would see her through whatever awaited her. My father and brother weren't so sure. I, the priest son, wasn't so sure. But she was. Her strength and faith were passed on to us that day and they helped to get us through the most harrowing ordeal we had experienced as a family.

Once again it was a lesson to me of the contagious power of faith. My mother was peaceful because of a spiritual haven she had cultivated through years of prayer and commitment. She drew strength from that center, a wellspring of fortitude and replenishment to which she returned when depleted. It was as if she had squirreled away grace for a rainy day, and when the rains came, the grace provided a place of dryness and warmth. I wanted such a place of my own. And I wanted to want to know how she had gotten there. Her example encouraged me to cultivate my own center, and to visit it more frequently. You don't learn that from theology school. You learn it by going there, after traveled people show you how.

When the time came for them to wheel her to the operating room, I asked for a few minutes alone with her. Everyone left the room, including my father and brother. I took out the relic. Robert, whose mother had been blessed with it in the 1940s when she had contracted a severe case of tuberculosis, had loaned it to me. It was a relic of St. Martin de Porres, a Peruvian saint known for his simplicity and willingness to attend to anyone in need who knocked at the monastery door. He was also a barber, a humorous coincidence not missed by my mother.

"Sure, he probably gave haircuts like the one I got now," she said.

The relic was a tiny piece of his bone, observable through a small glass window encased in a gold container. The container stood about five inches high, with the piece of bone attached to a red velvet background and placed underneath the small viewing window. Under the bone fragment was the name: +S. MARTIN DE PORRES.

"This is the relic I was telling you about from Father Bob."

"What do you mean 'relic'?"

"Remember, I told you his mother had been blessed with this when she was very sick in the hospital and they believe it really helped her? He was a great and powerful saint, and this is a piece of his bone."

"That's a piece of his bone? Under that glass? How did they get that?"

"I have no idea, Mother. I don't know much about these things. All I know is that it has helped some people and I want to pray that it helps you, too."

"So what do I have to do with it?"

"You don't have to do anything. I'm just going to bless you with it and pray for his intercession and help during the surgery."

"You better tell him that I have a Jewish doctor."

"I don't think that makes a difference, Mother."

I placed the relic on her forehead and she closed her eyes. I could tell she was going to that place deep inside of her that I had seen her travel to before Mass began, when she knelt and said her Rosary, moving her lips and bowing her head when she came to "blessed is the fruit of thy womb, Jesus."

"St. Martin de Porres," I prayed, "we turn to you at this hour of need and we pray for your help. Bless my mother during her surgery and guide the doctors in their care of her. Keep her strong and healthy and allow her a full recovery, if it be God's will. We know that, through your power and holiness, others have been blessed and cured. Help my mother."

My voice began to break toward the end of the prayer. "Help my mother" was probably the most heartfelt prayer I have ever prayed. My mother opened her big navy blue eyes and tears began to roll down the sides of her scrubbed cheeks. The surgical cap she wore made her look like she had just gotten out of the shower. I wanted to say something to her, some final words, but they were stuck in my throat. We were out of time.

I bent down on one knee, my eyes level with hers as she lay on the gurney.

"Mom, I just want you to know that . . . I love you."

I had never remembered saying those words before. Perhaps I had written them in a card, or uttered them hurriedly at the end of a phone conversation, but this was the real thing. I meant it.

She looked at me with gratitude and said, "I know. I love you, too."

They wheeled her into the hallway, where she had a final moment with my father and brother; then they pushed the gurney to the operating room for the eight-hour surgery.

Neurosurgery units are no picnic. Most of the people walking the corridors consider themselves lucky to be able to. During the hours in the waiting room, between walks to the bathroom and trips to the hospital concession to get coffee and snacks, we forged an unspoken bond with others who also awaited word on their loved ones. I noticed one couple whom I had seen each time I'd been in the unit. They were in their forties, seemingly pleasant, but often forcing a smile I could tell they weren't feeling.

On one of my trips downstairs for something to drink I said, "Can I get you two anything in the cafeteria?"

"No, we were just down a little while ago, thanks . . . but we would like to talk to you a moment." It was the wife, blond hair, sad, kind eyes, and that painful smile.

"Sure. What's up?"

"You're the priest, right?"

How did they know that?

"Um, yes, yes, I am. Edward, Edward Beck." I extended my hand. Hers felt limp, sapped of energy.

"It's so nice to meet you," she said. "We've seen you around the past couple of days. We've been here two weeks now. Our son is in the intensive care unit. He has a brain tumor, like your mother, but he also has an aneurysm that is blocking access to the tumor, so the doctors can't operate. He's in a coma right now and they say there's nothing they can do for him."

She took out a Kleenex and blotted her eyes, trying to salvage the little mascara that remained, while her husband sat looking at the floor, holding the sides of his head.

"Oh. I'm so sorry to hear that. It must be so hard for you." I wasn't sure I could deal with one more sad story. I didn't feel like ministering; I felt like being ministered to.

"Thank you. Father, my husband and I aren't Catholics. We're Baptists and our faith is very important to us, but we heard from one of the nurses that you blessed your mother with a *saint*? Did we get the story right?"

"Well, yes, not exactly with a saint, but I have a relic of St. Martin de Porres that a friend of mine loaned to me, and I blessed my mother with that. It's actually supposed to be a piece of his bone."

"Really . . . well, my husband and I were wondering if you would consider blessing our son with it, even though we're not Catholic. We're still very religious and we believe in the power of God, and, quite frankly, we're willing to try anything at this point."

"Of course, I'd be happy to. Let me get it. It's in my mother's room."

Although I would have preferred not being brought into another family's pain, how could I refuse? Blessing is to be shared, and I had the privilege of sharing it. I brought the relic to the waiting room. We had to wait about thirty minutes because admittance to the ICU was limited to ten minutes every hour, but when we finally entered I knew immediately which patient was Mark. He was about nineteen years old with sandy blond hair not unlike his mother's. He had tubes in his nose and mouth and countless IVs stuck in his arms. Even amid the medical intrusion, there was serenity in his face and peacefulness in his recline, as though he were dreaming of a time without needles and hospital gowns.

His parents and I stood around the bed. The nurse attending Mark stood with us, holding a tray she had been using to assist another patient. I joined hands with Mark's mother while she held the hand of her husband. The nurse holding the tray closed her eyes and joined us in our prayer as I placed the relic on Mark's forehead.

"St. Martin de Porres," I prayed, "you who are the protector and liberator of those in need, be with Mark and his family now. Bless them with your peace and intercede for them to Jesus in whom they strongly believe and place their faith. Bring healing to Mark and guide the doctors and nurses in their care of him."

I closed my eyes and prayed silently for the health of this young man, though a part of me felt his situation to be hopeless. The quiet of the room was suddenly interrupted by a loud crash, as if a handful of silverware had been thrown to the floor. I jumped, along with Mark's parents, displaced from the serenity of the prayer. I opened my eyes to see the nurse, who had been holding the tray with instruments, standing with both hands to her mouth, staring incredulously at Mark. When I turned to the bed, Mark was awake, out of the coma, conscious for the first time in two and a half weeks. He didn't say anything or make any movement, but his eyes were open and he appeared to be faintly smiling. His parents stood dumbfounded, their mouths agape, tears filling their eyes. I didn't know what to think, amazed myself at the synchronicity of Mark's awakening and the blessing with the relic. The nurse called for the doctor.

When Mark was tested later that day after emerging from the coma, the doctors discovered that the aneurysm had disappeared, making surgery on the brain tumor possible. The medical staff in the ICU termed it "a miracle." Mark's tumor was cancerous, and although the operation was successful, radiation treatment was needed and Mark was physically impaired as a result. He needed assistance walking and his speech was slurred, but he was alive and, to my knowledge, remains so. His parents were so grateful that they made a $500 donation to Covenant House in New York in my name and also eventually converted to Catholicism.

When I came out of the ICU unit, I went back to the waiting room, still shaken from the experience, to find my brother and father consulting with Dr. Ransohoff.

"How is she?" I said, perturbed that I had missed his arrival.

"She pulled through beautifully," Ransohoff said. "The tumor was much bigger, though, than I anticipated, about the size of a lemon. So we had to do a lot of cutting. I'm not sure what effects there'll be. But I think she'll be O.K."

"That's wonderful," I said. "But the tumor, was it benign?"

"Oh, yeah," he said. "Big, but benign. We got it all."

"Thank God." *And St. Martin.*

Word spread through the hospital that there was a holy relic on the premises. It was fascinating to witness people's reactions when they learned of the story. Jews and Muslims were as curious as the Christians. Blessing has no denomination. St. Martin quickly became a celebrity, fostering ecumenism in a hospital where suffering was the common faith experience.

I called Robert and told him that my mother, God, and the relic of St. Martin had all pulled through beautifully. I thanked him for the use of the relic.

"Oh, keep it as long as you want," he said. "Keep it by your mother as she heals."

That's what we did. We kept the relic on the table in my mother's hospital room as each day she grew stronger and more alert.

"Why do they give me these welfare tissues?" she said one afternoon, a few days after the surgery. "I can't even blow my nose in them without them ripping. Will somebody please go and buy me some Kleenex, for God's sake."

She was getting back to her old self.

The fourth day of her recovery I got to the hospital early and went up to her room. I immediately noticed that the relic was not on her nightstand.

"Mom, where's St. Martin?"

"In heaven, I hope."

"Mom, the relic. What did you do with the relic that was here on the table?"

"Oh, I put that in the closet at home. I didn't think it was safe here. Too many people were looking at it."

"In the closet at home? Mother, you haven't been home. You've been here in the hospital since the surgery. Now think, what did you do with the relic?"

"I told you, I put it in the closet at home."

She was obviously still hallucinating from the anesthesia. I assumed that someone had taken it, desperate to have his or her own miracle. I began interviewing the nurses and the janitorial staff, growing more impatient with every "No, I never saw it." By the end of the day, I was frustrated and embarrassed to call my friend and tell him that his prized relic had been lost.

When my mother had finished eating dinner that evening, my father and brother and I sat with her while the news hummed in the background on the TV suspended over our heads.

"Hand me a tissue," said my mother.

"Where are they?" asked my father.

"In the closet," my mother retorted.

"Gerri, *what* closet? All you have here is a bathroom. There's no closet."

"Well, I thought that's where I put them. Don't get so upset."

An orderly was clearing the hospital table on which my mother had been eating. It had been maneuvered over her bed for easy access. When the table was empty, I saw my mother lift up the top and retrieve herself a tissue and then close it again.

"Wait a minute," I said. "Let me see that table."

I lifted the top and there in the corner, safely ensconced be-

tween a Bible, some Rosary beads, and more tissues was the missing relic, shining like a new penny.

"Mother, the relic is right here in this table."

"I told you I put it in the closet. No one ever listens to me."

I'm not much for "magic religion." I've always been suspicious
of it. When people tell me they are flying all over the world to
visit shrines where Mary and other saints are supposedly appearing, I look at them with a jaundiced eye. I'm tempted to say, "Find
God where you are. The holy isn't something you seek outside
yourself. It's within." Or I feel like quoting the Scriptures to them
where Jesus says, "An evil and unfaithful generation seeks a sign,
but no sign will be given it except the sign of Jonah the prophet"
(Matthew 12:39). It seems obvious to me that the lack of "proof"
is what makes faith so cherished.

Yet, I cannot deny my experience of the relic and the way in
which it provided strength and hope for us in the midst of a harrowing ordeal. I believe it was our faith that ultimately provided
the power, but our connection to the holiness of this saint in the
relic represented a tangible expression for us of the inherent
power. Literally, it was something to hold on to. When the sick
were brought to Jesus, Matthew says they "begged him that they
might touch only the tassel on his cloak, and as many touched it
were healed" (Matthew 14:36). But the power wasn't in the tassel. The power was in their faith. It was in their belief that Jesus
embodied life for them and that if they could get close enough to
that life, they'd participate in its restorative power. Isn't that really
what incarnation is in the end—God becoming real, touchable,
alive? Whatever can mediate that to us is holy.

The real "miracle" of my family's experience continues to
make its power felt, more than ten years after the surgery. The
miracle for me was that I finally told my mother I loved her. The
miracle was that I spent weeks alone with my father and that we
talked openly, healing wounds of alienation and discord. The mir-

acle was that we all gained a new appreciation for the precious gift of life and its fragility. The miracle *is* that I know, in a way I have never known it, that God is the giver and sustainer of all life. Had things turned out differently, as they surely do, at times, for less fortunate people, could I still say this? I hope so. My mother says she isn't so sure.

CHAPTER FOURTEEN

A KUNG-FU GOD?

❧

Jesus said to them, "Amen, I say to you, tax collectors and sinners are entering the kingdom of God before you. When John came to you in the way of righteousness, you did not believe him; but tax collectors and prostitutes did."

—MATTHEW 21:31–32

He pulled up on his roaring Harley-Davidson like he owned the street. Though he lacked the de rigueur apparel of a true biker—leather cap, chaps, tattoos, and a scraggly beard—he possessed some of the attitude. Sitting on the motorcycle as if it was a throne, he was in control, surveying the street like the mayor in charge of cleanup. Surprisingly, he was dressed modestly, beige slacks, green and white polo shirt, and no helmet. His ruggedly handsome face showed some of the wear of too much sun; his stocky build and curly black hair made him look just a little dangerous. I knew before he opened his mouth that he could be charming.

"Hey, Father, what time's the next Mass?" he shouted across the sidewalk as he parked his motorcycle at the curb. I stood in front of the church in my vestments, greeting the people who were arriving for the next Mass.

"In about five minutes," I said curtly.

"Oh, man, that's not going to be any good. My wife's still at home with our kid—and she'd probably even be late for the Mass after this one, if I know her. Listen, we're going down the shore today, since it's such a beautiful day, and we can't get that late a start. O.K. if I just stop by with them before we go and you throw a little blessing on us?"

"You want me to bless you before you go to the shore? Why?"

"Well, I don't know, does someone need a reason to get a blessing these days? Maybe so we don't have an accident on the way down, and so my son's O.K. when he plays by the water. You know, there are lots of reasons. I don't have to explain that to *you*, do I?"

"Well, the best blessing you could possibly get," I said, "would be to bring your wife and child to Mass today and then, as a family, go down to the shore."

He paused momentarily, seemingly considering my proposition, and then said, "Father, by the time we get down there, I won't even need sunscreen anymore. C'mon, all we need is a blessing. We'll come to Mass next week. I don't think God will really mind."

"Look, I gave you my best advice. The decision is yours. I really have to start Mass now." I turned to walk into the church.

"You're new here, right?" he called after me.

"Yes, I'm here only a few months," I said, looking back at him.

"I think once you get the hang of this, you'll see that it would have been better just to give me the blessing."

"Well, since it seems there's a lot you have to explain to me, maybe you can teach me how to be a priest as I go along," I said, and walked into the church, leaving him smiling, standing in the street, shaking his head.

The next Sunday I presided at the ten o'clock Mass. About fifteen minutes into the service, just as I was starting my homily, he walked in the back of the church. Holding a child in one arm and escorting a blond woman on the other, he sauntered down the right-side aisle to the third pew. He was not unobtrusive about it. Chewing gum and walking down the aisle as though he were in a sports stadium, he arrived at the pew and climbed over the people at the end, dragging the child and woman behind him to the center.

Any disturbance, however minor, has always thrown me when I'm preaching. I easily lose my train of thought and then worry that everyone else is also being distracted and therefore, God forbid, not hanging on my every word. Usually the interruption involves tantrum-prone children who decide the central aisle of the church is the most advantageous venue in which to negotiate with their parents. This day, however, it was the motorcyclist beachcomber who was turning heads. I stopped the homily in midsentence and stared at him, waiting for him and his entourage to be seated. He looked around, oblivious to the delay, making faces at his son and smiling at the child's every move. If nothing else, this was a smitten father.

At the end of Mass, I stood in the back of the church, greeting the congregation as they exited. He came up to me with child and woman in tow.

"Hey, Father, that was a nice Mass. Thanks," he said as he extended his hand. I shook it and he said, "This is my wife, Annie, and our little son, Marco. This is Father . . . what's your name again?"

"Edward," I said, "Father Edward, nice to meet you." I nodded to his wife.

"Ah yes, Father Edward," he said, "Padre Eduardo. Oh, and I'm Henry, by the way. I don't think I ever really introduced myself last week."

"And how was your day at the shore?" I inquired, somewhat flippantly.

"It was great and we got there no problem, even without your blessing."

His wife, Annie, shook her head at him and looked at me sympathetically, as if to say, "Yes, he really is like this most of the time."

"Well, I'm glad," I said. "And I'm also glad you made it to church today—even if you were fifteen minutes late."

"Gee, you're worse than the nun I had in the third grade." He turned to leave. "Oh, by the way," he said, turning back, "I'm pretty handy and I could use some work, so if you need anything done around the church or in any of these buildings you have, let me know."

"O.K.," I said. "Do you have a card or anything—maybe something with your rates?"

"No, not with me, but I'll be seeing you around. And we can work out the payment stuff with the man upstairs." He pointed upward. "Oh, and one more thing, the homily was a little long today, especially for people with kids."

Henry began coming to church regularly. I learned later that he had made a secret pact with God: He would go to church and try to live a better life; in return, God had to make his business financially solvent, and maybe throw in a few perks here and there, like a better house than the basement apartment they were living in, and transportation that was more family-friendly than the Harley-Davidson he cruised around on. While it didn't seem the most sophisticated theological framework from which to reason, it apparently worked for him.

"Business is really picking up, Father Edward," he said one day, a few weeks after I had noticed his regular attendance on Sundays. "There's something to this God thing. I really think my Uncle Ralph, who I loved—the one who was killed—is helping me out. He's looking down on me and making it happen. Nobody's affected me in my life as much as him. I want to be good like he was."

Slowly, I watched Henry change. Although he still bounced checks like basketballs and racked up parking tickets like cherished heirlooms; though he still battled with the IRS and walked just this side of being behind bars; though he still flirted with girls, like Julio Iglesias in his prime, and drank more margaritas than was advisable for a short man, he began to change. I noticed it first in subtle ways.

Passing a homeless man on the street one day in Union City, he said to me, "How come you think God allows stuff like that?"

"Stuff like what?" I said.

"Well, people who are homeless, kids who are sick or abused, you know, stuff like that."

"I really don't know, Henry," I responded. "That's an age-old question. And I'm afraid we don't have the answers for it."

"Well, when I get up there—if I get up there—God better have some answers, because I sure got a lot of questions."

But rather than let the questions linger, like clothes on a line that you never pull in, Henry proffered his own answers. If centuries of biblical and theological investigation couldn't satisfy, Henry would give it a shot. He had a theory for everything.

"I think God's really cool about most of the stuff we do," he offered one day while we were driving in his truck to visit an apartment he was remodeling. "He can put up with all of it, except when we deliberately hurt somebody else, or if we don't take care of someone who can't take care of himself. That's when God turns into Bruce Lee."

Whenever we passed someone begging for money, he would rummage in his pockets, giving whatever he could spare, sometimes what he couldn't. But even more than the giving was the noticing. He was like a movie camera, taking it all in, always attentive to the one others passed by and missed. He engaged people on the fringe in his charming, offbeat way, making them feel that they too mattered.

Part of me felt that he was seeing himself in the marginalized. Born of parents who had to flee Cuba with him after Castro's takeover in 1959, Henry had always been the underdog, needing to prove himself, one step ahead of merely surviving. Unwittingly, he had developed a sophisticated, theological understanding that he was the struggling person he was passing by on the street, but he had none of the stilted inertia often accompanying highbrow intellectual acumen. He acted on what he believed; though he didn't know it, praxis was the motto by which he lived.

Unfortunately, acting according to his notion of justice sometimes proved morally ambiguous, even dangerous—for both of us.

His truck nearly got us killed one day. It was in a body shop, which some drug dealers had recommended, for repairs. I never bothered to ask what made him think drug dealers offered good references.

"Father Edward, I have to go and pick up my truck. Come take a ride with me," he said one day after I had just finished teaching religion class to the fourth grade.

"Henry, I'm working," I said. "I just can't take off in the middle of the day to tool around with you while you run errands."

"Hey, I'm a parishioner here. I *am* your work. And I'm telling you that I need you. What more do you have to hear?"

"You need me to go and pick up a truck?" I said. "Yeah, that sounds really important for me to put everything else on hold for."

"It shouldn't matter *what* I need you for. It should only matter that I need you. And I'm telling you that I do."

I stood shaking my head, exasperated that he was once more manipulating me into doing what he wanted. I had learned, however, that with Henry things were rarely how they appeared on the surface. There was always an underneath that you eventually got to—if you were tenacious enough to hang around for a while.

"Henry, let me get my jacket. I'll be right out. But I'm giving you one hour, not one minute more." I sounded like the third-grade nun to whom he had compared me.

As we rode to the body shop, he made chitchat about his business, his kids, and some crazy notion he had of making sunglasses out of wood, an idea he was convinced would produce a large windfall, since everyone would covet individually carved designer sunglasses. He speculated he could retire on the profits.

"Henry, why did I have to come with you to pick up this truck?" I finally asked, dismissing his get-rich scheme. "What's so important?"

"Well, I may have some problems with the guy, and I wanted someone else to be around. Well, actually, I wanted *you* around, since you have some pull with the man upstairs."

"What kind of problems?" I now was sure I had made a mistake in coming.

"Well, I don't think this guy did what he was supposed to with the truck, and I already paid him for it, so we may have some problems if he's not willing to make good and reimburse some of our money."

"*We?*" I said, "*We* may have some problems, Henry? No, *I* don't have any problems. So, unless you have a mouse in your pocket, I don't know who the *we* you're talking about is."

When we arrived at the shop, I told him I'd wait for him in the car.

"Man, you can't do that," he said. "The whole reason I brought you is so that this guy wouldn't start any trouble. You gotta come in."

"Oh, is that why you brought me? Henry, I'm really getting tired of your crap, and it's the last time I'm letting you get me into something like this. C'mon, let's go in and get it over with. I have to get back to the parish."

I would have laid down money that the man standing behind the counter in the shop knew the warden's name at Riker's Island. And, of course, it wasn't long before he and Henry were trading expletives while I stood on the sidelines, growing more alarmed with each screamed repartee.

"You can go to hell," the guy finally said. "We did what we were supposed to do to that crap truck. Now you, and it, get the hell out of here. I'm not giving you one dime. And take the reverend here with you."

The guy then went through a door behind the counter, leaving Henry and me standing there like reprimanded schoolboys who had no recourse but to take our knapsacks and go home. I would have gladly followed this docile, intelligent path, but not Henry. His sense of justice had been offended.

"I'm not letting that guy screw me," he said. "I want you to stand here and be a lookout. Yell to me if you see that bastard, or anyone else, coming."

"Henry, what are you talking about? What are you gonna do? Henry, let's just go."

Ignoring me, he moved to the rear of the body shop and came back holding an air gun, the kind used in construction and repair work.

"Henry, what are you doing?" I said.

"This is about worth what that moron owes me, so I'm taking it. Come on, let's go. You get in the car. I'll drive the truck."

"Henry, you can't just take that. It's not yours. File a complaint against the guy or something. You could get arrested for taking this. Are you crazy?"

"This guy's not going to have me arrested. He hangs around with drug dealers. And God knows what else he deals in."

"Henry, you can't . . ." And that's all I managed to get out before the guy suddenly came back through the door and saw Henry standing there with the air gun.

"Hey, what the hell you doing with my air gun, you Cuban spick," the guy said, jumping the counter and moving toward Henry, who stood there seemingly unfazed by this interruption to his larceny.

"I'm taking this to make up for what you owe me," said Henry calmly, as though he expected the man to throw in a drill and saw, too.

"The hell you are," the guy said, and from his pocket he pulled out an eight-inch switchblade that shimmered menacingly in the harsh fluorescent light of the garage.

"Henry, give the man back his air gun—*now!* And let's get out of here." My voice sounded higher than a castrato.

"He's not going to use that knife," said Henry. "He's just trying to scare us."

"Yeah, well, he succeeded," I said. "I want to go now, Henry. You want to come back and deal with this yourself, you do that, but I want out of here. *Now,* Henry!"

"Why don't you find out if I'm just trying to scare you, you son of a bitch? Come on, let me show you," the guy said.

Without appearing the least bit flustered, Henry dropped the air gun and said to me, "C'mon, let's go. It stinks in here." As we walked toward the exit, Henry turned back to the guy, who was still standing there with the knife, and said to him, "Oh, by the way, do you have a card or something? I may want to recommend you to my friends. You do such good work."

Though most of my experiences with Henry have been less dramatic, many have been as thought-provoking. His life is so different from mine. I pay all my bills on time, I usually get eight hours of sleep a night, and I never keep people waiting. Pretty boring. Yet sometimes I pass homeless people on the street and fail to notice; I don't always consult God on the minutiae of my daily life; and I rarely take the risks associated with major growth spurts. As a result, I miss some stuff along the way, and while I think I'm a fairly religious person, being a priest and all, I'm not always as spiritual as I might be. Henry lives there without knowing it.

He said to me recently, "You know, sometimes I'm afraid that, when *I* get up there, God *is* gonna turn into Bruce Lee."

"Why do you say that?" I asked.

"I don't know. Sometimes I just really screw up."

"Henry, we all screw up. That's what's so great. We have a God who loves us anyway."

"Yeah, well, I guess if God loves us as much as I love my kids, then I'll be all right. I couldn't kung-fu them no matter what they did."

I've learned to trust Henry's instincts, especially about God. Though he arrives at his conclusions in unorthodox ways, he's usually right on the money, except where his notion of distributive justice is concerned. And many years ago, Henry was right about something else: I should have just given him the blessing. But what he doesn't know is that I've gotten more benedictions than I've given. Henry dispenses them without ever lifting his hand.

CHAPTER FIFTEEN

A ROSE WITHOUT THORNS

There was a prophetess, Anna, the daughter of Phanuel, of the tribe of Asher. She was advanced in years . . . She never left the temple, but worshiped night and day with fasting and prayer. And coming forward, she gave thanks to God and spoke about the child to all who were awaiting the redemption of Jerusalem.

—LUKE 2:36–38

She looked unlike any woman I had ever seen before. I first met her when I had been in the parish only two days. Being the curious, new, young deacon, I was rummaging through drawers in the church sacristy, trying to familiarize myself with the layout. Excited to be exploring the surroundings of my first parish assignment, a preparation for my ordination to the priesthood six months later, I was taken with the churchy feels and smells of stuff that had been in there for years. As I opened a large wooden drawer that was home to ecclesiastical linens, she walked in the door of the sacristy.

"Oh, no, don't tell me someone else is going to be messing up my drawers now!" she said.

I looked up to see a woman hunched over and peering at me through pink-framed glasses, the arms of which sloped modishly downward before wrapping around her large ears. She wore a blue turban, a cover for the pink plastic rollers that peeked out from the front. Her face was as lined as any I have seen, a map of a life that no doubt had been full. Striking blue eyes, the color of a robin's egg, searched the room to see what else I may have messed up; the bottom lids drooped, revealing a conjunctivitis redness that looked painful.

"No, no, I'm not messing up the drawer," I said. "I'm just looking around to see what's in here. I'm the new deacon, Father Edward. I'm assigned here for at least the next couple of months."

I walked over to her and extended my hand as she moved toward me and lifted hers to mine. It was bony, with long fingers and purple and blue veins bulging at the top. It felt rough and calloused, no stranger to dishwater and brooms.

"Oh, darlin', I'm sorry. You look like one of the teenage boys from the youth group, God bless you. I'm Rose. Grandma Rose, that's who I am."

Her bent posture evidenced severe osteoporosis with curvature of the spine, creating a hump on her back, pushing her head downward, demanding she look at the ground when she walked. She wore a frayed blue and white housecoat, the kind women wear when cleaning or getting their hair dyed. Strong legs bound with thick layers of stocking became visible beneath the knee, ending in comfortable, orthopedic black tie-shoes.

"Hi, Rose. I'm really glad to meet you," I said. "Do you have some job in the sacristy?"

"Oh, darlin', I *am* the job in the sacristy. I wash all the linens, take care of the priests' vestments, and try to keep this place clean. But don't look at it today, because I haven't gotten to it yet. Lord, the dirt that piles up in here in just one week. It's unbelievable."

From our first moments together in the sacristy, Rose and I became quick friends. She took me under her wing, like the grandmother she called herself, and never held back from telling me exactly what she thought—about everything, especially the priests in the parish and the inevitable politics that disgusted her.

"It's all about serving God, isn't it, darlin'? I mean, why do these priests seem to care so much about money, and about pleasing this one over that one? Aren't they in this for God and to save their immortal souls? I'll just never understand it."

I listened carefully to the wisdom she spouted, raining down like pearls from an inexhaustible sky, born of life experience I had not yet begun to have.

She was instrumental in making my ordination to the priesthood ceremony memorable months later. Taking special pride that I had chosen to be ordained in "her church," she scrubbed every pew on her hands and knees, pausing periodically for a cup of tea she brewed in an electric pot that she kept hidden in the sacristy.

"Darlin', come join Grandma Rose for some tea. Set a spell with me and God." Rose was never alone. The long hours she passed cleaning the church became time spent with God. Sometimes I'd hear her talking to God when she thought no one was around.

"Lord, I'm trying my best to clean this place up for you. Don't ask me why people leave gum wrappers and tissues in your house. I'll never understand it. Wouldn't do that in their own house."

The week after my ordination we were sitting together in church for one of our three-way tea klatches. "That ordination was so 'bee-you-tee-ful,' darlin'. I actually felt the Holy Spirit come down on you and make you a priest. Thank you, God, that you let me live long enough to see that. Now maybe they'll let you stay here, Father Edward, so we can teach you how to be a good priest. Lord knows, we need more like you, darlin'. You have to be like God now."

It was a tough order from a tough lady, made tougher by the fact that she really believed it—and expected it.

One Saturday morning about six months later I had taken the opportunity to sleep in a little late, after having been called to the hospital in the middle of the previous night. I awoke to the incessant ringing of the doorbell. Not able to ignore it any longer, and wondering where all the other priests were hiding, I finally went downstairs in sweatpants and a T-shirt, to find Rose standing there in her housecoat and turban. A fashion statement we weren't.

"He's in prison," she said as soon as I opened the door.

"Rose, who's in prison?" I asked, trying to wake up. "What are you talking about?"

"They've put him in prison. How could they have done that?" she continued.

"Rose, calm down and tell me what you're talking about."

"Come with me. I'll show you." She took me by the hand, and we walked together to the church, and in the front door. "Look, look what they've done," she said. "They put God in prison."

She pointed to the front, right side of the church, where the newly installed metal dividers in front of the tabernacle that hosted the Blessed Sacrament glimmered like a celestial gate. The liturgical committee had approved this addition because the ironwork had been salvaged from the old monastery. It was a beautiful piece of a wrought-iron gate; thin pointed columns, painted gold and black, created a see-through divider between the congregation and the tabernacle.

"Rose, that's the metal gate from the old monastery church. We wanted to put that there to beautify the Blessed Sacrament area and create a sense of reverence."

"You mean, *you* knew about this?" she said. "You let them put God in prison?"

"Rose, God's not in prison. That's just there to create an effect."

"You've created an effect, all right, darlin'," she said, "a San Quentin effect."

She would hear none of my lofty theological and liturgical reasoning. As far as she was concerned, we had removed a God who was already distant, and pushed Him even further away.

"But, Rose, don't you think that the gate adds a sense of mystery to the space?"

"The only mystery, darlin', is how you ever allowed them to do it."

It wasn't until two years later when the ironwork finally came down that Rose could kneel there again, and not feel that she had to spring God from behind bars. Little did I realize that Rose herself was living behind bars, which is perhaps why she reacted so strongly to an incarcerated God.

One afternoon I was visiting at her small apartment down the street from the church. Walter, her husband, had died two years earlier and I had concelebrated at the funeral Mass and assisted at the graveside prayers. Rose had adjusted to living alone, but always appreciated company, especially around teatime in the afternoon. As we sat at her kitchen table, with Lipton tea brewing and the chocolate chip cookies she had made filling the air with a sweet aroma, she appeared unsettled, looking down at the table rather than at me. Playing with the end of her paper napkin, she finally said, "Father Edward, I have something to tell you that I've never told anyone else. And I think it's finally time. I've carried this with me my whole life and I feel I just have to lay it down now."

"What is it, Rose?" I said, wondering what an eighty-year-old woman could have carried her whole life without telling anyone.

"I'm telling you now, because you're like God to me and I don't want to get to heaven and have God say, 'How come you never told me this?' So now He can't say that because I'm telling Him through you."

"O.K., Rose, what is it?"

"When I was a little girl in upstate New York, you know I was one of thirteen young ones. And because there were so many of us, we had to help Momma take care of us. My older brother had to watch me and walk me back and forth to school each day."

"Yes," I said. "I remember your telling me that."

"Well, what I didn't tell you was that one day he was walking me home from school and we were about a half a mile from the house, walking through the woods, and we came to this ditch. And my brother pushed me into the ditch . . . and . . . he raped me."

"Oh, Rose . . . ," I said, reaching out for her hand. Her eyes began to fill up and she blotted them with the napkin. "How old were you?"

"I was seven . . . and he was about fourteen. But I've never been able to forgive him for it. And I know I have to before I die. He didn't know what he was doing. He was only a child himself. But I've always hated him for it. And I can't anymore. God says I can't." She started to cry softly, but was visibly relieved that she had finally released this burden.

As I held her hands, I said, "Rose, I am so sorry you had to go through that. It's so unfair. But why didn't you ever tell anyone about this, all these years?"

"I was always too embarrassed. I thought people would blame me, or think I did something wrong. I couldn't even tell Walter because I thought he'd think less of me. And he could never understand why I didn't enjoy making love. He thought it was him." She shook her head and held it in her hands. "I was just always afraid, that's all. But I know now I didn't do nothing wrong. My brother did. And when Momma saw the dirt and blood on my dress, she asked me if I had fallen down. And I just told her yes. So she took my dress and washed it. And that's the last time it was ever spoken of. And I was only seven . . ."

She cried cathartic tears that emerged from the shameful darkness of years of secrecy into the liberating light flooding through her kitchen window. I moved my chair next to hers and put my arm around her shoulder.

"Rose, it's O.K.," I said. "It's good that you told me. I'm just sorry you've had to carry this your whole life alone. And you're right. None of this was your fault. You didn't do anything wrong. Your brother did, and you suffered because of it."

"I know, but it made me mad at God for a long time, because I thought that God could have stopped it if He wanted to. I mean, if He can do anything, why didn't He stop it?"

"I don't know the answer to that, Rose, but I do believe that He was right there with you through the whole thing. And that He hasn't left you for one minute since."

"Even when I was mad at Him?"

"Especially then."

She was silent for a long while, seeming to consider what kind of God doesn't care if you get mad at Him.

I broke the silence by saying, "Rose, do you think this is why you minded so much about the gate, when you thought God was in prison, because you felt like you were, too?"

"No, darlin'. I minded so much because it looked like hell, and because I have people like you to help me, but who does poor God have? He'd still be behind bars if I hadn't made such a fuss."

"Oh" was all I said. So much for my psychologizing.

We talked a bit more and Rose assured me that we would speak about this again when she felt the need. I finally got up to leave, thanking her for her honesty and for placing such trust in me. As we walked to the front door of her apartment, I felt sad to leave her there alone, burdened by news I never could have guessed. Preoccupied, wondering if there was anything else I could do for her, I was looking down at the floor as I walked while Rose walked slowly behind me, hunched over.

"Darlin', don't look down like that," she said. "Don't ever walk and look at the ground. I have to look down, darlin', but you don't. Look up . . . because you can."

Two weeks later, I sprang a surprise on Rose. As a thank-you for all she had done for the parish, I took her to the Russian Tea Room for dinner and to Carnegie Hall to hear Liza Minnelli sing. (I guess I thought Liza was good for anyone ailing, since the last time I had taken someone to see her was just after Michael was released from the hospital in Chicago.) Rose took most of her meal home in a fancy doggy bag, not willing to let any of it go to waste "at those prices." After dinner, we sat in box seats at Carnegie Hall and she inched her way up to see clearly over the railing. When Ms. Minnelli belted a number so powerfully that we thought she was singing just to us, Rose turned to me and said, "When I was young, I saw her mother once. Same charisma, darlin'. I feel like I'm watching Judy again. I almost feel young again, too."

She turned back to the stage and I watched her shine the rest of the night, nodding her head with the music, tapping her foot to the melodies, and finally struggling to her feet to applaud an encore of "New York, New York." They were the perfect seats for her. Her back seemed less bent, her head less bowed. And holding her head higher than I had ever seen her do, I heard her say, "Because I can."

When Rose died about ten years later, I was in Florida in the middle of leading a parish retreat. Her daughter, Barbara, called me and told me that Rose had wanted me to say her funeral Mass and to preach the homily. Unfortunately, there was no way I could be there. If I had gotten there, I would have said that I was sure she had walked tall and straight through the pearly gates, teapot in hand, finally happy that there were no gates between her and God.

CHAPTER SIXTEEN

DRUNK DRIVER

David was distraught and went up to the room over the city gate to weep. He said as he wept, "My son Absalom! My son, my son Absalom! If only I had died instead of you, Absalom, my son, my son!"

—2 SAMUEL 19:1

It was two o'clock in the morning—not a time when my phone usually rang.

"Hello, is this Saints Joseph and Michael Church?"

"Yes, yes, it is," I managed, in my half-sleep state, sitting up in bed and turning on the lamp on the nightstand where the phone was.

"Is this one of the priests?" he said.

"Yes, this is Father Edward . . . Edward Beck. I'm one of the Associates here at the parish."

I had been ordained for two years and was just beginning to feel I was getting the hang of what it meant to be a priest.

"Who's this?" I said.

"Father, this is a state trooper in Vermont and I'm afraid I have some bad news for you and some of your parishioners."

"I'm sorry," I said, "you're going to have to repeat that. I didn't get what you said." I rubbed my eyes and stood up out of bed, not understanding why a trooper from Vermont was calling me in the middle of the night. I immediately began to think about whom I knew in Vermont, but came up empty.

"Father, do you know a Teresa Molinari, a Maureen Hogan, and a Linda Marturano?"

"Yes, I do. Well, I know Teresa and Maureen. They and their families are parishioners here in Union City. I'm not sure I know Linda, but the name sounds familiar." I remembered then that the girls had taken a trip to New England to see the fall foliage.

"Well, Father, I'm afraid they were all killed tonight in a car accident here by a drunk driver."

"Oh, my God, no . . ." I said as I sat back down on the bed.

"Father, we haven't been able to contact the families yet, but we did find the parish bulletin from your church in their possession, so we thought it might be better if you could help us break the news."

"You mean the families don't know yet?"

"Well, my men are working on contacting some of the siblings, but the parents don't know yet. And being Catholic myself, I know if it were my daughter, it would help me if the news came from my priest, rather than from some stranger over the phone."

I was silent, stunned for the moment. I didn't know what to say.

"Father . . . ? Father . . . ? Are you there?"

"Yes, I'm sorry. I just can't believe this has happened. I saw Terry and Maureen last week. They were so excited to be going on this trip to see the leaves and to visit Weston Priory . . . and now this."

As I was talking to the trooper on the phone, someone knocked on my bedroom door.

"Edward, Edward, are you there?"

It was Father Gregory, who lived in the room above me and who was also an Associate in the parish. When I opened the door, he was standing there barefoot, in his blue-and-white-striped pajamas, his hair standing straight up from interrupted sleep.

"Edward, there's been a terrible tragedy. I just got a phone call from Richie Hogan. The three girls . . ."

"I know, Gregory, I'm on the phone now with a state trooper from Vermont. Let me just finish with him."

I concluded my conversation with the trooper and assured him that we would take care of notifying the families of the tragedy, and that we would be in touch with the police later in the day for any details that needed attention. Gregory came into my room and sat on the sofa. Already nervous by temperament, he started shaking his leg and moving his hands in no discernible pattern. He wasn't helping my already agitated state.

"You know, the parents don't even know yet," he said, plastering his hair down with one hand.

"Yes, I know. They want us to tell them."

"Richie, Maureen's brother, asked if I could go with him to the Hogans'," he said, "and I told him I would. I think you should go to the Molinaris' house, since you know them better."

"Yeah, that's fine," I said, "but I don't want to go there alone. I don't even know which of the other children have been contacted."

I soon knew because my phone rang again and it was John Molinari, Teresa's brother. He had been notified about her death and wanted me to go with him to tell his other sister, Mary Ann. We would then all go together to his parents, who lived around the block from the church, and break the news to them. I told him I'd be ready in ten minutes and that he could pick me up in front of the church.

"Gregory, what about Linda's parents?" I said after getting off the phone. "I don't know them. Are they parishioners, too?"

"No," he said. "They're in Holy Family parish and I've already called Father Ashe and filled him in. He's going to take care of them."

Gregory left my room and I started to get ready for that which I could not prepare. Putting on my black shirt and white collar, I became the priest, as if the clothes would give me strength I wasn't feeling inside, and I prayed that God give me the words, that God give me emotional reserve that already seemed depleted. As I combed my hair in the bathroom, I tried to rehearse what I would say to Terry's parents. How could I tell them that their daughter was gone? And how could I tell my friend, Mary Ann, who had been one of the adult leaders in the youth group I had begun? We had worked so closely together for months, and now I would have to tell her that a drunk driver had killed her sister. What could I possibly say to soften the horror of the violence and loss? My stomach began to release acid and to churn, as feelings of inadequacy settled in like an invading opponent. Walking down the stairs of the rectory, on my way to the street to wait for John, I remember thinking: "I was ordained a priest to bring joy to people's lives, not sorrow."

When John and I got to Mary Ann's house, it was strangely quiet and peaceful, an ambience that seemed in discord with the news we had come to bring. The moon shone brightly over the condominium complex where she lived, illuminating the trees and carefully manicured gardens that were slowly dying with the advent of fall's chill. With leaves crunching beneath our feet, we walked in silence to the door. I couldn't help thinking that Mary Ann would never have considered the possibility of what we had come to tell her when she had gone to sleep just hours before. She still wouldn't believe it was possible. John had said little in the car, still reeling from the shock of losing a sister he had never imagined not seeing again.

"Father, I have no idea if Mary Ann's going to flip out on us or what," John said, "so we just have to be ready." He rang the doorbell.

When Mary Ann opened the door in her nightgown and soft pink slippers and saw us standing there, her face snapped to attention like she had been smacked. Putting her hand to her mouth, she said, "What? What happened? Is it Mommy or Daddy? John, did something happen to them? What is it!"

John put his arms around Mary Ann, began stroking her hair,

and said, "It's Terry, sweetie . . . she was killed in Vermont." And then he finally began to cry.

"No, no, no . . . not my sister . . . how?" She pulled back from John's embrace.

"A drunk driver crossed lanes . . . and hit them head-on," said John haltingly. "Maureen and Linda were killed, too."

Mary Ann began to cry in heaves, placing her head on John's shoulder, her body trembling with emotion. Then, as if she had an idea that would make it all go away, she suddenly lifted her head from John's shoulder and said, "What about Mommy and Daddy? Who told them?"

"We haven't told them yet," said John. "We wanted to come and get you first and now we're going to go there with Father Edward."

"Oh no," said Mary Ann. "Let me get dressed quick."

She emerged from her bedroom in control, assuming the stalwart demeanor I had seen her exhibit before, when trips with the youth group had gotten out of hand and a voice of reason and responsibility was needed. Being the eldest in her family, she was always the reliable one, the caretaker of her brothers and sisters—and now of her parents. She moved seamlessly into the role once more, as if on automatic pilot.

When we arrived at the Molinaris' house on Fourteenth Street, it was silent and dark, the moon having receded behind clouds, now thick and heavy.

"John, I can't do this," said Mary Ann in a voice almost pleading as we walked up the front steps of the house. "I just can't do this. How can I tell them Terry's gone? I can't . . ."

I wanted somehow to lift this burden from all of them, but I was helpless. Searching for words of comfort and meaning left me dry as a parched desert.

Mary Ann opened the door with her key and we walked through the hallway. Ann and Jim Molinari slept on a pullout in the living room, leaving the bedroom for Michael, a son who was learning-disabled. We stood for a moment at the doorway with the light from the hall illuminating the living room enough to see Ann and Jim sleeping. John and Mary Ann held each other, tears streaming down their faces, as they watched their parents' peaceful repose.

"Edward, you have to do this," whispered Mary Ann. "You have to tell them. I can't." She shook her head back and forth and began to rock slowly.

"Mom . . . Dad," John called from the doorway.

"What? What is it? Who is it?" said Ann from the bed. "What's going on . . . John?"

I moved toward the pullout bed as Ann reached up to turn on the lamp on the bedside table. When the light went on, I was standing above her. She looked at me like the intruder I was, violating the sanctuary of her quiescent slumber.

"Father Ed? Father Ed, what are you doing here?" She pulled the covers up to her neck. "What happened? John, Mary Ann, what's going on? Jim, Jim, wake up, Jim!" She shook her husband, until finally he too was sitting up, both of them looking at the three of us, standing mute with dread. I sat down on the edge of the bed and put my arm on Ann's shoulder.

"Ann, I'm afraid I have some bad news for you," I said. "It's Terry . . . she was killed in a car accident in Vermont. I'm so sorry."

I had never before, nor have I since, heard anything like the screams that came from Ann that early morning. They came from the depths of her soul—aching, yearning, unbelieving cries that shattered the stillness of that morning like the fire of a gunshot in a hushed church.

Mary Ann and John moved to the bed to comfort their parents. Jim, the father, was now shaking his head in disbelief and saying, "No, no, God, no . . ."

The five of us sat on the bed, holding one another, vainly trying to absorb the enormity of the horror we had come to speak.

As the parents and their son and daughter wept together, I turned a confused and accusatory interior glance toward God. "I don't understand how you let this happen," I prayed.

The Molinari family asked me to preside at Terry's funeral and to preach the homily. It was the last thing I wanted to do, but I knew it came with the job. What could I say: No, get some other priest who's less involved? But how could I speak of the senselessness of these deaths? Was there any meaning to be derived from this tragedy? The age-old theodicy question haunted my dreams in the days preceding the funeral. How does a good and loving God permit innocent suffering? As a Passionist priest, I'm supposed to deal effectively with suffering and to help others deal with it as well. Why then did I feel so helpless?

As the time to deliver the homily drew near, I was tempted to hide behind sonorous panegyric prose that would help me to remain emotionally distant and in control, but I decided I couldn't. Terry's other brothers and sister would be there, as would everyone else in the parish who knew my connection to the family. They would know I was cheating. So I decided not to try to explain away the tragedy and senselessness that covered the parish and lived in the minds and hearts of those who knew the girls. I couldn't anyway. I would instead allow my vulnerability to be transparent, as Sister Dianne had once encouraged me, and simply stand with the family in their suffering. Stand with my Jobian fist raised to the heavens in solidarity with theirs, demanding answers. It seemed a better response than trying to see this as "God's will," or as some piece of a Divine plan that someday we would come to understand. I just didn't believe that. I still don't.

The church was filled to capacity the day of the funeral—a community of faith gathered together to struggle for some meaning in the midst of absurdity. There was strength in the numbers, comfort in the unity we felt in praying for this hurting family and for the others ripped apart by loss, for the parents and siblings of the three girls who dragged themselves from wakes to funerals that week like wounded dogs.

As I walked to the pulpit to preach the homily, I looked out over the sea of people in the church and felt my knees grow weak with sadness. I could hardly look at the family in the first pew. Somehow I got through the words I had prepared, focusing on God's presence with us in the midst of our suffering, even if we couldn't understand it. It was all we had to hold on to. And then I reached for the text of the play *Agnes of God* by John Pielmeier. The closing words of that play had resonated with me and they seemed an elegiac way to conclude:

> *Why? . . . What kind of God can permit such a wonder one as her to come trampling through this well-ordered existence?! I don't know what I believe anymore. But I want to believe that she was . . . blessed. And I do miss her. And I hope that she has left something, some little part of herself with me. That would be miracle enough . . . Wouldn't it?*

CHAPTER SEVENTEEN

THIRTY DAYS
IN A HERMITAGE

The reports about Jesus spread all the more, and great crowds
assembled to listen to him and to be cured of their ailments, but he
would withdraw to deserted places to pray.

—LUKE 5:15–16

I couldn't decide what to do to commemorate turning thirty-three. I had missed my chance when turning thirty. Then, one friend had suggested taking a hot air balloon ride; another had advised taking a trip to Bali. (I'm sure my community would have *loved* my presenting that one.) Due to a variety of commitments, I was not able to entertain either suggestion at the time, but I was determined to do something to mark turning thirty-three. Traditionally known as the "Christic year," since it's believed Jesus was thirty-three when he died, the year possessed spiritual relevance to me. Though I had no delusions of modeling my life on Christ's, it seemed an apropos time to break step and examine my life more closely. Besides, I happened to be free that summer.

Eschewing balloons and Bali, I decided to retreat alone to a hut for thirty days (*thirty-three* days would have been taking it a little too far). I had long been counseled on the unparalleled spiritual benefits of a thirty-day retreat. When I received my master's degree in spirituality from Creighton University in Omaha, one of the recommendations to fulfill requirements for the degree was to make an Ignatian thirty-day retreat (a retreat following the Spiritual Exercises of St. Ignatius of Loyola). The university settled, however, for an eight-day retreat, the most that I could manage at the time. But at thirty-three, I decided to see what everyone was talking about and make the thirty days. The cosmic synchronicity and spiritual relevance of the plan was almost too much for my friends to take, causing one of them to remark, "It's so Oprah."

I began researching for a place to spend my thirty days in solitude. There were retreat houses in the mountains, spiritual life centers by the sea, and Esalen-like holistic communes where, I was informed, clothing was optional. (The last of the three would have been as difficult to sell to my religious superiors as Bali.) None of those possibilities really grabbed me. Having lived and worked in retreat houses and spiritual life centers for much of my religious life, I found them old hat; I wanted something novel and adventurous for my thirty days.

I recalled that, when I was in the novitiate, one of the brothers had come back from a trip to California and couldn't stop talking about Big Sur, California. "Oh, what a beautiful place. The mountains, the ocean, the wildlife . . . the hippies." He waxed lyrical for hours about his treks through the lush mountains and his solitary walks by the aqua-blue sea. I remember him saying that it was also a spiritual place to which seekers were drawn. The brother's stories had whetted my appetite, and I knew that someday I too wanted to go there, to seek the fabled wisdom of the mountains and the mythical truths of the sea. Turning thirty-three seemed as good a time as any.

I got some books about Big Sur, mostly travel material from the chamber of commerce. Though the pictures were enticing and the catalogues confirmed the high accolades of the brother, nothing I saw in the brochures appeared compatible with religious pilgrimage. There were plenty of expensive resorts and even a few hippie communes, but none resembled a spiritual oasis, except an obscure Buddhist monastery listed as being forty miles from Big

Sur. But I wasn't prepared to go that far afield, geographically or spiritually.

I happened to be talking to a friend about my fruitless search, when he said nonchalantly, "What about the Camaldolese Hermitage?"

"The *what*?"

"The Camaldolese Hermitage. I think it's called Immaculate Heart Hermitage or something like that. It's right in the mountains of Big Sur, overlooking the Pacific Ocean. The Camaldolese community of hermits lives there. It's supposed to be magnificent."

"And anyone can go?" I asked.

"Yeah, from what I've heard, they have some guest hermitages on the property for people who want to make retreats. I understand they're really stark, but beautifully situated. Call them and find out."

It seemed perfect. I reached a Brother John, who confirmed that there was such a place (he had lived there for fifteen years), and that they had three guest hermitages on the property for visitors. They were small, one-room trailer efficiencies situated in the woods, about a half-mile away from the community's hermitages.

"You have to understand," he said, "simplicity is the name of the game for us, so don't expect anything like a hotel. But you have everything you need in that one room."

"Well, it sounds like just what I've been looking for," I said. "Can I book it for thirty days?"

"Thirty days?" he asked, somewhat skeptically. "And this is your first time here?"

"Yes."

"Well, perhaps you should start with a week, just to see if you like it. Thirty days is a pretty big commitment for someone who has never done this before."

"But I've done eight-day silent retreats before with no problem. I think I'm ready for the thirty-day. It's kind of something I feel I have to do."

"Well, I'll pencil you in the book, but if you change your mind anytime before that, just give us a call. We'll look forward to seeing you."

I had decided I wouldn't take anything with me to the hermitage to distract me. I would bring my Bible and a notebook to write in—and that would be it. When I was in the airport awaiting my flight to San Francisco from New York, I stopped in one of the bookstores in the terminal to buy the *New York Times*. At the front of the store, there was a promotion stand with a newly published book by Paul Monette, *Last Watch of the Night*. I had read his bestselling and critically acclaimed book *Borrowed Time: An AIDS Memoir* for a class I had taken, and was deeply moved by it. In a review in the *New York Times*, William M. Hoffman had praised the book, saying, "Mr. Monette has etched a magnificent monument to his lover's bravery, their commitment to each other, and the plague of hatred and ignorance they had to endure."

While reading *Borrowed Time*, though touched by the fealty of Monette to his dying lover, Roger, I remember being disheartened by Monette's vitriolic criticism of institutional religion, especially of the Catholic Church. His understanding of the Church's anti-gay stand caused him to label the Church demonic, and its hierarchy "Vatican Nazis." While his rancor was not impossible to understand, given some of the harsh rhetoric of certain Vatican documents, I was saddened that he had dismissed *all* the hierarchy (which included all the priests, and, therefore, me) as hypocritical malefactors, writing that they were tacitly participating in another Holocaust and once again remaining silent. I remember wanting to write him and tell him he had generalized in a manner as discriminatory as were, supposedly, those he had chastised. I had wanted to write that we weren't all that way. Many of us were ministering to AIDS patients in compassionate ways and dealing pastorally with gay people who were struggling to live honorable and beneficent lives. But I never did write.

As I stood in the airport bookstore a number of years later, and picked up this new book, *Last Watch of the Night*, from the table,

I saw that the book had been written after Monette himself was diagnosed with full-blown AIDS. He had written it during his "last watch," though I had heard he was still living, defying all speculation that he might not even live to finish the book. I perused the Contents and noticed that Chapter Three was entitled "My Priests." The fact that Monette was writing about priests at all surprised me, but even more astonishing was his use of the pronoun "my." Had proximity to death encouraged a conversion of heart? I also wondered why I had stumbled upon the book. I paid the cashier for my *New York Times*—and the book—and boarded the plane for my hermitage. Now transporting the Bible, my notebook, and Monette, I was eager for a suitable time to begin *Last Watch of the Night* in the hallowedness of my solitude.

There are few vistas that compare to the coast of California as one drives south on Route 1 from San Francisco: the mountains to the left, sometimes green, sometimes desert-looking and parched, and the arrestingly blue sea to the right, with foamy whitecaps crashing against the rocks hewn through the centuries by the sea's power. The distracting beauty almost makes it dangerous for me to drive that route, and often beckons me to the scenic outlooks by the side of the road, where tourists aggregate to take pictures, stretch their legs, and guzzle down replenishing liquids. At one time, there were no guardrails along this serpentine road that weaves treacherously between the mountains and the sea. As I struggled to negotiate the hairpin turns in the clear light of day, I was glad someone had thought to finally include them.

When I reached Big Sur, I hardly knew I had arrived. There was no real town. A general store and a few shops that sold incense and wind chimes were there, but no discernible community. The community was found scattered in the woods, amid a few exclusive resorts, some squatters' cabins, campgrounds, and magnificent private homes carved into the cliffs that overlook the Pacific. It was a mix I wouldn't have anticipated, but the environmental equilibrium and a funky *je ne sais quoi* quality appeared magically harmonious, abolishing any thought of altering it. New Age spirituality floated in the air, palatable as the fog that hugs the coast on most mornings.

I stopped at some of the small shops and gas stations to ask if they knew where the hermitage was. I might as well have been asking if extraterrestrials frequented the area. One guy said, "We don't have anything like that around here. It's a little scary even to think about hermits holed up around here." The reactions surprised me, since I thought anything went in California. How unusual could a few hermits be compared to the legendary Californian gurus and shamans who have made fortunes promising eternal youth, beauty, and dynamite karma?

Driving farther down Route 1, I raced past a small sign on the left side of the road that I thought said IMMACULATE. How many signs like that could there be? I backtracked to discover that the diminutive sign—hardly one that shouted, "Come visit"—indeed marked the road entrance to IMMACULATE HEART HERMITAGE. I turned onto the dirt road and began my four-and-a-half-mile, circular ascent up the imposing mountain. With each turn, I rose higher and higher from the blue sea that loomed below like a giant beckoning pool.

The first thing I noticed was the absolute stillness. I could hear only birds and the rustling leaves and needles of the ubiquitous trees. Searching for any sign of human life, I finally discovered a small adobe building that had a carved wooden sign that said RECEPTION. A man behind a counter was taking inventory of some books on display. He appeared to be in his fifties and wore an unusual full-cut denim shirt with mufflike connecting pockets and a hood attached.

"Hi, I'm Edward Beck, the priest who's supposed to stay in one of the hermitages. I believe I spoke with a Brother John on the phone."

He looked up from the piles of books surrounding him and said, "Oh yes, yes, I've been expecting you. Passionist, right?"

"Yes."

"Brother John couldn't be here to meet you, but he asked me to take you down and get you settled in. Thirty days, huh?"

Raising his bushy eyebrows and lowering his head, he stared at me as if he were peering over the top of eyeglasses, only he wasn't wearing any.

"Yes," I said. "You say that with some doubt in your voice. Don't people stay thirty days?"

"Well, yes, some do, but not usually the first time, unless they're used to this kind of thing. But we'll see . . ."

I got my bags and he led me down a trail that disappeared into the woods. After about ten or fifteen minutes, we reached a clearing in the woods where a trailer sat, facing the wide expanse of the Pacific Ocean below.

"There's your home for the next thirty days," he said, and pointed.

"Wow, what a location," I said. "We're so high. The ocean goes on forever."

"Close to heaven, is what we like to say. Wait till the low morning clouds descend. You'll feel like you really are in heaven."

The white room was just as Brother John had described it to me on the phone: a twin bed, a small desk and chair, an efficiency kitchen (consisting of a two-burner electric stove, a small, square refrigerator, and a sink), a table, a sitting chair with a lamp, and a tiny bathroom with a stand-up shower. Sliding glass doors that faced west, affording a breathtaking view of the ocean, provided the only entrance to the Spartan space.

"So what do you think of your humble abode, Father Hermit?" he said.

"I think it's great. I don't suppose there's any cable TV?"

"That's funny," he said.

Initially enamored with my hut in the wilderness, and with the notion of being left with God to fend for myself for thirty days, I fancied myself akin to the desert monks who retreated to the wilderness to wrestle demons and purify themselves. Entering the experience as a "Lenten fast," I relished being thrown back on the basics in an effort to reconnect with God in a deeper way. Though I had lived the religious life for almost ten years at that point, I had allowed myself to be distracted from my original reasons for becoming a religious. Prayer, solitude, and penance—hallmarks of my religious community—were often compromised in my attempts to negotiate a busy professional life as a minister of the Gospel. Traveling from place to place, eating in nice restaurants, and being given the place of honor at banquet tables, I found myself living no differently from Wall Street friends I had left behind. I wondered: "Where is the witness value of my life?" My thirty days of solitude felt like a time of pruning during which I needed to hand God the scissors.

In the beginning I adapted well to my hermit life. Each morning, just before sunrise, I made the mile-and-a-half trek to the community chapel, where the hermits gathered from their individual cells to pray in common. Like everything else, the chapel was stark. It was built of white stone, similar to the kind omnipresent in Southwestern design. In its center, a beautifully carved crucifix hung over the altar, illuminated by the daylight that filtered in from the glass dome above it. Wooden choir stalls for the monks and benches for the visitors lined each side of the chapel.

Filing into their stalls in white choir robes with long, flowing sleeves, the monks stood attentively at their places, waiting for the first note of the Invitatory to sound, calling them to prayer. With eyes closed and heads bowed, they chanted beautifully; deep, sonorous voices lifted in praise of a God we had all gathered to worship. The visitors were given books to follow along and to participate in the chant, if they dared, but most who came made their prayer a silent one, deferring to the experts to give it voice. I found myself inspired by the reverence of the prayer and gradually felt myself slow down, releasing the busyness and distractions that I had carried there like a heavy knapsack.

Though I would return to the chapel at least twice more during the day, for Eucharist and for evening prayer, I did the re-

mainder of my praying in the woods, by the ocean, or in the solitude of my hut. I did, however, look forward to the common
prayer times, because it was the only time I got to see anyone.
Everything else, including eating, I did alone. I would either prepare my simple, meatless meal in my hermitage with supplies that
were dropped off weekly, or bring a mess kit to a room where
food had been left for visitors by one of the hermits. Slopping it
into the stainless-steel containers, I would then carry it back to my
hut. It was no-frills dining—except for the view, and the occasional candle I would light. The only music was that of the wind
and the wild animals who howled the sun to sleep.

My initial weeks at the hermitage at Big Sur passed slowly,
painfully so. Though I adapted to the praying and eating schedule
with relative ease, I found the time in between labored and sometimes hard to fill. I had my bags packed, ready to leave at the end
of my first week, but somehow found the fortitude and grace to
hang on. My attempted long walks in the mountains in the summer's heat were often abridged by a plague of flies, dive-bombing
for each of my exposed orifices. Their incessant buzzing drove me
crazy. Because we were in the midst of a severe drought, I was informed that the flies were thirsty and attracted to the oasis of my
mucous membranes. Not a willing host, I devised flyswatters out
of tube socks that I tucked under my hat so that they hung down,
covering my ears. When I ran, for exercise, the socks would flap
up and down like the ears of a benevolent dog, their movement
chasing even the most persistent kamikazes. I'm sure the hermits
wondered who the weird one dressed as Pluto was.

Aside from walks and running, I would sometimes journey the
miles required to sit by the ocean and breathe the salt air and rel-
ish the tidal timpani. Some of my best praying occurred there. I
was at a crucial juncture in my priesthood, realizing that, if I were
going to do this the rest of my life, I would have to come to peace
with certain aspects of my chosen life. As always, celibacy reared
its abstemious head as a paramount issue. Moving into my mid-
thirties, I had begun to confront the fact that my choices in this

regard were diminishing. Though I had already made my life choice at twenty-four when I took my Final Vows as a religious, I needed to reaffirm the commitment every day, not unlike married people need to do. I'm not sure if it was the seven-year itch or premidlife crisis, but I prayed about whether I could live celibately the rest of my life, and I asked God to bring peace to my turmoil. My unrest wasn't primarily about sex, though it certainly entered the equation. It was more about my desire for emotional intimacy and to be truly known by someone else. Egocentrically, I wanted to be most important in someone else's world. I prayed to God to make me feel that being the center of His was enough.

I was also having my struggles with the institutional Church to which I had implicitly vowed allegiance by becoming a religious and a priest. I just didn't agree with everything it said and did. Sexuality was again at the top of the list for consideration. While the Church seemed at the vanguard of revolutionary and progressive movements in the areas of social justice and human rights, it seemed in the Dark Ages with regard to human sexuality and the complexities of sexual morality and ethics. Though my agreement wasn't necessarily required, except maybe from a pulpit, as a priest I represented the authority. People looked at me and saw "institution," and everything that came with it. Privately I could appeal to one's informed conscience and could rely on the "internal forum" to minister pastorally, but publicly, unless told otherwise, people had every right to assume that I bought the whole ball of wax. That perception bothered me.

It seemed obvious we were living in a religious milieu where dissent was not appreciated and freethinking was dissuaded. Catholic universities are presently confronting this issue, as *"Ex corde ecclesiae"* (a Vatican document calling for an oath of allegiance of all theology teachers in Catholic universities) bears down, but some individual priests and religious have long been suffering the repercussions of active dissent. After signing public petitions not in accord with Church teaching, they have been ordered to recant or face expulsion from their religious communities, or even excommunication from the Church. I had read about two such cases a week before retreating to my hermitage. I found myself praying by the sea about these issues, longing for some peace and guidance.

In accord with the haunting title, *Last Watch of the Night,* I began reading Monette's book before going to bed each night. Sometimes that was a mistake. The power of his writing and the explosiveness of his emotions hardly led me to somnolence. His anger, incited by slowly dying a death he felt could be avoided if religious and political structures dropped their hypocrisy and did their part, was contagious. One night I tossed and turned relentlessly as Monette's arguments resounded in my head. I finally fell asleep when the first hints of dawn crept over the mountain and I missed morning prayers and breakfast.

I began to feel there was a purpose to my reading the book at that particular time, but I wasn't sure what it was, so I just kept reading. As I was about to turn the light out one night, tired from a day of battling flies and walking mountain trails that I had begun to navigate with the skill of a tour guide, I heard noise under my trailer—a mournful cry. Through the thin flooring, movement underneath caused my bed to jolt. I sat up frightened, and slowly got out of bed and crouched down to the floor to listen more closely. Then sounds unlike anything I had ever heard before emanated from under the floor: screeching, yelping, struggling cries, eclipsing the stillness of the night mountain air. They were not human cries. I had a full-fledged animal fight going on underneath my hermitage in the woods. Having no idea what kinds of animals were fighting, my pulse raced and my imagination soared. The hermits had told me that there were mountain lions in the area and that I should be careful walking alone, especially at dusk while carrying food back and forth. Could this be a mountain lion, or *two*? As the floor began to jostle and shake beneath me, I thought the animals would come right through it. What a way to end up, nighttime fare for a couple of feuding mountain cats.

After what seemed an interminable few minutes, I heard a final loud screech and then there was silence. Either an animal was dead, or one had run away waving the flag of surrender. I wasn't about to go out into the dark to find out. Sleep having been chased by the mammalian rendezvous under my bed, I made a cup of tea and sat down with Monette's book, which I was now more than halfway through. Feeling calmer after reading for about fifteen minutes, I was about to go back to bed when I came to page 193: "Two weeks after Canada we were on our way up the coast to Big Sur, the place I've returned to most, the one that never disappoints." I couldn't believe what I was reading. Monette had been here. He continued, "I went to Big Sur to convalesce a failing spirit, but knowing full well it would be no cure . . . I managed the full two miles to Molera Beach, where I sat propped on a driftwood log with Winston at the mouth of the Big Sur River." Not only had he been here, but it was his most special place. What weird cosmic synchronicity was this? Why had I seemingly been led to take this book here, and to read these pages while in this sanctuary of his? I didn't believe it was mere coincidence. Monette went on to speak of Molera Beach as "the place that has always stopped my heart." I knew where my excursion the next day would take me.

I rose early, expecting to find a dead animal under my hut, but there was nothing there, not even the slightest sign of a disturbance: The grass appeared smooth and unruffled, the cinder blocks on which the trailer sat were still perfectly aligned. I was mystified, but by then had more alluring pursuits occupying my attention. As I made my way down the mountain, the rising sun began to reflect on it in hues of orange and purple. I turned around occasionally, half-expecting to see a prowling mountain lion lapping at my heels, but my only companions down the serpentine decline were some rabbits and a few circling hawks. By the time I reached the road, dawn had emerged full-throttle, lighting the way for my ten-mile hike down Route 1 to Molera Beach. I prayed that God make the journey with me and help me to understand the significance of the events.

When I finally saw the sign for Molera Beach, I was hot, tired, and thirsty, my water having run out some miles previous. Walking the path from the road to the beach, I was already preoccupied with the arduous return to the hermitage. I began to feel that I had made a mistake in coming, not having adequately anticipated the distance or the stamina required to travel it. Nearing the end of the path, I turned around a bend of tall sea grass and sand dune, when suddenly it appeared before me. Royal blue surf towered between two large limestone formations, the water riding high, then crashing abruptly on the pinkish sand. The sound too emerged without warning. Unlike the calmer lapping I had enjoyed at the shore closer to the hermitage, this was a roaring tide, trumpeting the power of the waves that pummeled the shore relentlessly.

I stood transfixed for a moment, understanding why Monette had described this as "the place that has always stopped my heart." *But how could he question the existence of God after having seen this?* As I surveyed the beach, I noticed that high above the shore, ensconced in the rock formations, were benches from which to view this magnificent panorama. I carefully climbed the slippery steps cut into the side of the rock until I reached a bench high atop the beach, affording me a view not only of Molera, but also of a good bit of the coast beyond.

Prayer came immediately, without even trying. God seemed in every bit of what I was viewing from my bench post. And so did Monette. I sensed his presence in this place that had meant so much to him. His spirit lived there. I prayed about his anger and disenchantment toward religion and the Church and asked God what to make of it all.

When he received the Nobel Prize for Literature, the author Czeslaw Milosz said, "In a room where people unanimously maintain a conspiracy of silence, one word of truth sounds like a pistol shot." The longer I sat there, the more powerfully the shot sounded. I knew that Monette was right. I heard it as clearly as I saw the blue of the sea and felt the lash of the wind. An inner voice gently persuaded that Paul Monette had every reason to be angry and to demand that his life be respected with dignity. Who was the Church, or anyone, to say his love was inherently "disordered" and his actions "evil" when they were done in the name of love? The Church has always taught that celibacy is a special calling, a charism, which not everyone receives. How could it be demanded of those who profess no inclination to it?

As I sat watching the rhythms of nature move in delicious harmony, the prayer led to a consideration of the moral dilemma: Though certainly the Church has the responsibility to set moral standards and to call people to high levels of ethical response, it has no right to unilaterally dismiss the experience of a group of people whose lives are already burdened by the discrimination and hate perpetuated against them. It should rather focus its energies on alleviating the plight of those disenfranchised and ostracized. It should be their champion. I prayed about Jesus' response to the outcasts of society: to the prostitutes, the tax collectors, the women, and, I'm sure, to the gay people (if such an entity had been known at the time of Jesus). These were the recipients of Jesus' most lavish love and attention. I sat convinced that that same lavishness needed to be extended by those who continued the task of ministering in His name.

I looked down at the bench on which I was sitting and noticed it was chock-full of carvings into the wood. Most were initials surrounded by hearts, a few containing arrows, testaments of lovers who sat on this bench together or of lovers who sat missing the one they loved. I took out a pocketknife I had brought along for the journey and began my own carving with a slow and steady hand: PAUL MONETTE + WINSTON WILDE. I then etched a heart around their names.

I sat upon the bench for hours, a new heart added, breathing air that now smelled even cleaner. When dusk announced its first shadows, I took off all of my clothes and waded into the water, which had grown calmer with the low tide. Plunging into the cold blue was a baptism of sorts, a commitment to be washed clean of my own prejudice and discrimination, and to be a better minister of lavish love to those who feel loveless or feel betrayed by institutions whose only right to exist is in testimony to the One who loved.

When I returned to my hermitage that night, I wrote Paul Monette a letter. I told him of my experience and of carving his and Winston's name in a bench in that sacred spot that had "always stopped [his] heart." I assured him that I was now one of those "fighter-priests" of whom he spoke, part of the Resistance, in the ranks of those wanting to counter hate and discrimination and replace them with the compassionate and healing power of Jesus—even if Monette didn't believe in Him. I sent the letter the next day in care of Harcourt Brace, the publisher of *Last Watch of the Night*. Sometime later, I received this response:

Dear Edward—

How pleased I was to have your letter, and especially with its alignment of us all at Molera Beach. It happened that Winston and I spent four nights at Ventana (Big Sur) the next week after I got your letter. It was 100 degrees all week, too hot to hike even to that holy of holies. In my book of poems, Love Alone, *there's a long poem called "Last Day at Molera Beach," which I'm still proud of. How to thank you for adding our initials to the bench— a bench I've sat on a dozen times. You are clearly my kind of priest, and I wish you courage in the fight for a truly loving church. And thank you for your prayers.*

All best wishes, brother to brother,
Paul Monette

I made it through the whole thirty days, though I had my moments when a nice restaurant and the warm hand of a close friend would have tempted me to abandon it all. But I'm glad I stayed. Sometimes it's hard for me to believe that the most significant event of my time there occurred because of a book I stumbled upon before boarding a plane. I suppose God uses whatever

God can, wherever we happen to be. Though many memorable things happened during my stay at the hermitage, none have had as lasting an effect as what occurred that day by the water. God spoke in a way I never would have anticipated, not unlike the gentle breeze spoken of in the Book of Kings. I left the mountain changed, and that change has perdured.

And yet, I continue to struggle with this issue. As a priest of the Church and as a preacher of the Word from a public pulpit, I am obliged to convey the Church teaching with regard to homosexuality and sexual ethics. And I do. But I feel the teaching reflects an ideal based on some tenuous predications. All Church teaching with regard to human sexuality hinges on whether or not the sexual act is open to procreation. This teaching seems limited when one considers that some sterile, disabled, and elderly people have sex with no hope of procreation, yet it's viewed as acceptable because they are not *choosing* not to procreate. But all reputable studies confirm that homosexuality is not a choice either. Even the Church agrees with that. Why would anyone *choose* a life marred by discrimination, hate, and social ostracism? Although it agrees that homosexuality is not a choice, the Church demands the homosexual live a life of absolute chastity. But how can chastity, supposedly a special grace, be demanded of those who don't feel they've received it, especially when it's not demanded of others in similar nonprocreative situations?

There may come a time in the Church's not too distant future when the procreation linchpin can no longer hold the weight bearing down upon it, and the teaching will be reevaluated in light of people's lived experience rather than a lofty ideal. In the meantime, I welcome the opportunity to deal with individuals in their private struggles and to counsel them on the Church teaching regarding "informed conscience" as the highest moral barometer. The Vatican II document *Constitution on the Church in the Modern World* (*Gaudium et Spes*) says that our conscience goes to the heart of who we are, to our human dignity. Our absolute moral obligation is always to follow our conscience, and never to act against it. This presumes we take time to inform our conscience, which includes knowing the Church teaching, approaching it with respect, and being open to it. But it doesn't mean we will always literally follow that teaching. Church teaching informs our decision; it does not replace it. "For man has in his heart a law written by God. To obey it is the very dignity of man; according to it he will be judged" (*Gaudium et Spes*, Sec. 16).

In a confessional or a counseling room I can appeal to people's conscience in light of their lived experience in a way not possible from a pulpit. Extending the compassionate love of Jesus to those struggling to make spiritual sense out of seemingly conflicting messages is my obligation and my privilege. I do that more authentically today because once on a mountain, I responded to an inner call to withdraw to a deserted place to pray.

On February 13, 1995, the *New York Times* headline of the obituary read: PAUL MONETTE, 49; WRITER HUMANIZED AIDS. The obituary ended with a quote from Monette's book *Becoming a Man: Half a Life Story*, his memoir that had won the 1992 National Book Award for Nonfiction. It read:

> *This is what I am sifting for, to know what a man is finally, no matter the tribe or gender. I can't conceive the hidden life anymore, don't think of it as life. When you finally come out, there's a pain that stops, and you know it will never hurt like that again, no matter how much you lose or how bad you die.*

I still have a picture of the bench with the initials emblazoned clear as day. I keep it close to remember that the fight is not over.

CHAPTER EIGHTEEN

IT DIDN'T PLAY IN PEORIA

～⌘～

The disciples entered a Samaritan village to make ready for Je-
sus; but the people would not receive him, because his face was set
toward Jerusalem. And when his disciples James and John saw it,
they said, "Lord, do you want us to call fire down from heaven to
consume them?" But Jesus turned and rebuked them. And they
went on to another village.

—LUKE 9:52–56

I still don't know how I wound up there. I had never been to
Peoria, never knew anyone from Peoria, never had any desire
to go to Peoria. But one day as I sat at my desk in the Bronx, the
phone rang. It was the pastor of a parish there requesting me to
come and lead a retreat.

"I've heard some good things about you," he said. "We'd like
you to come in the fall."

I was available for the dates he requested, so I agreed. I could
not have predicted what awaited me.

After making two air connections from New York, I landed in
Peoria on a pristinely clear Saturday in September. It was the kind
of fall day that produces clarity in the air seldom experienced in
the other seasons. A Midwest blue sky hosted a sun that continued
to dispense the warmth of a summer already past. It felt good to
be out of the city for a while. The Middle America ambience of
Illinois seemed a nice low-key introduction to another season of

itinerant preaching. This would be my first retreat of the year, after a summer of working to hone a new theme into what I hoped would be inspiring presentations.

I needed to be at the parish by early afternoon, in time to preach at the evening Vigil Mass. The pastor had suggested I rent a car at the airport and drive to the church, as no one was available to pick me up at the airport. After getting lost on back roads and being helped by an obliging man whose confession I heard as we stood by the service pump at a Hess station outside Peoria, I arrived at the church. Hoisting my green backpack on my shoulders, I walked down a finely landscaped path flanked with burgundy chrysanthemums to the rectory and rang the bell. A priest dressed in a crisply ironed cassock opened a large, carved wooden door that supported a lion's head knocker in its center.

"You must be Father Beck," he said solemnly.

He had short-cropped black hair and round wire-rimmed glasses that made him appear older than his thirty-some years. After glancing accusingly at the jeans I was wearing, he motioned me in. We stood in a foyer with kelly green tapestry walls and a large chandelier hanging from an intricately carved plaster relief reminiscent of old world architecture. It was an antechamber that suggested what followed would be impressive—a prelude to one of the most lavishly decorated rectories I have ever seen.

I later learned that one of the associate priests had been given the task of overseeing the remodeling of the rectory, to "make it a more fitting home for the priests." In addition to renovating all of the rooms in an ostentatious baroque style, he had installed a fountain in the central courtyard in which he kept Japanese koi fish. He seemed particularly proud of them, commenting on their rarity and expense and their need to be brought indoors during the colder months. He didn't seem to appreciate it when I referred to them as the goldfish I thought they were.

The priest who answered the door, who I later learned was the pastor, ushered me into the guest room. It was a beautifully appointed suite with a private marble bath and a plush queen-size bed with a tasseled comforter and an array of various-size down pillows. I couldn't help wonder where one procured such elaborate decorative accoutrements in Peoria, of all places, but I didn't complain. I reasoned it would make up for all the pullouts I've slept on in other Rectories. The pastor checked that the housekeeper had put a fresh supply of towels in the bathroom and then quickly excused himself, citing the need to hear confessions in the church before the Vigil Mass.

"If there's anything you need, please don't hesitate to ask. And we're delighted you're with us, Father."

He turned hastily, his cassock billowing in a trail behind him, and he was gone. I attributed his seeming discomfort to first-meeting awkwardness and unpacked my bags. While rereading the Scriptures in preparation for the homily I would preach that evening at the Mass, I fell into a deep sleep and awoke just in time to hurry over to the church.

Constructed sometime in the '70s, the church was a simple edifice of dark brick and wood, a sharp contrast to the sybaritic Rectory. My immediate impression was that more light was needed, but I soon realized mere electricity couldn't provide it. The sanctuary, more ornate than the rest of the church, contained ecclesiastical appointments placed precisely according to liturgical guidelines. The one exception to this was the tabernacle. Instead of being situated at a side altar or in a Blessed Sacrament chapel, as the norms suggested, it loomed large in the center of the sanctuary with two large floral arrangements of white and yellow roses adorning each side. I was told later that this was the intentional choice of the priests, who felt the tabernacle should be central in the worship space.

More than its architecture or furniture, however, I noticed the lack of welcome present in the church. There were no greeters, no ministers of hospitality, no one to invite the congregation to this celebration of thanksgiving. It was cold. As I stood at the back door in my Passionist habit and began to introduce myself to the people as they entered, some hurried by me without so much as a glance; others took time to say they were glad I had come and were looking forward to the retreat.

One elderly woman, who entered with a walker, pulled my ear down to her mouth and whispered, "See if you can do anything to get these guys here to loosen up a bit."

I smiled without knowing quite how to respond. Wondering if her request reflected a common sentiment in the congregation, I walked back into the church and was surprised to see it was completely full by the time Mass began.

One of the associate priests presided at the Eucharist. He too was in his mid to late thirties but of Asian decent. This was the interior decorator with the penchant for esoteric fish. He uttered the prayers of the Mass slowly in a monotone voice that had an accent not recognizably Asian at all. I soon realized it was his "priest's voice," deliberate and precise, but employing what sounded like a Boston pronunciation of "a" words, even though I was informed he was reared in the Midwest.

" 'Faarther,' we come to you in praise and thanksgiving, for your love is 'everlawsting.' " *Why was he speaking like this? When I spoke to him in the sacristy before Mass he didn't sound this way. He sounded then like he was from Illinois.*

He sat in the presider's chair like a satrap surveying his worshipping subjects. As the "alleluias" were sung to signal the proclamation of the Gospel, I walked to his chair from my seat on the side of the sanctuary to receive his blessing. With eyes closed and hands outstretched over my head, he mumbled a prayer in Latin. Surprised by the use of a liturgical language the Church has not used for more than thirty years, I assumed it was the usual blessing prayer, but I had no way of knowing. I proclaimed the Gospel and then, breaking tradition, stepped from the pulpit into the center aisle of the church to deliver the homily, no longer able to see the priest who sat at the high presider's chair behind me.

Preaching in my usual fashion, I incorporated stories and humor to develop my homily. I began by telling them a bit about myself, and then proceeded to speak about the retreat, using the just-proclaimed Scriptures as the framework for my invitation. The congregation seemed receptive but not overly enthusiastic, cooler than I had experienced at other places. They nodded half-heartedly, almost suspiciously, as if something were preventing them from responding more fervently.

At the conclusion of the Mass I went into the sacristy so that I could accompany the Asian priest back to the rectory for dinner. When I entered, he refused to meet my gaze and answered me with one-word responses—a cool reception, to say the least. While it was obvious he had not been bowled over by my presentation, I wondered what in particular had disturbed him, but I knew it wasn't the time to inquire.

He fiddled around with some papers on a table by the door and then, without looking up, finally said, "I still have to say my thanksgiving prayers after Mass. Why don't you just go over to the rectory and I'll be along in a few minutes. I'm sure we're about ready to start dinner."

"O.K.," I said nonchalantly. "I'll tell the others you're on your way."

I left wondering if these prayers too would be uttered in Latin—and if God even understood Latin anymore.

The meal proved to be a classic rectory experience, one that I imagine was more common in the 1930s than today. We sat at our assigned places in a dining room of marmoreal beauty, suitably appointed to feed a papal delegation. The three priests, all dressed in cassocks, and I, once again in my jeans, prayed a perfunctory grace before the meal, and then the pastor rang a bell which had been placed by his chair. Wheeling a silver cart, the cook-server entered the room with her eyes downcast and a slight shuffle to her walk. Her hair pulled back in a bun, she wore a black-and-white serving uniform that I playfully thought made her look like an inmate. Engaged in vapid conversation about some parish fund-raiser to be held the following week, the priests appeared to ignore her as she labored to put everything on the table in its proper place. She seemed jumpy, struggling to carefully place butterballs on the bread plates. I tried to engage her with a smile but she never looked at me. "Yes, Father. No, Father. Is everything to your liking, Father?" These were the only words I heard her utter during a long and strained meal in which I too was ignored.

On Sunday morning I rose early to prepare myself for what I knew would be a long and arduous day. My task was to continue to preach at all of the Masses in an attempt to initiate interest in the retreat that was to begin that evening. I was met with the same chilly reception from the other two priests who presided at the Masses, though I sensed a growing interest in the retreat from the Sunday morning congregations.

Upon leaving the church after the Masses, many said, "We'll see you tonight, Father." I was encouraged.

One woman with an eyebrow raised and an amused smirk shook my hand and proffered, "We'll see if you can succeed where others have failed."

Succeed? Failed? What did she mean?

I anticipated the approach of dusk—with mounting trepidation.

Arriving in the church one hour before the service was scheduled to begin, I wanted to leisurely set up and to quiet myself with prayer before beginning. Usually the priests of a parish offer to assist me with the many pre-retreat tasks, but none of my dinner companions from the previous evening was anywhere to be found. I secretly hoped they would skip the service altogether, thus lessening my anxiety level. The last thing I needed was three suspicious clerics sitting in the congregation with evaluating pen and paper in hand.

About fifteen minutes before we were scheduled to begin, the people started to arrive. It started as a slow trickle from the parking lot, but soon they were crowding the doors to enter. By the time I walked down the center aisle to the organ playing and voices lifting a robust rendition of "Amazing Grace," the church was filled to capacity with more than a thousand people in the pews for our first evening of retreat. As I approached the sanctuary, I could see the black shadows lurking in the sacristy just out of view. My brother priests may have been opting not to visibly attend the evening service, but they would be listening.

After some introductory and welcoming remarks, I ascended the pulpit to proclaim the Gospel text I had chosen for the evening, the story of Nicodemus (John 3:1–21), a wonderful example of John the evangelist's theology at its best. It highlights John's concern that we be attentive to not only our physical selves, but our spiritual ones as well. "No one can enter the kingdom of God without being born of water and the Spirit. What is born of flesh is flesh and what is born of spirit is spirit" (John 3:5–6). In this Gospel, Jesus attempts to teach an obdurate Nicodemus about the world of Spirit, suggesting that, as a teacher, Nicodemus must become more conversant with this world before he presumes to teach others about it (John 3:10). And then in a theologically groundbreaking conclusion to this prodding encounter, Jesus speaks of a God whose love is so vast, "He sent his Son into the world, not to condemn the world, but that the world might be saved through him" (John 3:17). John speaks of a God without judgment, of a God who needn't judge because we ourselves are so adept at it. "This is the judgment, that the light came into the world, but people preferred darkness to light . . ." (John 3:19).

Walking into the center aisle after proclaiming this Gospel, I felt the Spirit present in the church. The resistance that had concerned me up to this point seemed to melt away. I became calm and focused. As I began my talk, many in the congregation sat expectantly, hungrily, unlike some other congregations, where the beginning of the homily is often a cue to start reading the parish bulletin. Still, some others sat suspiciously, with arms folded, daring me to convince them I had something worthwhile to say. I was brimming with a desire to convey John's healing and liberating words to a congregation that I sensed needed both, and I was soon oblivious to the dark shadows skulking behind me. As the promise of John's Gospel took hold in the listeners, I was concerned only with the emerging light I perceived flooding hearts that had for too long been denied. I felt so privileged to be a conduit that evening, as an aphotic church seemed to grow in luminosity.

When I was done preaching, I walked to the baptistery and blessed water as a reminder of our baptismal call to be born of Spirit, as Jesus had suggested in the Gospel. Then eight laypeople, with whom I had spoken before the service, came to the font and I blessed them with the water. Commissioning them to now go forward and bless their sisters and brothers, I handed them bowls filled with the water as they dispersed throughout the church. Taking my seat in the sanctuary, I watched a thousand thirsty people come to the water and be signed on their foreheads as a reminder of our birth "from above."

By the time the service ended, I knew that many of those who had come left feeling nourished. As I said good night to people at the church doors, some went out of their way to express gratitude.

"Father, I can't tell you how long I've waited for something like this to come to our church," said one of the women who had helped with the blessing ritual. "I feel that there's some real hope for us. Thank you."

A young father with four children in tow came up to me and said, "I was about to start going to the other side of town to church because I just didn't like what was happening here, but maybe I can hang on." I nodded in affirmation, wanting to respond even further.

Of course, not everyone was ebullient. Some passed by me at the church doors without even looking in my direction. I extended my hand to one middle-aged woman who had been sitting in the first pew with her mother and she turned away from me. There was nothing lukewarm about this group—clearly heeding the Gospel directive to be either hot or cold.

Once everyone had gone, I emptied the water from the baptistery and collected some of the programs left behind. One of the associate priests appeared from the sacristy and informed me that he would turn out the lights and lock the church, saying nothing about the service. I thanked him and left.

When I arrived at the rectory, I went directly to my room, eager to unwind and to get some sleep. I was feeling the repercussions of the long, stress-filled day and just wanted some time alone. I had searched Peoria that afternoon for a newsstand that carried the Sunday *New York Times* and finally located it in a Barnes & Noble that had one copy left. Sipping a glass of cold lemonade, I stretched out on the couch in the sitting room of my suite with the paper on my lap. As I opened the first page of the Arts and Leisure section of the paper, there was a knock on my door. I hesitated opening it, but when I did, the pastor, still in his cassock, was standing there with a pen and notebook.

"May I come in?"

It was 10:40 P.M.

"Well, sure, but I was just getting ready for bed. Can it wait till morning?"

"No, I'm afraid it can't."

"Well, then come in."

What could I say? It was his house. I invited him to sit down on a chair opposite the couch and I waited for him to speak. He looked down at the coffee table and fumbled with his papers. His already serious face grew even more so as he seemingly struggled to find the words.

"I'm going to need a transcript of everything you plan to say from now till the end of the retreat."

"What?"

"A transcript. You know, your manuscripts. I can't let you continue unless I review what you're going to say before each service."

I sat stunned, sure that he couldn't be serious.

I finally said, "I don't have any manuscripts. I don't preach that way. I have some words written on index cards in an outline form to keep me on track and that's it. I like to leave some room for the inspiration of the Spirit. And even if I did have a manuscript, I wouldn't give it to you. What is this, the Church police?"

He shifted in his chair and started to rub his temples, sensing this wasn't going to be an easy late-night visit.

"That remark was uncalled for," he said quietly. "We simply had some problems with some of what you said and did tonight, and the other associates and myself feel that we need to know what's coming so that we can head off any problems."

"And what exactly did you object to?"

"Three things that I can name in particular for you, but in general, it's just your style. Well, more than just style . . . we think you're too liberal for this community. And we've worked too hard to get the people to where they are to let one retreat cause all kinds of dissension again."

So now we're getting to the real issue. I knew these guys were conservative, but I never thought they'd go this far. He would actually end the retreat?

I picked up my glass of lemonade from the table and drank slowly, giving myself time to decide how to respond.

"Well, you're going to have to tell me what it is exactly that you had a problem with and maybe we can talk about it. But as far as my being too liberal for this community, I think that's perhaps better phrased 'too liberal for you and your associates.' There were a thousand people in church tonight—most of whom seemed pretty pleased with what happened. So I don't know *what* community you're talking about."

He took off his wire-rimmed glasses and shot back, "Sometimes the people don't know what's best for them theologically or liturgically. They depend on us to make sure they get teaching that is in accord with the magisterium of the Church."

"And you feel that what I said was in opposition to that? Where? What did I say? Tell me what you're talking about." I was honestly perplexed.

He said, "First of all, we feel you dismissed Catholic education in this country by your comments about how what the nuns taught us in catechism was errant and guilt-inducing. We feel as though the sisters deserve more respect than that for the many years of service that they've given the Church."

I couldn't believe how he was twisting what I had said.

I took a deep breath, exhaled, and said, "I never said that. What I said was that *some* of what we learned about a punitive God who was waiting with bated breath to punish us was not helpful. And that we have an awful lot of guilt-ridden people as a result who don't know what it means to have a loving relationship with God because they're so afraid of God."

Ignoring my apologia, he consulted his notes and pressed on.

"Secondly, we feel that you undermined the priesthood by allowing laypeople to usurp our role as the ordinary dispensers of blessing."

"And how did I do that?" I asked, dumbfounded.

"You let laypeople bless with holy water when you had three capable priests here, readily available, who could have assisted you. It wasn't clear what you were trying to accomplish and many were confused because it so resembled baptism."

"Resembled baptism?" I asked. "Well, yes, it was supposed to resemble baptism in calling that sacrament to mind, but I hardly think anyone in the church tonight thought laypeople were baptizing. And I wouldn't exactly call three priests hiding in the sacristy 'readily available.'"

My voice was rising and my anger coming to the fore. I was indignant that he was misrepresenting what had happened in the church, and I couldn't believe him not being more supportive of an experience so obviously well received by his community. And then it occurred to me that he and his associates were threatened. They wanted me out of their parish—and out of Peoria.

"Are you afraid the people are actually going to like what I'm saying and relate to it more than they relate to you and your preaching?"

The pastor was now sitting on the edge of his chair, leaning forward while he consulted his notebook.

"And thirdly," he said, ignoring my question, "you casually dismissed the judgment capacity of God and heretically undermined what we say to be true about God every Sunday when we recite the Creed."

"And that is . . . ?" I ventured, knowing this could only get more absurd.

"That God is the *judge* of the living and the dead," he practically shouted. "It's right there in what we say we believe as Roman Catholics and you dismissed it."

I was totally frustrated. It seemed useless to attempt to explain I was communicating John's theology in a specific text and not the catechism of the Roman Catholic Church.

"Look," I said. "I can see we're worlds apart in what we believe to be significant about our faith. It's eleven-thirty at night and I'm tired and getting angry, so there's probably no use discussing any of this further tonight. So what are we going to do about the retreat?"

He hesitated a moment as if not totally sure what to say. "My associates feel it would be best if we just cancel the retreat and just send the people home when they come tomorrow night."

"And *you?*" I said. "Is that what *you* want to do?"

I could tell he wasn't totally convinced yet and probably worried about how he would explain the cancellation of the retreat to a thousand expectant people, who were certain to return on Monday night.

"I'm not sure. I'd like to sleep on it and let you know in the morning," he said. I was tempted to say that *I* no longer wanted to continue the retreat under such circumstances, but I was convinced it could be helpful to the community, so I resisted the impulse to cancel it myself.

"O.K.," I said. "You sleep on it and you let me know. But I'd like you to consider something. These aren't children you're dealing with here. These are intelligent, discerning adults who have the right to choose what they want to listen to and whether or not they want to accept what they hear. They don't need 'Big Daddy,' or in this case 'Daddies,' to protect them from some imagined heresy. The Holy Spirit just might be working in this community through this retreat and you don't have the right to squelch that through censorship."

"Thank you for your wise advice, Father," he retorted. "I will certainly take it into consideration as I make my decision."

He then rose wearily from his chair, extended his hand to me, which I shook, and walked out the door, leaving me with my *New York Times* to distract me from the surreal conversation. Although it bothered me that this was now all his decision, it was, and there was nothing I could do about it.

I managed to fall asleep after an hour or so and awakened about seven the next morning. When I walked into the sitting room of my suite, I noticed a white legal size envelope had been shoved under the door. Retrieving it, I saw FR. BECK written on the front. It was a letter from the pastor, signed by him and the two associates, informing me that he was canceling the retreat and that my services would no longer be required. He went on to say that he would monetarily reimburse the Passionist community for my time and also pay any airfare fees incurred through changing my ticket for an earlier departure.

By ten o'clock that morning, I was on a plane back to New York City, understanding more fully what they mean when they say, "If you can make it in Peoria . . ." I didn't.

I learned from parishioners who called me in New York that when the people arrived that evening for the second night of retreat, there was a note attached to the church door which read: DUE TO THEOLOGICAL DIFFERENCES, FR. BECK FEELS HE CAN NO LONGER CONTINUE TO PREACH OUR RETREAT. THE REMAINDER HAS BEEN CANCELED. My brother priests didn't have the guts to accept responsibility for their own decision. I was also told that when people went to the rectory to demand an explanation, the building was dark, the blinds drawn, and the clerics nowhere to be found.

To his credit, the pastor subsequently wrote me and admitted his actions may have been hasty; he also requested that we enter into a theological conversation by letter to continue to explore our differences. I wrote back once out of fraternal obligation and because I still needed to process the experience for myself, but I soon saw that the conversation was fruitless and chose to discontinue it. The whole incident saddened me. I was hurt and angry but also concerned at what I perceived to be unwarranted censorship. And in my perception, the people of the parish were the ones who suffered.

But not only the people of the parish. I can't help but think that we all suffered as a result of my experience in Peoria. I am, of course, aware that there are vast theological differences within our universal Roman Catholic Church. *Conservative* and *liberal* are words too easily used to describe distinctions that are multifarious and complex. They are words I sometimes use myself to dismiss others who are not in accord with my theological or ecclesiastical perspectives. When the pastor suggested that I was too "liberal" for his community, what was he really saying? My theology was certainly orthodox and could be supported by many respected theologians and Scripture scholars. But it wasn't *his* preferred perspective. He would have consulted different scholars and presented just as orthodox a theology, albeit a different one. Does that make one right and one wrong? Or is there room for both?

I also think he viewed me as representing a priesthood that threatened his understanding of Church and priestly ministry. From his perspective, "liberal priests" like me are the cause of much of the confusion the Church is currently experiencing. We are weakening the link to revered doctrine and rubrics that extend from Rome to all the daughter churches throughout the world. But does his being threatened give him the right to extinguish my message?

Similarly, when I assigned the label "conservative" to him and his associates, it wasn't merely that their theological views seemed stiflingly rigid, but also that they wore cassocks at the dinner table and kept *L'Osservatore Romano* on the coffee table. The *droit du seigneur* attitude with which they embodied the role of "priest" irked me, although much of it was stylistic, not inherently evil. They had been trained in Rome and had developed a theology and understanding of priesthood very different from mine; that difference caused me to be less receptive to them from the moment of our initial meeting. I quickly intuited that, for them, a priest dressed a certain way; spoke a certain way; said Mass a certain way. Their way was obviously not mine. But is there only one right way?

While some could argue that it was a "professional difference of opinion" that occasioned my departure, I couldn't help but feel personally rejected as well, feeling that their actions and attitudes were implying that my priesthood was unacceptable. And yet, I was thinking the same about them. What most disturbed me was that such young men had definitively decided what was theologically and ecclesiastically normative, and were leaving no room for any variance. They had so soon arrived at "the truth," but with so little pastoral ministry experience to guide them. The intolerance and hubris exemplified appeared to me contrary to the call of the Gospel. Upon further reflection, however, I realized that I too was recalcitrant in my positions. I also believe strongly in my vision of the Church and I am, at times, unwavering and intolerant in communicating it. So my brother clerics and I were arm-wrestling theologies and ecclesiologies, with neither side willing to say "uncle." But what about the congregation witnessing the match? Shouldn't they have some say?

It seems obvious that the issue is power. These guys didn't want the laity to participate in the blessing because they feared their role as priests was being usurped. I wanted the laity to participate to demonstrate my belief in the universal call to holiness that Vatican II propagated. We both were holding tightly to reins we fear may be taken from our hands, I by conservative Vatican autocrats, and they by liberal disrespecting laity and clergy. Both responses are rooted in fear, but such fear cannot be of the Spirit. Who mediates the divergence and facilitates the Spirit getting the upper hand?

In the Gospels, Jesus is a man of empowerment and inclusion, always seeking to advance the cause of the disenfranchised, but never by strong-arming. Jesus honored the various religious perspectives in his midst and encouraged people to seek the common ground of universal truths. Although his disdain of the Pharisees and Sadducees is not concealed, he never gives up on trying to reason with them from within their own theological milieu. While respecting their religious commitment, he attempts to take them deeper into the world of a God who transcends rules and theological assignations. My fear is that unless we learn to do the same, we are all diminished, as is the Church we unanimously purport to love so dearly.

CHAPTER NINETEEN

THE DANCE OF CELIBACY

Jesus said, "Some are incapable of marriage because they were born so; some, because they were made so by others; some, because they have renounced marriage for the sake of the kingdom of heaven. Whoever can accept this, ought to accept it."

—MATTHEW 19:12

She sat in the front pew for the first two nights of the retreat. I couldn't miss her: statuesque as a runway model, straight, shimmering brown hair with blond highlights, which the church lights danced off of, and an attentive gaze that suggested she was hanging on every word I said.

The retreat was going well and I was confident, judging by the nodding of heads, that my attempts to communicate the biblical spirituality of the Scripture passages were paying off. People were also laughing at my jokes, another good barometer. As always, individuals seemed to be experiencing the week in uniquely personal ways, as if God had tailored the experience for them. I was often amazed during a retreat how some seemed to receive what they needed at that particular time in their lives. It was as if God had chosen the retreat week to make His move. Sometimes people would quote back to me decisively transformative words that I had supposedly uttered, but I often had no recollection of saying any such thing. I guess the Spirit can bamboozle her way through no matter what.

On the third day of this particular retreat, I got a call from the receptionist at the rectory, who said a woman was waiting to see me. I was surprised because I hadn't scheduled any appointments. When I walked into the rectory waiting room, the woman from the front row in church was sitting there, dressed like she was anticipating dinner at a tony restaurant with dancing afterward.

"Hello, Father," she said, standing up, her black wrap falling to the chair. "My name is Zoë. I've been making the retreat you've been giving here at the parish, and I'm really enjoying it."

She was even more beautiful close-up than from a distance. She had large, doelike brown eyes and pore-less, translucent skin that radiated healthiness. While she looked like a woman who couldn't have a care in the world, upon closer inspection, I perceived a traceable sadness in her eyes and a forced quality to her smile. I was curious as to why she had come to see me.

"Hi, it's nice to meet you, Zoë," I said. "I'm glad you're enjoying the retreat. Please sit down. What can I do for you?"

One hour later, I was still sitting there, having listened to much of her life story. With tears and histrionics, she talked about being a victim in just about every situation, about her poor relationship with a domineering father, and about her failures with men who never measured up. She bemoaned the irony of being a successful executive, running a major corporation, but not being able to run her own life. Strangely, her self-pitying lamenting only served to mar her beauty. I wanted her to be stronger, more self-assured. But then, of course, she wouldn't have needed me.

"I tell you all of that," she said, "and I'm sorry I went on so, because I really feel that I need spiritual direction. I think my problem is that I haven't been spiritually centered. But in listening to you, I'm sure you could help me. I totally agree with your approach to spirituality. I need to make God more the center of my life, because I'm not finding fulfillment in my relationships, in my job, or in anything else. It's just like you said, 'We have to find our center in something deeper.' "

Despite her enthusiasm, I wasn't so sure Zoë's problem could be solved simply spiritually. Everything I had heard her say pointed to serious relationship issues that needed more than prayer to fix them. It was not just that God wasn't her center. She also needed to figure out why all the significant relationships in her life, particularly with men, seemed to go awry. Hearing only what she wanted, she had seized on my comments during the retreat as an easy solution, but there was no easy answer. I wanted to tell her that God works in and through our attempts to help ourselves, and to encourage her not to hide behind overspiritualizing everything.

Although God often uses other people to help us as well, I wasn't sure that I was the person to help Zoë. Feeling that perhaps she was attracted to me in ways that went beyond the realm of spiritual direction, I started to feel uneasy. It was the way she held her glances just a bit too long; it was her leaning forward in rapt attention, as though my words were elixir for all her ills; it was her constant tossing forward of her shiny hair in a way that betrayed a self-consciousness peculiar for a spiritual direction session. Instinctively sensing the complexities, I intuited that someone else would better accompany Zoë on her journey with God—and all the other journeys that I knew would be involved.

"Well, I appreciate your saying that, Zoë, thank you. But as you know, I travel from place to place every week giving these retreats, so it's really impossible for me to have an ongoing spiritual direction relationship with someone."

"Yes, but you do a lot of work in this diocese, and I don't mind traveling to come to see you whenever you're in a parish around here. That would be somewhat regularly, by the looks of your schedule."

I was feeling pressured. Aside from being uncomfortable in the situation, and not being sure all her needs were spiritual, I also suspected her problems required long-term psychological counseling, something I wasn't qualified to give. While there was something attractive about her vulnerability, enticing me to rescue her, the "need" that poured out of her scared me, making me feel I could become so absorbed by her that I'd never find my way out.

"Zoë, I'm just not sure that I can really help you. I . . ."

"Father, I think I'm the one to decide what's helpful to me," she said curtly. "And I'm telling you that you would be. All I'm asking is that you let me come see you to talk about my spiritual life and how that's affecting the rest of my life. Isn't that what you do? It's certainly what you've been preaching about this week."

"Yes, of course, it's what I *try* to do, but because of my schedule and the travel involved, I can't commit to an ongoing relationship."

"I'm not asking for a commitment, Father. I'd just like to call you once in a while and maybe come in and talk—when it's convenient for you. But if it's too much trouble . . ."

I was silent for a moment, not knowing how to respond. She made me feel like I'd be a bad priest if I turned her down. And while she made her request seem innocuous, I envisioned the minefields. I had been down this road before, when suddenly I had found myself the primary support system for someone I didn't have the time for. Also, I worried about her seeming attraction to me. Past experience had taught me that attraction and need could be a lethal combination—on both sides.

My own initial feelings toward her were similarly complex. Though not based primarily in a physical attraction, I was attracted. I found myself engaging in a bizarre fantasy, imagining I was the strong man who could solve all her problems. Although I knew that was unrealistic, there was something appealing about being so wanted and needed. The male ego can be a dangerous thing. I also wasn't sure how to refuse her without seeming cold and heartless. She had played the "good priest" trump card, one that always caused me to cash in my chips.

"O.K., Zoë, fine," I finally said. "If you feel the need to talk again, and we can arrange it when I'm in this area, then we'll do it. Give me a call." I secretly hoped that the call would never come.

But of course, it did. Over the next few months, whenever I was in the vicinity, she would call, sometimes two and three times

a week. I explained to her that my first obligation was to see people in the parish who were making the retreat, and that if I had
any time available after that, I could meet with her. Suspecting my
resistance, she would often make appointments with the secre-
taries at the Rectories without saying who she was. Clueless, I
would walk into the office and she would be sitting there.

"Oh, I didn't want to give my name to the receptionist on the
phone," she would say playfully. "I just figured I'd surprise you."
She'd then smile, exposing straight white teeth that appeared the
result of years of orthodontia.

I was aware the appointments were becoming too frequent,
and I sensed her growing dependence on me, but I wasn't sure
how to control it, or if I wanted to. She insisted that God had led
her to me. A part of me liked that. She was effusive in her praise
of my advice and insights, assuring me that she couldn't have sur-
vived this strenuous period in her life without my counsel. An attractive, successful woman, whom everyone seemingly admired
and desired, kept telling me that my presence in her life was allowing her to cope. It was pretty heady stuff. And there was more.
Entering religious life at a young age, I had never had the opportunity to have an adult relationship with a woman who depended
on me. I enjoyed being the center of someone's world. It made me
feel important, needed, and even loved. Though I knew a more
intimate relationship was not possible because of my vows, and because I really didn't want it, I enjoyed skirting the edges. It was arrested, adolescent dating—only I wasn't an adolescent anymore.

But it all began to come crashing down one day at lunchtime
when she called for an appointment. She said she preferred not to
come to the rectory because she knew the receptionist. Could I
possibly meet her somewhere else? She suggested a restaurant not
far from the parish where I was giving the retreat. Without giving me time to digest her request, she told me she'd be waiting
there and hung up.

It felt wrong to see her in a social setting, but I convinced myself it was harmless. After all, we could talk at a table in a restau-

rant as easily as in the counseling room at the rectory. And I did need to eat lunch, so seeing her there would also be time-effective; I'd then have more availability for other appointments in the afternoon. I changed clothes and went to the restaurant.

She was sitting at a corner table, dressed as elegantly as I had ever seen her. She wore a blue silk dress and a multicolored scarf, gathered around her shoulders and held in place by a gold nautilus brooch. Her shoes were dyed the same color blue as her dress and had long, thin heels that looked difficult to walk on. When I arrived at the table, she kissed me lightly on the cheek—a first—and said how happy she was that I had come. I looked around quickly to see if anyone I knew was in the restaurant, strangely feeling that I was having an illicit tryst. A waiter brought a cold bottle of Santa Margherita Pinot Grigio, the bottle sweating with condensation. I started to sweat, too, feeling that I was being set up, maybe even seduced. But rather than feeling flattered, I resented it.

"Zoë, what's this?" I said, pointing at the bottle, once the waiter had poured some wine and left the remainder in a silver ice bucket next to the table.

"Oh, I thought wine would be nice with lunch. This one's really refreshing—not too sweet. I remember your saying you liked dry white wines."

"Zoë, I don't want any wine. It's the middle of the day and I still have three appointments this afternoon. I'll be falling asleep on people."

"Oh, don't be ridiculous," she said. "A little wine won't hurt you. You priests drink it all the time." She raised her glass for a toast.

I hesitantly picked up my glass, clinked it against hers, and said, "Zoë, what is it you need to speak about, because I only have an hour. I have an appointment back at the rectory."

"Well, first of all, I have some really great news, some *amazing* news. Talk about God working! I've been transferred, at least for the immediate future, to the same city where you're living! Can you believe that? They want me to get our corporate office there up and running."

My face must have fallen. I didn't know what to say, but I felt an immediate unease, like the restaurant was closing in on me.

"Well, don't look so happy about it," she said. "Isn't it amazing that I've been wondering how I could do spiritual direction more regularly with you, given your schedule, and now we're going to be living in the same city? So when you're not traveling, I'll be able to see you. I mean, isn't that unbelievable?"

I was thinking that was the perfect adjective.

"Zoë, did you ask for this transfer?" I said.

"No, no, I was completely floored by it when the vice president presented me with it. I mean, he gave me an option to stay here, but I really think the change would be good for a while. I'm excited by it. Obviously, you're not."

"It just seems like too much of a coincidence."

"I know," said Zoë. "That's why I'm absolutely positive God's hand is in it."

I was positive that she was beginning to confuse her hand with God's.

Zoë moved after coyly enlisting my help to find an apartment. She was apologetic about needing to involve me with her relocation, but she said she didn't know anyone else in the city, and it overwhelmed her to anticipate looking for housing in a strange place. I was hesitant to accede to her request, but I didn't know how to say no. On the surface, helping her move seemed the "Christian thing" to do. In actuality, she was once again playing the helpless damsel in distress, and I was the knight in shining armor on the charging horse.

My initial attraction to her was beginning to wane, however. Her manipulation and incessant neediness were squelching that, but it was being replaced by something else. In retrospect, I unconsciously enjoyed looking for an apartment with her and helping her to set it up. I was getting to "play" at something I would never have the opportunity to do for real as a religious and a priest. I had always wanted a place of my own, so it fed a domestic, nesting need; I willingly helped to gather the straw, even though I knew it misleading, and even a little dangerous.

While I tried to come to peace with the realization that our relationship had become something more than professional, that transition wasn't as emotionally charged for me as it seemed to be for Zoë. I was still puzzled as to how the evolution had even occurred. Had one restaurant meeting abruptly shifted the tenor? Suddenly we were shopping for curtains together, but I wasn't sure I even wanted a friendship with her. For a while, my hesitancy didn't alter my external behavior because I was enjoying some of the perks: nice dinners, intelligent conversation, admiring glances from other couples. The relationship was feeding my ego and my need to be wanted; and it was feeding her need to have a man in her life who didn't abuse her. I did begin to wonder, however, if we had anything in common, other than her problems. And although I resisted it, I knew it was time to discuss our relationship and our expectations—without the distraction of restaurants or home-goods stores.

That conversation and another I never anticipated occurred one evening at the Passionist Residence where I lived. She arrived early, as the community members and I were finishing dinner. Escorting her to the library, I excused myself, and went back to the dining room to help finish clearing the table.

"So who's the woman in the red dress?" asked Columkille, one of the senior priests, and a friend.

"Oh, that's Zoë," I said. "We have an appointment this evening, but she's early, so I told her I'd be with her in a few minutes."

"Is that the same woman that you helped to move here?"

"Yeah," I said. "Why?"

"Oh, nothing. It's just that, the way you talked about that, I sensed some hesitancy in you about the relationship, like you were feeling pressured. I'd just be careful if I were you."

"Careful of what?"

"Well, it's just that I've met some Zoës in my day, and sometimes they can expect more than you can give. A white collar can be a magnet, you know. You don't want to get yourself into something you'll regret."

I knew he was hitting the mark, but I didn't want to let on. I wasn't ready to admit how complicated it had become, or to fess up to my own complicity, although it was becoming harder to pretend that I didn't have a full-fledged problem on my hands.

"O.K., I'll be careful. Thanks."

I returned to the library on the second floor and found Zoë holding a copy of *The Confessions of St. Augustine.*

"May I borrow this?" she asked. "I've always wanted to read it. I remember you quoting him in one of your talks. You like him, right?"

"Yeah, I think he's a great writer and thinker. It's a wonderful book. Sure, you can borrow it."

"He was quite the Don Juan in his youth, wasn't he?" she said.

"Yeah, he certainly broke his share of hearts, and caused his mother to shed a lot of tears, too."

"I hope that's not why you like him," she said, slightly smiling.

"What do you mean?"

"Well, you know, sometimes I have the feeling that you want to be more open with me and closer, but that you resist it. It just hurts sometimes."

Now *I* was hurting her, like every other man in her life. My built-up resentment surfaced immediately, and was the impetus I needed to initiate the conversation I knew had been long coming.

"Zoë, could you sit down? We really need to talk about this, because I don't think we're on the same wavelength here. For a while now, I've been feeling that you have a lot of expectations of our relationship, and frankly, I'm not sure I can meet them. In fact, I know I can't. I mean, we began this relationship as a professional one, and I know it has evolved more into . . . like a friendship. But

I think maybe we're at a point where we need to set some boundaries."

She looked at me without blinking and said, "Edward, you don't have to pretend with me any longer. I know that you want more from our relationship, and so do I, and I'm prepared to give it. I've thought a lot about this. I've listened to your talks very closely, and I sense the struggle you have with your priesthood. But it's O.K. You don't have to hide it with me. Maybe it's not what you're supposed to do for the rest of your life. I mean, God can call some people to serve for just a while and then have them do something else, can't He?"

"What are you talking about? Zoë, you've got this all wrong. I'm very happy as a priest, and I plan to stay one the rest of my life. You may have heard me express some dissatisfaction with certain aspects of my life, or talk about stuff I wish was different, but that's normal. Everyone does that. But I don't have any intentions of doing anything else. Is that what you think?"

"Are you going to sit there and pretend that you haven't led me to expect that we could have a more intimate relationship?" She leaned forward in her chair, reaching out and touching my knees with her hands. My body tightened and I pushed back slightly.

"No, I haven't led you to expect that. Zoë, I don't know what signals you've picked up, but I can tell you they're the wrong ones. I've tried to be a good counselor to you and I've also tried to be a friend. And that's all. Now, maybe I've been remiss in allowing the friendship part, but it was only after your continued urging and relentless pursuit."

"Oh sure, now it's all my fault," she said, shaking her head, and lifting her hands up into the air. "I can't believe you. You're like every other man. We women are just manipulating shrews, trying to get you men to do what we want. The nerve of you even suggesting that. How misogynistic."

She folded her arms and sat back in the chair, staring out the window behind me. Her eyes started to fill with tears and then her bottom lip began to quiver. My initial instinct was to rescue her again, to apologize, and say we could work this all out. But I knew it would be the wrong move. After sitting in silence for what seemed to be five minutes, I finally said, "Zoë, I don't think we can see each other anymore—at all." I felt liberated as I said the words.

She looked at me in disbelief, her mouth opening slightly, her eyes squinting, as if trying to see if this were the same man she thought she knew so well.

"What are you talking about? Of course we can continue to see one another. We'll work this out. We just need a little time."

"No, I don't think you understand. I don't need any more time. I don't *want* any more time. I don't think I could ever be comfortable with our relationship, knowing we have such different expectations. I'm sorry. It won't work."

"I can't believe you're saying this. You? You who preach such a great message about love and intimacy and sharing one's feelings and being vulnerable. And now I sit here and try to tell you how I'm really feeling, and you can't deal with it?"

"Zoë, you did more than tell me how *you* feel. You told me how *I* feel. And you're wrong. You've misread it. You've interpreted attempted kindness for something else. And I'm not trying to blame you for it. I'm just saying I don't think we should continue in a relationship that has gone down such a misguided path. I'm sorry. And if I've done anything to send you mixed signals, I'm sorry about that, too. Because I never intended to."

She was silent again, back to staring out the window, shaking her head back and forth. When she finally spoke, it was haltingly, apologetically, as if she knew this was her last chance to redeem a quickly disintegrating situation.

"Edward, I know you're . . . a little . . . upset right now. And so am I. So why don't we just take a few days to calm down. And then maybe we could talk again. We could . . ."

"Zoë," I interrupted, "let me walk you downstairs. I need for you to go. I'm really sorry."

She stared at me with pleading eyes, then stood up slowly, adjusting the belt around her red dress, which shimmered under the lights in the library. As she put on her black and red plaid coat, and pulled her hair out from inside the collar, sadness seemed to descend on her like a heavy weight, her shoulders drooping, her head bowing down. She turned toward the door and then, sobbing, turned back toward me, rushing me and throwing her arms around my neck.

"Don't do this, please don't do this," she cried. "I'm sorry I said what I did. We can go back to just spiritual direction. I promise. Please . . ."

I felt awful, like I was kicking a wounded animal whose cries I had shut out. My heart ached, not just for her but also for me, the result of pain we both could have avoided, but chose not to.

"Zoë, I promise this will get better in time, for both of us. Please trust that. We have to do this."

I disengaged myself from her hold and opened the door. She reluctantly followed, blotting her eyes with a tissue, and blowing her nose. As we descended the stairs in silence, Columkille, the priest who had helped me clear the table, sat in the living room with a newspaper, never lifting his head to acknowledge our descent. When we got to the front door of the house, Zoë turned and looked at me once more with wounded, bloodshot eyes. I looked away, opened the door, and waited for her to move over the threshold. She did so slowly, deliberately, giving me time to change my mind. Finally, opening the screen door and stepping onto the front porch, she turned back and stood staring at me through the screen. I shut the door, and locked it while she stood there. As I slowly walked back up the stairs to my room, Columkille called to me from the living room, "Edward, I feel like some ice cream. Let's go to that great place on Main Street."

I stood at the top of the landing, tears streaming down my face, and said, "Give me a minute. I'll be right down."

Celibacy is a tough nut sometimes. And it's not usually about sex. It's about the undercurrents and the push and pull I experience with people dear to me. It's walking the fine line between intimacy and exclusivity. It's a dance many of us know well.

A recent Broadway show, *Contact,* tells its story through a trio of dance sequences that reveal three pairs of intimate relationships in various stages. Dance, however, is more than the medium by which the stories are told. The relationships become the dance. Revealed as swirling movements of intimacy, connections are forged between people lifted by the call of the music. Sometimes, the dance is hot and frenetic, exhausting, but it ends. The last dip is savored, the *pas de deux* relished, but the music stops.

Not so with every dance. One of the pieces suggests that some dances of intimacy continue for a lifetime; the steps grow surer, the choreography more imaginative. The rhythmic movements deepen the bond and illuminate the partners, who come to know themselves in relation to the one with whom they sway. They move as one.

I like to think I participate in this dance with terpsichorean skill mastered through years of practice—even with a vow of chastity. And yet, I know I've often fallen flat on my face. Relationships don't always fit into the neat categories that exist in my head. They're a lot messier. It's hard for me to compartmentalize intimacy into: acceptable and unacceptable, appropriate and inappropriate, because I don't love that way—and I don't know many people who do. I have one heart and its chambers aren't labeled. And sometimes that gets me into trouble.

While it is clear that my vow limits sexual expression and exclusivity in relationships, I often find myself in the foggy gray area of that limitation. Who decides what's exclusive? What constitutes sexual expression? How much intimacy is too much?

Taking vows at twenty-one, I was barely beyond adolescence. Chastity seemed an admirable pursuit then—and an easy one. Romantic notions filled my head: I would save myself for God. God alone would be my love. God would fill that empty place inside of me. It didn't seem murky at all. And while I still believe those sentiments contain truth, striving for such ideals has proven to be wrought with complexity and heartache.

My experience with Zoë hurt a lot. I handled it poorly, and we both suffered because of it. Yet, even though it was a wrenching episode, it was easier to negotiate than some I've had, because I didn't want what she wanted. I was settled and fulfilled in my priesthood at the time, desiring simply to be her friend—and maybe to pretend I had an apartment I could call my own. But she wanted more.

There have been other times, however, when I too have wanted more, when the loneliness and disconnectedness of celibacy have weighed upon me, threatening to squeeze life and vitality from me. Realizing that God's desire for me is happiness and fulfillment, I have pursued intimacy. But in that pursuit, I've made mistakes, and I've made compromises. I've hurt people because I led them to believe I could give more than I was able. And I've been hurt, pursuing what I never had a right to.

But it is also in this amorphous dance of intimacy that I've come to appreciate the deepest longings of my heart. It's been here that I've known the gift of a chaste heart; here where I've learned that even a priest can share love and intimacy; here where I've realized that the deep friendships of my life make up most of who I am. Those ties are what sustain me, as does the intimate dance I share with God. They've been worth the struggle. And while there may be others along the way who facilitate my stumbling again, I know there is also Someone else reaching out, lifting me from the floor, hand around my waist, poised to step again to a slower, steadier dance, to music only we hear.

CHAPTER TWENTY

THE STUFF THAT DREAMS ARE MADE OF

"This is the work of God. I recall the dream I had about these very things, and not a single detail has been left unfulfilled—the tiny spring that grew into a river, the light of the sun, the many waters."

—ESTHER 10(F):1–3

"Then afterward I will pour out my spirit upon all humankind. Your sons and daughters shall prophesy, your old men shall dream dreams, your young men shall see visions."

—JOEL 3:1

My cousin Denise says that when we were kids we played a game called "Who Do You Want to Meet?" You had to name three famous people you wanted to meet and tell why. The others then had to guess whom of the three you secretly wanted to meet the most. Denise remembers me picking Carly Simon as one of my three wannabe encounters. She doesn't remember if Carly made it into the final "meet most" category. Neither do I. But I'm not surprised that she was on my short list.

I was first introduced to her music when I was in grammar school, probably around the fifth grade. "That's the Way I've Always Heard It Should Be" had become a big hit, and I remember listening to it on the radio in my room, where I often spent long hours listening to music and sometimes making recordings of my own. Using a black Panasonic tape recorder with silver push buttons, I would hang a microphone from the bookcase of World Book Encyclopedia volumes, positioned over the stereo, and then sing along with records—with my mother occasionally singing backup. We did a mean "(I'll Be with You in) Apple Blossom Time," my mother favoring the Andrews Sisters to my more pubescent, contemporary mix. Sometimes I'd arrange empty coffee cans on the stereo, and we'd sing into those, attempting to duplicate the echo-synthesized effect that made singing in the shower sound so much better. For a while, I even tried using the bathroom as a recording studio, capitalizing on the enhanced sound of everything bouncing off the shiny yellow tiles. Since it was the only bathroom in the house, that didn't last long.

I never tried to sing along with Carly, though. With her, I only wanted to listen. Her haunting, mournful alto settled me in a way no other music did. She sang from her soul, and, intuitively, I resonated with the manifold emotions she vocalized. Impressed that she wrote her own words and music, I felt that each song was a heart-baring confession of a rich inner world to which she was allowing me entrée. She didn't sing about *other* people's yearnings and dreams. Her music was all her, trenchant poetry and soaring melodies converging to impart poignant insights about life and love—and God. With the release of each new album, the more I listened, the more I felt that I knew her: her soul, her dreams. I knew her secrets, even when she sang that there weren't any. And somehow I felt that her soul, with its secrets and dreams, was connected to mine.

By the time the album *No Secrets* was released and "You're So Vain," a single from that album, became the anthem for a generation of young people, she was my favorite musical artist, a detail not hidden from anyone who knew me. I anticipated the release of every new album, like such major events as Christmas and birthdays. After playing a newly purchased disc over and over, by the end of the first day, I knew the words by heart and heard the music in my head like a never-ending rondo. I used to gaze at the cover photo of *No Secrets*—with Carly in her floppy magenta hat, and braless in her simple blue pullover—and wonder what went on behind those sly eyes. Where did she get the inspiration to write words that captured the emotions of my heart, a heart she didn't know? And *who* was "You're So Vain" really about?

I was packing my bags for yet one more retreat, this one in Little Ferry, New Jersey. I had to be there by late Saturday afternoon to preach at the Vigil Mass and try to get people interested in attending the retreat. The phone rang. It was Robert.

"Hey, what are you doing?"

"Packing, what else?" I said. "I start in Little Ferry this afternoon," I said.

"What time do you start?" asked Robert.

"I have to preach at the five o'clock Mass."

"Would you be up for taking a little detour on your way to Little Ferry?"

"Detour? What are you talking about?" I was wrapping a shampoo container in plastic, having learned that lesson from traveling with a bottle of Neutrogena that had leaked, providing a prewash soaping to all my clean clothes.

"Did you see the *New York Times* today?" he said.

"No, I've been too busy getting myself together."

"Go get today's and open up to page twenty-two."

I went to the kitchen and hunted through all of the Sunday sections that we subscribers are privileged to get a day early. I finally found the Saturday Arts section and opened to an ad which read:

CARLY SIMON SIGNING COPIES OF HER NEW BOX SET: CLOUDS IN MY COFFEE. BARNES & NOBLE BOOKSTORE, LINCOLN CENTER. 2 P.M.

"Do you see it?" asked Robert.

"Yeah. How do you like that? I already have that CD set, you know. I bought it a few weeks ago." It sat on the floor by my stereo; the cover photo of the three-CD collection (a retrospective of thirty years of recording) was a youthful picture of Carly smiling, with her head tilted and eyes cast down. The stereo and CDs were under the big picture window in my room, which faced the Hudson River and the majestic Palisades of New Jersey.

"Well, are you going to go?" Robert asked.

"No! Why would I go there? To stand in line with a bunch of crazy fans to get an autograph? That's not what it's about for me with her."

"I know, but this would be a chance to meet her, and to see if this spiritual connection thing that you think you have is really anything."

"Nah, I don't think so. I'd feel stupid. It's not how I want our meeting to be, if it's ever gonna happen." I walked over to the window and looked down at the CD box set with the picture of Carly smiling. Her young and scrubbed face intimated innocence not yet tested by the rough-and-tumble world of recording stardom.

"All right, but I think you should do it," Robert persisted. "You could always just write her a letter and give it to her, and not get into the autograph stuff or any of that. At least then you'd be sure that she gets it."

"Nah, I don't think so, but thanks for letting me know."

I hung up the phone and put on the first of the CDs from the set, listening as I finished the last of my packing. "Let the river run. Let all the dreamers wake the nation. Come the new Jerusalem." The mellifluence of her voice and the driving percussion filled my small bedroom. While staring out at the river she may have been singing about, I conceded that my curiosity had been piqued. I wondered what those record signings were like. *Did you really get to speak to the person, or were you just shuttled along to make way for the next breathless devotee? What if someone I knew saw*

me standing on that line? I'd be embarrassed. "Oh, hi, Father, are you
going to get her to sign the Playing Possum *cover, where she's wearing
the skimpy underwear? Pretty sexy, Father."* I could just write the letter,
tell her why I felt this connection, drop it off, and leave it at that. It was
kind of on my way to New Jersey, if I took the Lincoln Tunnel, instead
of the George Washington Bridge.*

I wasn't sure exactly why, but I sat down and wrote the letter.
I told Carly of my long feeling of connection to her and why her
music struck spiritual chords in me. Encouraging her to continue
to write about beauty and truth, I assured her that I sent blessings
and peace her way. Deciding not to hand-deliver the letter at the
record signing, though, I stuck it in my knapsack and planned to
mail it from New Jersey, care of Arista Record Company, confident that she'd eventually get it. At least I had finally taken the
time to communicate my feelings, after thirty years of emoting
from afar, unbeknownst to Carly.

My car would not go over the George Washington Bridge. I
missed the turnoff from the West Side Highway and soon found
myself looking for a parking space in the crowded mess that is the
Lincoln Center neighborhood on a Saturday afternoon. Hundreds
of people were racing like lemmings into the state-of-the-art Sony
movie theaters and hundreds more were descending upon Tower
Records, Gracious Home, and the Barnes & Noble that sat on the
corner like a welcoming aunt.

Parking came easily. Walking into the bookstore did not. I cir-
cled the block twice, looking into store windows I had no interest in, distracted by my nervousness and the running script that
played in my head of what I would say to her. I hated the thought
of having to stand on line with everyone else, as if I were just another besotted fan who wanted to brush up against stardust and sa-
vor the glitter for the rest of my sorry life. Would she be able to
tell that this was something different? Would she sense that this
was ingenuous spirit and not ersatz pop apotheosis?

By the time I jettisoned my overweening pride and walked
through the revolving doors of the store on Broadway, the line

was already snaking through fiction, nonfiction, biography, and travel. How odd to see all of those people standing in a bookstore, not reading books, but clutching box sets of Carly's CD and every kind of fan-club paraphernalia imaginable. I joined the line behind a delirious set of twin girls from Long Island, who were embracing album covers, magazine pictures, and a "Carly doll" they had made from what looked like a Barbie, to which they had added fuller lips. Their conversation was so full of "totallys" and "awesomes" that I feared that from my listening to them *ad nauseam*, the modifiers might unwittingly slip into my homily that evening, like an unruly mantra I couldn't refrain from repeating. Then there would be no concealing that I had been hobnobbing with the erudite youth of Levittown.

Although the twin teenagers were obviously obsessed, there were others on line who appeared quite normal, making me feel somewhat less conspicuous: some men and women my age, a handful of mothers, a sprinkling of couples, even a few grandparents—all waiting patiently for the line to start moving, signaling that the songstress had taken her place and had begun signing. Every once in a while I contemplated hightailing it out of there, but something deeper told me to stay; I felt there was a reason I had gone.

With my letter safely ensconced in my black leather knapsack, I had just pulled out a book that I had brought with me to pass the time, when a security guard approached me.

"Have you bought your CD yet?" he asked. He was short and fat, the kind of guard who doesn't carry a gun, but acts like he does.

"No, I already have one at home. I'm just here to give Ms. Simon a letter."

"No, you'll have to get off the line. You can't do that." He shook his head authoritatively, having given the final word and then awaiting my compliance.

"I can't give her a letter?"

"She's signing CDs only. You have to have a CD in order to

go up there. You'll have to get out of the line." Folding his arms, he drew his own line in the sand.

I considered my options. I didn't want to spend the money, not exactly throw-away change, on another box set. Yet, if I didn't have one, I wasn't going to be permitted to proceed. So I devised a plan to buy the box set to show the security guard, and then to bring it back for a refund after I had seen Carly and delivered my letter. It seemed like an amenable compromise. I assuaged my conscience by telling myself that I had already shelled out my money for the CD set weeks before—even though I had bought it at a discount at DiscoRama, and not at Barnes & Noble. But hey, most of the proceeds went to Arista anyway, and I assumed Carly got her cut no matter where it was bought.

The line began to inch up slowly, but I still couldn't see anything. They had positioned Carly around a bend of books, so she wasn't visible until one neared the front of the line. The closer I got, the more I feared I had made a mistake in coming. Although I convinced myself that my reasons for being there differed vastly from those of everyone standing around me, my chance to meet a soul friend was turning into a surreal pop promotion scene that was leaving a bad taste in my mouth. Even after waiting an hour, with only a few people in front of me, I pondered bolting. But then I finally rounded the bend of books and saw her sitting there.

She was smiling that legendary, expansive smile, well known from having graced magazine and album covers for over three decades. It was a mouth you wouldn't pass without noticing, voluptuous and sensual, a pretty version of Mick Jagger's orifice. Carly was nodding her head at the woman standing in front of her, having already signed her CD, and then offering some parting words before the next lucky enthusiast stumbled starstruck to the table. She looked younger than I had imagined, almost coquettish, with her hair pulled up and her tall lean physique leaning in intently. With her wearing a pastel sundress and little makeup, a scintilla of winsomeness was evident even from a distance. Although she was smiling, I sensed she wasn't totally comfortable with the shenanigans unfolding around her, as if she knew the hype was merely part of the requisite game she had to play, given the current state of music promotion. Shyness covered her like a pall of protection—an ally of her then-manager, Brian, who sat protectively next to her for comfort—and to keep the line moving.

While a few aficionados were still ahead of me, she looked up at me and caught me staring, and smiled. Warmth wafted across the room. I took it as a sign that she would affirm our connection and intuit our encounter as distinct from those she would have with the others waiting on the serpentine line, which by then extended out the door.

When at last it was my turn, I wasn't at all nervous. I felt like I was greeting a lifelong friend to whom I'd finally come home. Walking up to the table, I paused and knelt down. Not a posture of worship, it just seemed more comfortable than her having to look up at me. Gazing into eyes that shone with interest, I said, "Hi, I'm Father Edward Beck, a Passionist priest. And I have a letter that I'd like to give you. I hope you'll read it sometime."

She took the letter and passed it to Brian, without ever breaking eye contact with me, and said, "Yes, of course, I'll read it later. Where are you from?"

"Riverdale. Our monastery and retreat house is there, on the Hudson, right next to the Hebrew Home for the Aged."

She looked startled. "I grew up in Riverdale and went to school there."

"Yeah," I said, "I know. When your mother was dying, her housekeeper, Mary, called our monastery for prayers for her. I didn't believe it was mere coincidence because, as you will read, I have for so long felt connected to you. It was just one more confirmation."

Her smallish blue eyes started to fill with tears. Perhaps the mention of her mother had touched an emotional chord she had not expected to be played. She tossed the bangs of her hair for ward with a flick of her head, the way a filly uses a mane to shoo away flies. "I can't talk about this now. I'm too overwhelmed. And there are all these people waiting. Perhaps we could speak at another time, in less distracting circumstances?" She seemed so open, so vulnerable.

"Sure, my phone number and address are in the letter. Feel free anytime to get in touch with me. I'd welcome it, Carly."

"I surely will. And, Father Edward, thank you sooo much for coming to see me. I really am searching spiritually, and maybe this is the beginning of an answer."

She smiled broadly and reached out for my hand. I placed it in hers, feeling her warmth, knowing it wouldn't be the last time our hands would touch or the last time our eyes would peer into soul space that we intuitively shared.

"Oh, here, let me sign your CD before you leave." She put out her hand, waiting for me to deposit my unopened, "soon to be returned" box set.

"Oh, no, that's O.K. I don't want to hold up the line anymore."

"No, don't be silly. You waited all that time. It's the least I could do."

She took it from my hands, unwrapped it, and wrote: TO EDWARD—WITH LOVE—CARLY SIMON, MAY 18, 1996.

A good friend got the box set on the floor in my room.

Within days, I had a note from her, written on fine white parchment that had her initials embossed on the front. She wrote how much she appreciated our brief meeting and of the desire to get together the next time she was in New York City. She included her Martha's Vineyard phone number and address, in case I was going to be in that area before she would be in New York again. I thought it an exposed and brave thing to do, considering that she didn't know me.

The following month we sat in her homey New York kitchen for three hours and shared our personal stories and journeys of faith. Jim, Carly's husband, arrived halfway through and contributed his own keen theological perspective, having been a Franciscan seminarian in his youth, and still a definite searcher. We chatted like old friends over green tea and homemade scones, while Carly's cat, Ursula, prowled quietly on the table and then fell asleep in my lap. I realized sometime in the middle of that afternoon that God had brought us together for a reason. It still wasn't clear to me exactly why, but the ease of rapport and the commonality of our spiritual quests confirmed a convergence that was more than serendipitous. Our paths were meant to cross.

We kept in touch through letters and occasional phone calls over the ensuing months. Carly moved from being a celebrity to whom I had felt connected from afar, to a trusted friend with whom I felt comfortable to be myself. While she respected my priesthood and the spiritual nature of our relationship, she also treated me like a real person in whom she could confide, sharing with me the intimacies of her life, her joys and struggles, and the pressures of the sometimes bizarre three-ring circus that is stardom.

To facilitate her spiritual unfolding, she and Jim made a weekend retreat at our Passionist Residence in Riverdale. I directed the retreat, along with a religious sister who had inspired Carly and Jim on a TV show on which the sister had appeared with the Dalai Lama. Although my partner wound up talking incessantly during the weekend (and mostly about herself), it was a graced time for Jim and Carly to connect spiritually and, when they could get a word in, to talk to each other about issues not easily negotiated when they were alone. I thought we had our best moments once the gabby nun had left, but then, maybe I just didn't like the competition.

The following summer, in yet another coincidence, I was asked to give a retreat for the parishes of Martha's Vineyard, where Carly lived. She attended with her friends Jake, Mindy, and Robin. During the week, we got to visit at her storybook house on the Vineyard—a magical edifice, complete with towers, wildflower gardens, and beautifully appointed rooms, one of them called the E.T. room after Elizabeth Taylor, because its lavender color was said to resemble the shade of her eyes.

After having dinner with Carly and Jim, I had a preview of the music she was writing for a new album. While lying on her bedroom floor, listening to her clear alto emanate from miniature Bose speakers that sounded like concert amplifiers, I reflected on how far we had come in our relationship. It was hard to fathom that the familiar voice, shimmering like polished silver and filling the bedroom with resplendence, belonged to the woman who had just cooked dinner and cleaned up. But in another way, it was sublimely congruous, juxtaposing Carly's luminous talent with her down-to-earth accessibility. I began to feel as though we had always been connected.

Some months later, Carly called me in New York. Her tone of voice, lacking its usual fervid quality, indicated that something was very wrong. She had found a lump on her breast and needed to have a biopsy done. I felt awful that she was being presented with such a frightening ordeal. Though she was confident everything would be fine, she said my prayers would bring her further peace. I assured her I would begin praying that day and not cease until I had more news from her.

"More news" came via my answering machine one evening after I had returned home from food shopping.

"Hello, Edward dear. It's Carly. I just wanted to call and let you know that I got the results of the biopsy back . . . and I do have breast cancer . . ." She paused, her voice breaking with emotion. "I'm finding it really hard . . . but I'm trying to be positive about it. I know that this can be the golden key to the next phase of my life, if I let it be. I'm really going to try. Please keep me in your prayers. I know you will. I send you my love."

I was stunned. I looked at the answering machine as if the next message was going to say that it was all a mistake. But there were no other messages. I pressed "repeat" and listened to her hurting voice again, then I sat in my glider chair and prayed for her peace.

Sadness filled my bedroom, like a fog that rolls in uninvited, clouding everything embodying color and life. But one bright beacon shone through: As I prayed, it became clear that this was the reason why Carly and I had finally met. I was to assist her through this ordeal and offer spiritual solace, the only kind that really mattered at a time like this. I had always told Carly that I never wanted anything from her. My desire was to give something back to her after the many years of feeling that she had given me so much through her music. Now was my opportunity to make good on my promise.

"St. Martin de Porres?" said Carly. "I've never heard of him." She sat in her kitchen on a stool pulled up to the marble table that rose from the floor like a shiny mushroom.

"He's a Peruvian saint," I said. "I'm sure Jim has heard of him. I have a relic of his. It's the one I told you I blessed my mother with when she had a brain tumor. I'd like to bless you with it and also anoint you with oil of healing."

"Oh, Edward, that would be wonderful. It would help me so much. Do I have to do anything to prepare?"

"No, nothing at all. Just be open—which I know you already are. Let Spirit and grace move through you with ease and without fear, and you'll be just fine. We can do the blessing here in your apartment tomorrow night, if you like. I can be here about seven-thirty."

Jim, Robin (Carly's assistant), and I gathered the next evening in the dining room while Carly lay on a daybed on the far side of the room. Reposed in a peaceful posture of receptivity, she lay perfectly still, her eyes closed and her hands folded in prayer. The serenity on her slightly smiling face was almost beatific. Someone walking in cold might have thought she was being laid out. I reverently unwrapped the relic of St. Martin de Porres, removing it from its black leather case, and unfolding the red felt that protected the gold container. Carly never even opened her eyes to look at it.

Burning candles of all sizes and shapes illuminated the room in a tranquil glow as Jim and Robin joined silently in the prayer from their seats at the dining room table. Placing the relic on Carly's chest, I prayed for the intercession of this efficacious saint. I called on his power to heal, his power to comfort, his power to instill peace; a tradition of holiness was symbolized in this tangible piece of sacredness that we held on to. I then blessed Carly with the holy oil, asking God for healing and for the blessing of tranquillity. I anointed her forehead, her hands, and her chest, making the unctuous signs of the cross with a forceful thumb, as if transmitting definitive commands that I expected to be obeyed. She lay quietly the whole time, seemingly absorbing the import of this moment of beseeching.

When I was finished, I sat in a chair beside the daybed and silently joined the others in prayer. And then without warning, I found myself singing an a cappella rendition of "Amazing Grace," slow and deliberate, making each syllable a prayer. "Amazing Grace, how sweet the sound, that saved and set me free. I once was lost but now am found, was blind, but now I see." As soon as I was finished, I realized the height of my audacity in singing while Carly Simon lay there. But I know it was inspired, because I never would have done it of my own accord. Amazing grace indeed seemed to be liberating.

We sat for a few moments more in silent prayer, not wanting to interrupt the sacredness of the moment that blanketed the room, until Carly finally said, "That was the most amazing experience. I feel so peaceful. I feel like I've been healed. I don't want to move." She kept her eyes closed, present to the moment, at one with a deeper place.

"Well, I hope it *is* the beginning of a healing," I said finally. "There are many kinds of healing. For now, your feeling of peacefulness is a wonderful start. I want you to keep the relic of St.

Martin de Porres close during this period. Pray to him when you feel frightened and alone. He'll bring you comfort. He can be your way to God, if you need one."

Carly kept the relic during her surgery and subsequent convalescence, along with a prayer book and biography of Martin de Porres. She was fascinated to discover that he was of the same mulatto lineage as her mother. I also gave her a finely rendered statue of St. Martin, which she still keeps in a prominent place in her home, near her other religious articles, a collection of spiritual paraphernalia from every imaginable religious tradition. For Carly, born of a Jewish father and a Catholic mother, ecumenism is a way of life. She dabbles in it all and finds meaning and succor wherever she can.

In another remarkable convergence of events, I was privileged to accompany Carly to her first chemotherapy session at Sloan-Kettering Cancer Center. Jim, her husband, was sick with a cold and proximity to Carly could have compromised her immune system, so he had to stay away. Ben and Sally, her two children, were out of state, and therefore not available to go with Carly either.

As I was speaking with her on the phone, I said, "Well, who's going to go with you for the session then?"

"I'm not sure," she said. "I of course have friends I can ask, and my sisters, but I don't know . . . for some reason, it doesn't seem quite right to ask any of them."

"This may be a little presumptuous of me, but would you like me to go with you?"

"Would you? Are you free?"

"Of course, Carly. I'd be honored."

"Oh, Edward, I would love that. You would bring me such peace."

After quietly being ushered in a back door, Carly and I were safely ensconced in a treatment room at Sloan-Kettering—a small cubicle, one of many, situated around a brightly lit and plant-laden atrium. Carly's anxiety immediately kicked into high gear and manifested itself through constant talking, about anything at all.

She asked lots of questions of the staff and started to think out loud ideas that were pure fantasy.

"Maybe we can all go to Ireland together and I can shoot a video of 'Touched by the Sun' as a public service announcement for breast cancer. Jim Sheridan, the director, is interested in doing it. Wouldn't it be great to do it there? Edward, you could come as spiritual adviser."

"Yeah, sure, that would be great," I said, humoring her playful imagining.

"Would you like to come, too?" she said to the nurse who was preparing the IV.

"Sweetheart, I'm from Ireland. I go back every year with my husband."

"Oh, that's great. What's your husband's name?" the inquisitive Carly asked.

"Martin, my husband's name is Martin."

Carly and I looked at each other.

"But Martin isn't an Irish name, is it?" said Carly.

"No, not really, but he was named after a saint—Martin de Porres. He's very popular in Ireland."

Carly closed her eyes and settled in for the hour or so of slow dripping, with not another peep out of her.

Her surgery and treatment were successful, and today Carly lives cancer-free. She is at the height of her creative powers, having recently released an album that I also first heard while lying on her bedroom floor last summer. It bursts with imagination, feeling, and most of all, soul. It's obvious in listening that she has allowed her harrowing experience to be "a golden key to the next phase of [her] life," just as she said. Coincidentally, the album is called *The Bedroom Tapes*.

I don't know if Carly's cancer is the only reason we met. We continue to keep in touch with one another, though our connection ebbs and flows, depending on where we are and what's happening in our lives. Whenever I see her, on those rare occasions when our disparate worlds converge, it's as if no time has passed and nothing has been lost. There is a bond that has been forged by our experiences together that no time or distance can ever dissolve. Soul solder is everlasting.

I assume Carly would have gotten through her ordeal without St. Martin and me. But the experience would have been a different one. She said that she has never met someone at a public event like a signing and kept in contact as we did. When I asked her why she trusted it, she responded, "I just knew it was O.K. I could tell that you were different, and that I'd be safe with you." I believe it was because I was meant to share a small piece of her trek with her. That's the beauty of faith: the belief that God gives us what we need, when we need it. And although Carly may not realize it, I needed her, too. She wound up strengthening my faith by the witness of her unflagging spirit in the midst of a potentially paralyzing experience. And she helped me to believe that sometimes the dreams of little boys really do come true. Assisting one another in this magical life odyssey, we allowed grace to do its job, appreciating that it's the nature of grace to beget more grace. Who knows what comes next?

On her album *Coming Around Again*, Carly sings a song entitled "The Stuff That Dreams Are Made Of." Its refrain goes "It's the stuff that dreams are made of. It's the slow and steady fire. It's your heart and soul's desire. It's the reason we are alive." Whether the young or the old dream them, Carly (and Shakespeare) knew that the stuff of dreams makes our lives worth living. In the Scriptures, God often appears in dreams—warning, prompting, wrestling. Dreams are God's gift to us: pieces taken from our lives, refracted and reshaped, returning to us with ferment and new possibility. Some of the dreams of my youth, once existing only in my imagination, have become authentic and palpable, fulfilling my heart and soul's desire. The dreams have carried me through, exposing me to worlds to which I might never have dared venture. Carly keeps me dreaming—and venturing. And for that, I am forever beholden.

CHAPTER TWENTY-ONE

FORTY AND
STILL COUNTING

*Love never fails. If there are prophesies, they will be brought to
nothing; if tongues, they will cease; if knowledge, it will be brought
to nothing . . . So faith, hope, and love remain, these three. But the
greatest of these is love.*

1 CORINTHIANS 13:8, 13

I turned forty last year, had a small celebratory dinner with
some close friends, and resolved to live my remaining years
worrying less about what other people think of me. I read in
some magazine that in our forties we rediscover the interests we
had when we were young and take greater pleasure in them. The
writer maintained that, from our teens to middle age, we put
aside doing what we like in favor of doing things that will get us
liked. In our forties, however, we start doing what we really like
again, and care less about what others think. It would be nice if
that was true.

Much of my life as a priest has been spent trying to do what
people like, or at least what I thought they expected of me. I figure it comes with the job. That's not to say that I haven't done
what I wanted along the way, too, but always while conscious of
the expectations and perceptions of others. Never wanting to shatter people's image of what a priest should be, I wound up reveal-

ing only the parts of me I deemed compatible with a white collar, while expunging the human foibles I thought might scandalize the fainthearted. But I've begun to rethink all that.

My reevaluation has been prompted not so much because I turned forty, but because that event happened to coincide with my year's sabbatical, during which I wrote this book. Writing memoirs has encouraged me to reveal more than I ever thought possible. Perhaps after reading the preceding pages, some may view the priest's collar differently, maybe even as besmirched. But now that people have gotten a glimpse of a truer me, I feel that I don't have to pretend as much anymore. Maybe I *can* worry less about being liked and start doing the things I like more.

Actually, I'm not sure what I'd do differently. Some maintain that I've always done what I wanted anyway. Maybe it's just that my attitude seems to be shifting. I'm becoming more comfortable being myself, as I witness an increasing number of people more amenable to seeing priests as human—with the same needs, dreams, and propensity to mess up as everybody else. I feel that I can open my besmirched collar and breathe a little easier. It's liberating to have others accept that, just because we priests speak from a pulpit about life's spiritual journey, it doesn't necessarily mean we've mastered it or that we never veer from the straight and narrow. Some of us stumble big-time. Just read the headlines. (When the writer Anne Lamott gets confessional, she says, "I worry that Jesus drinks himself to sleep when he hears me talk like this." Ditto.) But the inner transformation I've been experiencing is about more than just my vocation to the priesthood. It's about how I believe the deepest desires of my heart are going to be satisfied.

My reflections have caused me to think about how I got here in the first place. I had a first-grade nun who warned us to be suspect of our desires. I remember her saying, "Figure out what *you* want to do, and then do the opposite." She encouraged us to "offer up" our predilections, with the belief that somehow others would benefit from our self-abnegation. She's no doubt responsible for some major guilt I've incurred along the way, but I would forgive her anything.

Sister Mary Alicene sure had a way with the boys. She would walk into the classroom in her starched serge habit and flowing black veil and wink at the lad who sat closest to the heavy wooden door. Sometimes that was I, since she didn't believe in assigned seats and rotated us like a supermarket stock boy moving the oldest yogurt to the front. Whenever she whisked past me, I could smell the sweetness and purity of what it meant to be a nun in 1965. What *was* that smell? It wasn't perfume, heaven forbid, but rather a mixture of unadulterated soap, bleach pressed into the meticulously ironed habit, and a natural skin scent that seemed reserved for women who wrapped themselves in reams of cloth. I used to want to follow her up the aisle to revel in her scent a bit longer. When she stood by my desk to read to us from books that related the adventures of Dick and Jane, it was an olfactory delight—to say nothing of what it did for my other senses. I think I was in love with her.

"Edward, I want to see you for a few minutes after school tomorrow," Sister Mary Alicene said to me one day at the end of the school day. "So tell your mother that she should come ten minutes later."

"Yes, Sister."

I couldn't imagine what I had done. Intent on having her love me back, I had endeavored to be a model first-grade student: sitting with my hands perfectly folded when books were put away, hanging my coat up on my assigned hook, rather than throwing it on the floor like most of the boys did, making sure my clip-on tie was always straight, and endlessly practicing my printing so I would be awarded a gold star at the top of my page. But now she wanted to see me alone. No more gold stars for me.

"What's the matter with you?" my mother asked that night at dinner.

"Sister Mary Alicene wants to see me tomorrow after school, so you have to come later to pick me up."

"See you about what?"

"I don't know. She didn't say."

"And you didn't ask her?"

"No."

"Why not?"

"I figured I'd find out tomorrow."

"What did you do?"

"I don't know."

"So you *did* do something. How many times do I have to tell you that we're paying good money for you to be in that school, and we're not going to waste it on your carrying on."

"I'm not carrying on. I don't know why she wants to see me."

"Well, when we find out tomorrow, you are in trouble, mister. Wait until your father gets home."

I had initiated a family crisis and didn't even know how or why. I tossed and turned that night. Pirouetting nuns, twirling their veils by bending their torsos and necks, danced through my dreams. Sister Mary Alicene came to me with no veil, in a haze of clouds, and I saw her hair for the first time—long, beautiful blond hair that swirled perfectly, shiny and bouncy, and with that wonderful smell. How did she fit it all under that black veil?

When she walked into the classroom the next day, I wasn't seated by the door, so I was deprived of the rush of all that material against my arm as she made her way to her barren desk, adorned with only a crucifix and, sometimes, with a polished apple that some student, usually a girl, had deposited there. I watched Sister Mary Alicene throughout the day for any sign of what might follow after school. When she called on me to come to the board to practice my letters, I was so nervous that I couldn't write straight. By the time I was finished, it looked as though an octogenarian with Parkinson's had scribbled the characters.

"Edward, you haven't been practicing," she said, more softly than I had expected.

"Yes, I have, Sister, but it's not working today."

"Why not?"

"I don't know, Sister."

"Well, sit down now and we can talk about this later."

Maybe that was what this was about. She didn't like the way I printed. But I was usually better than this.

The rest of the day passed slowly. I was quiet at lunch, leading one of the monitors to ask me if I wanted to see the school nurse. I declined, but did consider the possibility of getting sent home sick, rather than having to bear the disappointment of my dear Sister Mary Alicene.

The end of the school day finally came. I sat with my hands folded on my desk, a solitary figure left behind by my squealing classmates, who had apparently mastered penmanship in a way that eluded me. My eyes were downcast, studying the grain in the dark wood of the desk that shone like my dear nun's cheeks. Sister Mary Alicene sat at her desk, too, marking papers that we had submitted before recess. Now I was sure there would be no more gold stars for me.

"Edward, could you come up here, please?" she finally said.

"Yes, Sister."

I moved from my desk slowly, like a death row prisoner taking his last walk. I couldn't look at her and stared instead at the parquet tiles, which shone almost as brightly as the desks that I passed. When at last I reached her desk, I could smell her once again, clean as a newly washed baby. I watched her arm resting on her desk, the perfect crease of her starched sleeve, still standing at attention, even after a day of animated teaching.

"Edward, I've been considering this for some time, and there's something I want to ask you."

My hands were wet; my right leg began to quiver.

"I need someone to help me a few days after school each week, cleaning up and clapping out the erasers. You seem dependable, and I wonder if you'd be willing to make the sacrifice to help me."

I looked up to see if she was smiling, to see if this might be the prelude to some cruel joke, but there was no hint of duplicity on her face. Her warm brown eyes looked at me expectantly, her head tilted to one side, her clear skin pulled tight by the stiff material surrounding her beatific face.

"You want me to help you?"

"Yes, I know it would mean your mother coming a bit later a few days a week. Do you think she would mind?"

"No, no, I don't think so."

"And you wouldn't mind?" she asked.

"No, I'd love to help you. I could do it every day, if you want."

"Well, that won't be necessary, but thank you for the offer. You're a good boy."

"Thank you, Sister."

"We'll start tomorrow, so let your mother know tonight. And bring some old clothes, so you won't get your uniform all dirty with chalk dust. That, your mother would not appreciate."

I floated out of the classroom and sailed down the steps to the schoolyard, where my mother waited at the gate. She had pink rollers in her hair, which she had attempted to camouflage with a green kerchief, and was smoking a cigarette.

"Well?" she said. "What did she want?"

"She wants me to help her after school a few days a week."

"As a punishment? What did you do?"

"No. I didn't do nothing. She says I'm dependable and a good boy."

"Yeah, right. Have her take you home to the convent for a few days, and see if she still feels that way. You better be telling me the truth."

We walked out of the schoolyard and waited at the bus stop, my mother stealing periodic glances at me to see if a latent confession was imminent.

Thirty-four years later, I was giving a retreat at a parish in Cambridge, Massachusetts. At the end of the first evening, I stood at the exit of the church, saying good night to those who had attended. A woman with permed gray hair, a black leisure suit, and comfortable rubber-bottomed tan shoes stood in front of me with her head tilted and a familiar smile on her face.

"Edward Beck. I can't believe it. You became a priest."

And then I smelled her. It was still there, like some odor of sanctity.

"Sister Mary Alicene?" She had the same kind eyes, and a familiar mole on the left side of her chin.

"Yes, believe it or not, it's me. Only I'm not Sister Mary Alicene anymore. I went back to my real name, so I'm Sister Virginia Mary now. My goodness, after all these years, here you are." She shook her head in what seemed like tandem appreciation and disbelief.

"How could you possibly remember me?" I asked. "All those students you had."

"Oh, I remember you. You used to help me after school. You were one of my best students."

"I was?"

"Yes, you were. You would look at me with your sad blue eyes as if you thought I was God or something."

"I did think you were God, or at least close to it."

"No, far from it, I'm afraid," she said.

"So you're still a nun?" I asked.

"Oh, yes, but I live with my mother now to take care of her, and I tutor problem children in the afternoons. Sort of semiretired. But I do miss the classroom."

"And I'm sure it misses you, too." Then I asked her what I had been waiting to ask for thirty-four years. "Sister, you used to tell us to figure out what *we* wanted to do, and then do the opposite. What did you mean?"

"Funny you should remember that. I guess I meant that we want so many different things, mostly superficial, and that those things don't have lasting value. So that, if we could find some way not to let those things control our lives, maybe we'd get to the deeper place, the place that really does matter. Of course, I say that after thirty more years of living. I'm not sure I knew any of that back then. Maybe I just wanted to keep all you ruffians in line."

We talked for a few minutes more, before she departed into the night air as miraculously as she had appeared. She attended every night of the retreat that week, and sat in the front pew, beaming with pride, tacitly taking some credit that I had become a priest. And she was right to. Those days in her classroom had left me with feelings of serenity and security that have rarely been matched. I wanted to *be* Sister Mary Alicene, or at least the male version of her. Maybe years later when I took my own vows and donned my own habit, it was in some way due to her example and to that wonderful smell.

This book has been an attempt to find God in the significant experiences and people in my life. Sister Mary Alicene seems a fine person to end with, since she was an important part of the beginning. My belief throughout has been that God has been part of my experiences and relationships, even when I wasn't aware of it at the time. My underlying supposition has been that the spiritual is infinitely more significant and empowering than the physical. I'm at a time in my life when I yearn to live the truth of that declaration more authentically.

Sebastian Moore claims that desire is the heart of who we are. True enough, none of us are exempt from desire's Herculean grasp. Desire comes from God to bring us back to God. But it also can waylay us, as Sister Mary Alicene once suggested, because we sometimes attempt to satisfy our desire with things or people that never can. We forget where we've come from and to whom we are returning. And once we do, the door is open for desire to eat us up like an insatiable predator.

In the third century, St. Augustine wrote, "Oh God, our hearts are restless until they rest in Thee." The ineffable truth of this prayer sees me through and makes bidding farewell to the ephemeral easier. Reminding myself of the prayer's certitude and clinging to its wisdom are salubrious for my body and spirit. As I gather daily to pray with and be supported by like-minded people in a faith community, we tell each other that we believe in a power and richness beyond ourselves—a love born of desire that transcends the physical and rises above what we can see, feel, taste, and touch. We point to a reality that is unseen, but nonetheless real. We acknowledge the transforming potency of a God whose origin is love and whose desire is that we live more in accord with that love. Best of all, it's a free gift.

No doubt plenty in our lives conspires to prevent us from receiving that gift. For some, perhaps a preoccupation with their physical looks or appearance gets in the way. For others, it may be what they own, or how much money they have in the bank, or whom they love possessively, or the job that they depend on for their self-esteem, or the headiness of their sexual prowess, or their talent in some coveted field. While none of that stuff is bad, it's just that—stuff. It passes away, as will all of us. So, in the end, what has really mattered? To what have we given our lives? With whom have we cast our lot? Whom have we loved—really loved? I'm not sure much else matters.

> *To keep one sacred flame*
> *Through life, unchilled, unmoved,*
> *To love in wintry age the same*
> *As first in youth we loved,*
> *To feel that we adore*
> *Even to fond excess,*
> *That though the heart would break with more*
> *It could not live with less.*
>
> —UNKNOWN

Amen.

About the Author

EDWARD L. BECK, C.P., is a Roman Catholic priest and a member of the Passionist community. A onetime parish priest, director of seminarians, and campus minister, he travels throughout the country preaching and organizing retreats and workshops. He has experience in theater, radio, and television. He lives in New York City.

www.godunderneath.com

www.edwardlbeck.com